2/10

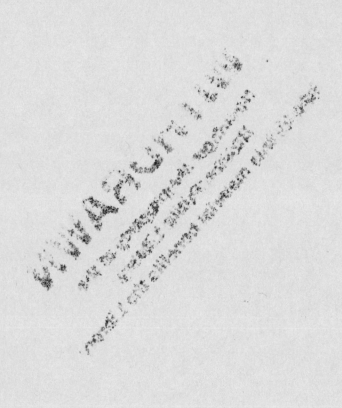

DARK DAYS, BRIGHT NIGHTS

DARK DAYS, BRIGHT NIGHTS

FROM BLACK POWER TO BARACK OBAMA

Peniel E. Joseph

BASIC
CIVITAS
BOOKS

A Member of the Perseus Books Group
New York

Published by Basic*Civitas* Books,
A Member of the Perseus Books Group

Books published by Basic*Civitas* are available at special discounts for bulk purchases in the United States by corporations, institutions, and other organizations. For more information, please contact the Special Markets Department at the Perseus Books Group, 2300 Chestnut Street, Suite 200, Philadelphia, PA 19103, or call (800) 810-4145, ext. 5000, or e-mail special.markets@perseusbooks.com.

Designed by Trish Wilkinson
Set in 11 point Adobe Garamond

Library of Congress Cataloging-in-Publication Data
Joseph, Peniel E.
    Dark days, bright nights : from Black power to Barack Obama / Peniel E. Joseph.
        p.   cm.
    Includes bibliographical references and index.
    ISBN 978-0-465-01366-1 (alk. paper)
    1. Black power—United States. 2. African Americans—History—1964–
3. African Americans—Politics and government. 4. African Americans—Civil rights. 5. African American leadership. 6. X, Malcolm, 1925-1965—Political and social views. 7. Carmichael, Stokely—Political and social views. 8. Obama, Barack—Political and social views. 9. Democracy—United States. 10. United States—Race relations—Political aspects. I. Title.
E185.615.J677 2010
323.1196'073—dc22   2009037946

10 9 8 7 6 5 4 3 2 1

CONTENTS

INTRODUCTION

From Malcolm X's vivid denunciations of racism outside of Harlem's gritty storefronts, to Stokely Carmichael's dramatic call for Black Power in Mississippi, radical black political activists during the civil rights and Black Power era openly questioned America's capacity to extend full citizenship to African Americans. However, Malcolm's and Carmichael's confrontational styles and combative words have obscured their pivotal roles in transforming American democracy. Hailed as bold oracles of racial militancy, their defiant identification with underdogs, ranging from prisoners to sharecroppers, made them particularly attuned to democracy's shortcomings and jagged edges. The image of Malcolm, his fingers stabbing the air to make a point about racial oppression in America, remains searing. Likewise, the vision of Carmichael, eyes blazing on a humid Mississippi evening as he asserted that only raw political power could definitively protect the lives of African Americans living in the South, persists in our cultural history. Like ancient museum artifacts, these images offer a powerful—if flattened— image of the past. But the popular memory of Malcolm and Carmichael remains misunderstood, focused as it is more on their fiery rhetorical style than the substantive meaning behind their words. Despite their volatile images, Malcolm and Carmichael played crucial roles in America's extraordinary journey from Black Power to Barack Obama.

Since the nation's inception, black Americans have been among the most vocal, eloquent, and longstanding proponents of American democracy. Yet due to their status as chattel slavery until 1865 and their subsequent legal disenfranchisement during the Jim Crow era that followed, African Americans' relationship to democracy remains star-crossed.

In spite of the obstacles, however, black political leaders have held steadfast to a belief in the redemptive values of citizenship in pursuit of larger goals of racial, political, and economic equality. This has remained true from Frederick Douglass's famous 1852 speech extolling the paradoxical nature of Fourth of July celebrations in a nation scarred by slavery, to Ida B. Wells's passionate antilynching crusade, and to W. E. B. Du Bois's groundbreaking work as a founder of the NAACP. It is now common knowledge that the civil rights movement went a long way toward turning the rhetoric of democracy into a living reality for African Americans. The struggle for civil rights is characterized by a *heroic* period between the May 17, 1954, *Brown* Supreme Court decision and the August 6, 1965, passage of the Voting Rights Act. Out of this period, iconic images of activists have become enshrined in American memory, such as those who persevered through a long-shot bus boycott in Montgomery, Alabama, braved snarling German Shepherds and fire hoses in Birmingham, Alabama, and endured mob violence in Little Rock, Arkansas, and Oxford, Mississippi, all before reaching a symbolic mountaintop at the August 28, 1963, March On Washington. As a poetic capstone to this era, the November 4, 2008, presidential election of Barack Obama has become instant folklore: "Rosa sat, so Martin could walk, so Barack could run, so that your children can fly."

As emotionally powerful as these words may be, they make for poor history. America's civil rights era remains a far more complex, scattered story. The struggles for justice that animated the modern movement's high point predated the 1954 *Brown* decision, just as they also endured beyond the 1965 passage of voting rights legislation.

It is important to keep in mind that struggles for civil rights were not merely confined to isolated bastions of racism in the South. Geographically, Northern civil rights activists likewise began crucial struggles for racial justice. For example, New York City activists waged rent-strikes and demonstrated for open-housing, while Detroit organizers labeled urban renewal programs "Negro removal" and started a brutal fight for school desegregation. Efforts for racial justice in New York, Ohio, Michigan, Illinois, and New Jersey were particularly acute as these five states contained the largest number of blacks living outside of Dixie.[1]

Like a children's bedtime story, our national civil rights history demands a happy ending. The movement is remembered as a political and moral good, employing nonviolence to achieve unimpeachable, deserved rights. However, the movement's resolute and sometimes militant challenge to American democracy's fundamental flaws remains less visible, and its relationship to the Black Power era continues to be dangerously combustible.

The story requires a suitable hero, and Martin Luther King Jr., stripped of his complexities and ambiguities, is presented as a straight-out-of-central-casting leading man. Our memory of Martin Luther King Jr. remains incomplete when the activist's increasingly radical critiques of American racism, poverty, and military adventures are eclipsed. Indeed, in the last three years leading up to his Thursday, April 4, 1968, assassination in Memphis, Tennessee, most national observers regarded King as more of a pariah than a prophet. Having spent the vast reserves of his moral and political capital criticizing the Vietnam War and urban and rural poverty, King gambled the remains of his reputation on a Poor People's Campaign that attempted to shame elected officials into passing sweeping antipoverty legislation. Yet even King retained faith in the redeeming nature of American democracy. Others, however, remained more skeptical.

King's all-consuming heroism requires not only one, but two major villains. Most often cast in the role of disgruntled spoiler to King's dreamer, Malcolm X led a local, national, and global movement for Black Power that pointedly questioned democracy's capacity to extend justice, opportunity, and equality to African Americans. As a local political and religious organizer in Harlem during the 1950s, Malcolm joined forces with labor, political, civic, and religious leaders to confront the police brutality, poverty, and violence plaguing urban black communities.

A national figure by the late 1950s, Malcolm participated in a long-running dialogue regarding the very nature of American democracy. In speech after speech during the early 1960s, Malcolm challenged the Kennedy administration to protect civil rights workers, punish racist law breakers, and protect the integrity of America's Constitution. After breaking with the Nation of Islam in 1964, Malcolm expressed admiration for the Declaration of Independence's lofty idealism while also castigating America for its failure to put that democratic theory into practice. Thus, Malcolm's critique of American democracy defined the contours of the movement to come.

Most often remembered for coining the phrase "Black Power," Stokely Carmichael was a civil rights militant turned Black Power activist who embodied the civil rights movement's redemptive form and tone. As a member of the Student Non Violent Coordinating Committee (SNCC, pronounced "snick"), Carmichael braved rural prison farms, tear gas, and routine violence in his painstaking efforts to secure poor sharecroppers the right to vote. By 1966, Carmichael argued that Black Power—the belief in self-determination, racial and cultural pride, and the global nature of domestic antiracist activism—held the key to the promotion of genuine democracy.

With his unabashedly confrontational public statements, Carmichael managed to scandalize the American public and press. Yet over four decades after "Black Power" entered the national lexicon, Carmichael's complex challenge to American society remains vital to still raging debates over race, war, and democracy.

Black Power remains the most misunderstood social movement of the postwar era. It was demonized as the civil rights movement's "evil twin" and stereotyped as a politics of rage practiced by gun-toting Black Panthers. Because of this, the movement's supple intellectual provocations, pragmatic local character, and domestic- and foreign-policy critiques remain on the fringes of America's memory of the 1960s. Nonetheless, Black Power's cultural and political flourishes, militant posture, and provocative rhetoric permanently altered the contours of American identity, citizenship, and democracy.

It was at the neighborhood level, where activists blended radical and at times revolutionary rhetoric with political pragmatism, where Black Power's quiet side emerged. Although some militants steadfastly promoted violent revolution to the bitter end, others proved more flexible, adopting strategies that helped the movement make enduring marks in education, art, and politics. Black Power-era politicians such as Maynard Jackson and Harold Washington embraced the movement, but with a moderate perspective that was attuned, they argued, to prevailing political realities.

As a result, the real and symbolic struggles that animated much of this postwar black activism have culminated in Barack Obama's presidential election. For most Americans, Obama's ascension to the pinnacle of political power vindicates King's vision of a color-blind democracy. The image of the nation's first African American president-elect instantly reverberated around the world as a triumphant testament to historic struggles for racial justice. However, Obama's election also called into question the civil rights-era understanding of domestic race relations and the continued viability of the politics of racial solidarity. Conservative pundits put the matter more crudely, arguing that Obama's election would end the politics of "racial grievances" practiced by "professional agitators" such as Jesse Jackson and Al Sharpton.

The truth is that Obama's climb to the top of American politics does not so much illustrate the end but rather the evolution of black politics. Americans old enough to have lived through the 1960s collectively marveled at Obama's election, a sight that many believed they would not witness in their lifetime. Yet the powerful symbolism attached to Obama's election can do little to end generations of racially based poverty or restore income and wealth lost during slavery and Jim Crow. Nor can it wipe away national scars of slavery and lynching. Obama's election does, however, offer hope in the concept of democracy, one that African Americans, more than any other group, have always taken to heart. This does not mean, on the other hand, that it guarantees a more sophisticated approach to foreign policy toward Africa and the larger Third World. As Obama's July 11, 2009, speech to the Ghanaian Parliament made painfully clear, American policy toward Africa (even with a black president) remains mired in a Janus-faced strategy that simultaneously acknowledges the brutal legacy of slavery and colonialism as a historical burden while it also ultimately locates blame for the continent's present troubles on government corruption. Obama's enormous popularity overseas and especially in Africa has helped gloss over such consistencies in U.S. policy after the transition to a black president. The politics of racial identification and solidarity implicit in Obama's international appeal have made his every move outside of American soil a historic event, one in which symbolism, as in the case of Africa, at times overpowers substance.

Six months after his inauguration and fresh from his trip to Ghana, Obama addressed America's racial legacy directly in a July 16 speech to the National Association for the Advancement of Colored People (NAACP). It was an event that, from all reports, the president and the White House took seriously. Aides reported that Obama worked on the speech for two weeks and continued to make revisions right up until the last minute.[2]

In New York City to celebrate the venerable civil rights group's one hundredth anniversary, Obama gave his most lucid domestic speech about race since being inaugurated. In discussing the NAACP's origins amid a particularly low period in black history—when unabated racial strife seemed to escalate with each passing day—Obama confronted part of America's history that remains a sensitive national subject. In front of a well-heeled crowd of African American civic, political, and business leaders, he offered a brief history lesson that acknowledged the rough road traveled by generations of blacks in order to achieve the kind of racial progress that his very presence—as the nation's first black president addressing a body devoted to ending racial discrimination—so powerfully symbolized. As he is fond of doing, Obama mentioned some of the epic battles fought during the civil rights era's heroic period, including the Freedom Rides, the sit-in movement in Greensboro, North Carolina, and efforts to register black sharecroppers in Mississippi. Following a quick tour through the contemporary ills that find blacks more likely than any other group in the nation to face unemployment, incarceration, and health crises, Obama discussed the need to challenge blacks to take on more personal responsibility.

In a passage from his speech that would be interrupted by applause four times, Obama transformed himself from statesman to preacher, admonishing black parents to teach their kids that, in spite of long odds, they could in fact succeed: "No one has written your destiny for you. Your destiny is in your hands—you cannot forget that. That's what we have to teach all of our children." For good measure and in a departure from his prepared text, the president continued: "No excuses. No excuses."[3]

Before he closed his speech, Obama recalled his recent trip to Ghana's Cape Coast Castle, a critical way station on the arduous journey from West Africa to the New World taken by untold numbers of Africans. He reminded those present of the courage displayed by blacks on their journey from slavery to freedom and challenged his audience to display the same tenacity as recent generations did during the civil rights movement in the 1950s and 1960s.

Part Sunday-morning sermon, part university lecture, and part autobiographical memoir, President Obama's thirty-four minute speech navigated a racial tightrope made all the more difficult by his own political ascendance. While characterizing America as having "less discrimination" than at any other time in its history, by forthrightly discussing the litany of racially based challenges still confronting the black community, Obama's address implicitly refuted the notion that his own election had thrust the nation into a "post-racial" future.

Portions of Obama's speech that touched upon racism's institutional legacy undoubtedly comforted black activists and organizers who were fearful that the nation's first black president remained too reticent to directly address the most pernicious racial matters. Other parts of Obama's NAACP speech—especially the "tough love" message to wayward black parents—galvanized the now accepted feeling within large swaths of the black community that the once-strong bonds of family, civility, love, and respect that sustained African Americans through slavery, Jim Crow, and poverty have become strained in the civil rights movement's aftermath. The dissolving of the tight-knit relationships that preserved black folks during some of the nation's darkest days is perhaps an unintended legacy of America's post-Jim Crow regime. This message also resonates with moderate and conservative whites, who applauded the president's words as a much needed message of personal responsibility—one that no white politicians could have gotten away with.

On the subject of race, Obama, out of political necessity, continues to outline a rough and at times improvisational vision of America that combines a candid understanding of America's tragic racial past with a clear-eyed vision of its future. Yet some people nurture a pervasive nostalgia for a communal past and shared identity among blacks, one forged through the crucible of Jim Crow segregation and whose brutality transcended class distinctions. Unfortunately, this nostalgia can be dangerous. It romanticizes America's Jim Crow years as an era in which family values flourished while it also indicts the contemporary black poor for failing to take advantage of the sacrifices made during that period.

When he discussed renewing an ethic of parental discipline in black communities, Obama validates a sepia-toned black past that, in turn, encourages a two-dimensional portrait of the present. He stated that, "We need to go back to the time, back to the day when we parents saw somebody, saw some kid fooling around and—it wasn't your child, but they'll whup you anyway." This line evoked laughter and applause from the audience—a sentiment shared by press coverage of the speech, which largely ignored the complex discussion of race and democracy in favor of the soundbites of Obama's address that spoke to black responsibility.[4]

The abbreviated press coverage glossed over the subtler complexities of Obama's message. By not widely reporting portions of Obama's NAACP address that lingered over America's racial past and criticized the nation's democratic shortcomings, the press stripped the president's speech of some of its rich complexity. In doing so, popular media was able to maintain a more simple and patronizing image of the first black president as a racial healer who, in certain instances, is willing to air out the African American community's dirty laundry. This false image ignores the subtle dimensions of Obama's NAACP speech wherein he positioned problems of poor health care and crumbling schools as *American* rather than *black* issues.[5]

Obama's strategy amounts to an acknowledgment that race-based solutions to historic discrimination no longer carry the moral weight and political urgency that they did only a generation ago. Instead, Obama's rhetorical call to arms situates issues that, in the past, have been largely framed in racial terms—and for good reason—as now being universal problems that impact the entire country and thus merit national action. If such a perspective becomes conventional wisdom, it will turn centuries of racial thinking on its head.

This will be more difficult than most people assumed after Obama's election. On the same day that Obama delivered his NAACP speech, Harvard

University professor Henry Louis Gates Jr. was arrested at his home by local police in Cambridge after being mistaken as an intruder. Gates's arrest quickly triggered a national firestorm over the eminent African American Studies professor. Gates accused the Cambridge police of racial profiling while the arresting officer's report characterized the fifty-eight-year-old Gates as an academic-turned-thug whose belligerence led to his own arrest. Obama weighed in on the Gates controversy a week later during a July 23, 2009, press conference designed to promote his ambitious universal health care proposal. The president characterized the Cambridge police as acting "stupidly" on the one hand while acknowledging his own election as an example of the nation's enormous racial progress on the other. A majority of white Americans polled found Obama's words to be offensive, as did police unions across the nation. Within a short time, Obama admitted that he chose his words poorly. He then invited Professor Gates and Sergeant James Crawley to the White House for a meeting over drinks, which journalists dubbed the "Beer Summit." Obama's first racial firestorm provides a window into the current state of race relations. Despite euphoria over the nation's election of its first black president, America remains a long way from embracing the kind of racial maturity that allows for an open and honest dialogue about racism's historic legacy and contemporary persistence.[6]

This country has a long history of considering blacks a "problem" for American democracy, rather than asking why democracy itself has such difficulty accounting for their equal citizenship—W. E. B. Du Bois called this phenomenon "the unasked question." Obama's most transformative achievement as president may rest on his ability, through speeches and concrete policy, to bridge this chasm of perception between black folk and the rest of the nation. This chasm still frustrates the everyday hopes, dreams, and yearning faced by too many African Americans. Only when black issues are taken seriously as both historically specific and nationally substantive—rather than racial grievances, complaints, or pathologies—will institutionally based racial disparities begin the long road toward recovery.

Obama embraces a tradition of black activism that recognizes that the inherent tension between race and democracy remains at the heart of the American saga. But where Malcolm X and Stokely Carmichael grew disillusioned with the gap between America's high ideals and practical realities, Obama remains convinced of its transformative capacity. Because of this, he frequently hails his own election as proof of democracy's enormous possibilities.

But even in the Age of Obama, the racial and political turmoil rooted in the social and political movements of the 1960s persists. Indeed, one conservative news commentator went so far as to compare First Lady Michelle Obama to "Stokely Carmichael in a designer dress"[7] shortly after the inauguration of America's first black president. The comparison stemmed from two factors. First, Mrs. Obama made widely publicized comments during the election season ("for the first time in my adult life I am proud of my country") that opponents seized on as proof of a glaring lack of patriotism. Secondly, a larger stereotype, caricaturizing her as strident, arrogant, and angry, is perpetuated through much popular media. Anger remains the characteristic that Stokely Carmichael is best remembered for, despite the fact that, in the face of racism and dangerous resistance, he spent years heroically organizing in the small towns and hamlets that dotted Mississippi and Alabama's rural black belt.

Attempts to link Michelle Obama to Black Power militancy resounded across the ideological spectrum. This effort ranged from the conservative Fox News Channel to even the liberal *New Yorker*, which portrayed her as an Angela Davis-type radical, complete with bandolier (and with Obama as a turban-wearing terrorist). Underlying these puerile and profane efforts to identify Michelle Obama—and by association her husband—as a reincarnation of 1960s-based racial militancy is the fact that their ascension to the highest realm of American politics represents an example of black power once thought inconceivable.

The difficulties in accepting the Obamas as "mainstream Americans" is partially related to misconceptions about the civil rights era that have flourished over the past several decades. Historians and the larger public have been slow to recognize and acknowledge the role of the intersection between race and democracy in dramatically reshaping the national character. Despite the importance given to the civil rights movement, the changes wrought by the sixties are too often thought of as the product of white, middle-class Baby Boomers bucking their parents' generation. This is an important historical turn, to be sure, but one that pales in comparison to the impact of the black social revolutions on our contemporary understanding of democracy and American society.

The failure to identify radical black activism with efforts to expand democracy further diminishes and isolates both historic and contemporary racial justice movements. Malcolm X, Stokely Carmichael, and the Black Power Movement attempted to, in complex and at times contradictory ways, transform American democracy. Black Power's penchant for verbal pyrotechnics has obscured its concrete efforts—from the neighborhood level to American foreign policy toward Africa—to confront, challenge, and reform democratic institutions. Although Barack Obama's unprecedented rise to power represents progress for the black freedom struggle's long quest for racial justice, its reception throughout the media also illustrates the limits of contemporary American race relations.

Dark Days, Bright Nights is not a linear story of social and political struggle culminating in political triumph. The chapters that follow promise no happy ending. Instead, they probe the transformations in postwar America since the civil rights era through key historical figures who found common ground in trying to reimagine American democracy. Black militants during the 1960s did this primarily through protests that looked toward the political arena as a tool for social and political justice. However, they also made efforts at the grassroots level that pushed the boundaries of citizenship, democracy, and civic action to their outer limits.

Thus, American democracy's unprecedented postwar expansion can be directly traced back to African American political activism during the civil rights–Black Power era. But the swirling controversies of Hurricane Katrina and Louisiana's Jena 6 stand as poignant twenty-first-century testaments to the nation's unfinished quest for racial and economic justice—even as Obama's historic election offers bittersweet hope for a more just future. Blacks continue in their insistence that democracy matters and that it remains at the core of movements for social, economic, and racial justice. But what democracy means, precisely, continues to be a matter of debate, one whose tenor has changed quite dramatically over time.

This book is animated by the examples of grassroots black activists of the postwar era who recognized that the vast spectrum of movements for racial justice were, in fact, all movements for democracy. Without such an understanding, it is doubtful that twenty-first-century America, whose racial landscape promises to be even more socially and politically charged, will be able to cope with the challenges it faces in its efforts to achieve justice for all of its people.

1

REIMAGINING THE
BLACK POWER MOVEMENT

In an era before multiculturalism and diversity, the Black Power movement introduced a new political landscape that permanently altered black identity. The politics of Black Power scandalized race relations in the United States and transformed American democracy. The daring and provocative rhetoric of activists like Malcolm X and Stokely Carmichael unleashed passionate debates and sparked enduring controversy over the very meaning of black identity, American citizenship, and the prospect of a social, political, and cultural revolution. Malcolm and Carmichael questioned the legitimacy of democratic institutions whose doors were closed off to African Americans. In their lifetimes, both turned to community organizing as a vehicle for empowering black people—Malcolm on some of New York City's toughest street corners and Carmichael in America's Southern black-belt region. As their notoriety grew, both men publicly criticized presidential leadership in regard to domestic race relations, blasted America's participation in Vietnam, and linked struggles against Jim Crow in the United States with anticolonial movements that were raging throughout the world. In doing so, both of these Black Power icons helped to expand the boundaries of American democracy. Black Power activists, no less than their more celebrated civil rights counterparts, contributed to postwar America's transformed landscape. In order to understand the American journey from Black Power to Barack Obama's election as the nation's first black president, we must cast a spotlight on the movement's at-times star-crossed relationship with democratic institutions. Although Obama's election has sparked widespread nostalgia about America's civil rights years, it has offered scant analysis of this watershed historical moment's relationship to Black Power.

But today many still wonder: What exactly was Black Power? At its peak during the late 1960s and early 1970s, Black Power touched every aspect of African American life in the United States. A wide range of the citizenship advocated a political program rooted in Black Power ideology, such as Black sharecroppers in Lowndes County, Alabama; urban militants in Harlem, New York; trade unionists in Detroit; Black Panthers in Oakland, California; and welfare and tenants' rights activists in Baltimore. A broad range of students, intellectuals, poets, artists, and politicians followed suit, turning the term "Black Power" into a generational touchstone that evoked hope and anger, despair and determination. But, in time, this aspect of Black Power was forgotten.

Now, Black Power is most often remembered as the civil rights era's ruthless twin. In most historical accounts of the 1960s, the civil rights movement represents the collective black consciousness of the postwar era. In these accounts, Black Power is then relegated as its evil doppelganger, having engaged in thoughtless acts of violence and rampaging sexism, and provoking a white backlash before it was finally brought to an end by its own self-destructive rage. The movement therefore emerges as the destructive coda of a hopeful era, a fever-dream filled with violent images and excessive rhetoric that ultimately undermined Martin Luther King Jr.'s prophetic vision of interracial democracy.[1]

Black Power represents the manifestation of the brute force and physical rage of the African American underclass. Because it is seen as being devoid of intellectual power, uncomfortable with nuanced debate, and wracked by miseries both seen and unseen, the movement's legacy is considered inconsequential at best and mindlessly destructive at its worst. Yet for a movement that is now reviled, Black Power's impact spanned America's local, regional, and national borders and beyond. It galvanized political activists in the Caribbean, Europe, Africa, Latin America, and much of the world. Regardless of this influence, much of Black Power's history remains obscure and undocumented. Skewed memory too often serves as a substitute for actual history.

Historians have only recently begun the long overdue process of rescuing the Black Power era, separating history from myth, fact from fiction. Black Power's origins and geography, activists and ideology, as well as its relationship to the civil rights movement remain pivotal to understanding postwar America.[2] Black Power activists not only operated in the civil rights movement's long shadow, they at times also participated simultaneously in both arenas. In fact, America's Black Power years (1954–1975) paralleled the golden age of modern civil rights activism, a period that witnessed the rise of iconic political leaders; triggered enduring debates over race, violence, war, and democracy; featured the publication of seminal intellectual works; and propelled the evolution of radical social movements that took place against a backdrop of epic historic events. Indeed, black militancy and moderation often fed one another, producing a combative ongoing dialogue between the two that provoked inspiration and anxiety as it also inspired both begrudging admiration as well as mutual recriminations.[3]

Black Power offered a fresh approach to struggles for racial justice. It redefined national racial politics even as local activists used it as a template for regional struggles. These efforts spanned Northern metropolises, Midwestern cities, Southern towns, hamlets out West, to California's eclectic political landscape. The movement's scope broadly impacted world affairs, and Black Power activists found inspiration in Cuba, hope in Africa, support in Europe, and the promise of redemption in the larger Third World. Moreover, the movement's call for social justice and robust self-determination appealed to a wide variety of multiracial and multiethnic groups, who patterned their own militancy after Black Power's rhetorical and aesthetic flourishes. Black Power's influence traversed oceans to impact struggles for racial justice and national liberation around the world.

Rethinking the contours of the Black Power era requires expanding the narrative of civil rights struggles in postwar American history. Conventional histories of the era concentrate on the years 1954 to 1965. These are the years that are bookended by the 1954 *Brown* Supreme Court decision and the 1965 Voting Rights Act, and they are seen as encompassing the whole—rather than part—of a messy and complicated history. This perspective, one that is now enshrined as public memory of the era, envisions these years as the movement's *heroic* period. For instance, it is during this period that cultural memory locates courageous civil rights workers who risked beatings, incarceration, and their lives to register blacks to vote. The truth is that both civil rights and Black Power contain a larger historical trajectory and a richer cast of characters than previously assumed.[4] In order to understand the complexity of this historical progression, we must revisit that journey and cast of players.

Both civil rights and Black Power have immediate roots in the Great Depression and the Second World War. If World War II signaled the defeat of fascism and the decline of European colonial empires as it also extended new freedoms to far corners of the globe, it also imbued black U.S. veterans and ordinary citizens with a sense of hard-fought political entitlement. Black Americans were among the fiercest partisans in the efforts to harness the political energies unleashed during wartime so as to secure new rights at home as well as abroad.

Spurred by massive migration, African Americans relocated to urban metropolises in staggering numbers, which turned New York's Harlem neighborhood into a black metropolis during the 1920s. Then, in the 1940s, the Great Migration's second act exploded in a rush of energy that was as ferocious as it was hopeful. In addition to this new energy, it was also in bracing numbers that eclipsed its earlier incarnation. Because of this, it was during this time that black Americans led a national movement for social justice that stretched from urban inner cities, to rural Southern labor factories out West, and all the way to the Bay Area cities of Oakland and San Francisco.[5]

National political activists such as Paul Robeson and W. E. B. Du Bois became icons of this age, which combined dynamic political action with cultural organizing that made the prospect for radical democracy in the United States seem inevitable. The war's freedom surge created unprecedented political alliances that featured the venerable National Association for the Advancement of Colored People (NAACP) in cooperation with Robeson's militant Council on African Affairs. Walking in lockstep with these new times was the eminent black scholar and civil rights activist William Edward Burghardt Du Bois. He headlined a broad coalition of human rights activists who placed optimistic faith in the United Nations as a harbinger for a new world.[6] Robeson and Du Bois served as internationally known luminaries of racial justice, even as grassroots movements were led at the local level by activists like Ella Baker, the NAACP branch director and future founder of the Student Non Violent Coordinating Committee (SNCC).

The black radicals who came of political age during the Great Depression and the war years preached a gospel of freedom whose resolute and at times strident message seemed inspired by Old Testament prophets. For instance, Asa Phillip Randolph emerged as the era's most powerful black labor activist, sparking a March On Washington Movement. He then used the threat of mass demonstration to coerce President Franklin Delano Roosevelt into issuing an executive order—though largely symbolic—banning segregation in the armed forces. This action then provided the historical context for a second March On Washington two decades later. Collectively, the black radicals of this time set an agenda for a new world order that sprang from aligning domestic struggles against Jim Crow with international crusades against fascism and colonialism.[7] But the advent of the Cold War would disappoint them.

Those early civil rights organizations who interpreted racism as an international issue looked toward the United Nations for help in defining human rights as a global movement that encompassed racial equality.[8] However, the 1948 Truman Doctrine's promise of a global movement to spread democracy engendered a hard peace through the threat of a worldwide atomic war. Cold War politics stymied the effectiveness of civil rights militancy and blunted the cohesiveness of civil rights coalitions. It was then during the years between 1954 and 1965 that America's new political center offered the carrot of desegregation and voting rights against the stick of red-baiting to a burgeoning Southern civil rights movement. Over time, African independence movements and the Cuban Revolution would complicate this arrangement. Both the civil rights and Black Power Movements drew inspiration from postwar freedom surges. The difference between them, however, was that while the Southern civil rights movement navigated within Cold War-designated boundaries, Black Power activists were inspired by the radical political struggles that abounded during the Great Depression and war years. Against the backdrop of the Cold War's political constraints that smeared desegregation efforts in the South was anti-Communist propaganda claiming that Black Power activists embarked on a dangerous course that openly embraced association with left-wing political forces both domestically and overseas.

Placing Black Power activism within the same contested political climate as civil rights struggles alters our standard conception of postwar African American history. Although civil rights and Black Power activists occupied distinct branches, they nevertheless remain part of the same historical family tree.[9]

Over the past three decades, America's postwar civil rights movement has become increasingly well known. Its signal events have been incorporated into the fabric of the nation's political and cultural institutions and historical memory through popular and academic histories, the King national holiday, and commemorative museums, films, documentaries, and television programs.

The Black Power Movement, on the other hand, has received far less attention, which should come as no surprise. Conventional wisdom indicts Black Power activists and organizations for, among other things, fueling a white backlash, aiding and abetting an electoral realignment built on Middle American resentment, and inspiring violent self-destruction of the New Left in the late1960s and early 1970s.[10] However, if we tap into the lower frequencies of the postwar era, we can see glimpses of a panoramic black freedom struggle in which Black Power militancy paralleled—and at times overlapped with—the heroic period of the civil rights era.

Early Black Power activists were simultaneously inspired and repulsed by those Southern civil rights struggles that served as a violent flash point for racial transformation. These early black activists laid the groundwork for the spectacular displays of racial militancy, cultural transformation, and political organizing that came to fruition during the late 1960s and early 1970s, when Black Power occupied the national stage. A generation of Black Power activists came of age and gained their first taste of organizing during the civil rights movement's high tide from 1954 to 1965. Though the grandeur and travails of their stories remain outside our national civil rights history, their influence profoundly affects the popular narrative nonetheless. In order to understand this movement's rich tapestry, it is important to see the underlying threads of its production.

The *Brown* Supreme Court desegregation decision in 1954 marked the beginning of two decades of political, social, and cultural revolution both within and beyond America's borders. More than a half century after this pivotal turning point, these years of domestic unrest and international transformation remain locked in a time warp. Popular history fondly remembers the first decade after *Brown* as a sepia-toned era ushered in by the prophetic witness of ordinary black citizens whose stubborn resolve was personified by Martin Luther King Jr. From this perspective, the years between 1954 and 1965 represent a uniquely American story of race, rebellion, and redemption. This period, then, was Reconstruction's more successful sequel where dreams of freedom, despite violent opposition, could prosper, grow, and reinvigorate the nation's extraordinary democratic experiment.[11]

In much of this narrative, King is cast as the doomed protagonist whose personal sacrifice illustrates American democracy's enormous resilience. America's mythology surrounding the civil rights era burdens King to the point of caricature and—perhaps even worse—abstraction. Unfortunately, King's eloquent calls for economic equality, his cosmopolitan worldview, and his courageous stances against war, militarism, and exploitation are all but forgotten.[12] Instead, we remember King as a stalwart Christian soldier whose dignified pleas for racial justice and genuine democracy signaled Jim Crow's death rattle.

As such, Malcolm X, Black Power's most enduring symbol, serves as King's historical counterpart and political foil. Malcolm's fiery denunciations of King as a feckless leader and the March On Washington as a "farce" have been presented as the complete portrait of his activism. Because of this, Malcolm's grassroots community organizing, supple political instincts, and brilliant intellectual analysis of race, democracy, and American domestic and foreign policy are ignored. Furthermore, Malcolm's very real relationship with civil rights-era radicals is rendered invisible, thus turning him into a one-dimensional and even cartoonish hero, isolated by his own rage and an artifact of a justly forgotten era. It is important to note that this characterization of Malcolm impacts King as well. While Malcolm's genius is discounted, Dr. King's political complexities are conveniently discarded so that he can assume the role of doomed hero. Though the simplification of Malcolm and Martin makes for a neat story, it's bad history.

The decade after the passage of the 1965 Voting Rights Act witnessed massive and at times brutally disruptive democratic movements in a style that continues to defy historical explanation and pat analysis. This political explosion emerged most visibly in the Black Power Movement. Although it was the cry for "Black Power" that broke through the commotion of ordinary politics in 1966, the sentiment behind the slogan long preceded Stokely Carmichael's defiant declaration.

Even before there was a group of self-identified "Black Power activists," African American radicals such as Paul Robeson, Lorraine Hansberry, Malcolm X, Robert Williams, Gloria Richardson, and William Worthy existed alongside more well-known civil rights activists in the black freedom movement. Although these Black Power activists subscribed to different interpretations of American history, racial slavery, and economic exploitation than their civil rights counterparts, the two movements grew organically out of the same era and thus they simultaneously inspired, critiqued, and antagonized each other.

Of the two movements, Black Power was more vocal and robust in its criticism of American racism and the failure of democracy. Black Power activists remained skeptical of democracy's capacity to extend full citizenship to African Americans while civil rights activists expressed steadfast faith in America's transformative abilities. Stokely Carmichael and scholar Charles Hamilton, in their classic 1967 treatise, *Black Power*, defined the movement as a series of political experiments that would produce black political, economic, and cultural power. Black Power's reach was global, spanning continents and crossing oceans, and its iconic personalities and organizations (some of whom were key civil rights activists) shaped debates about race, war, and democracy that still rage today.

The beginning of the Black Power Movement is usually seen as the mid-1960s. The 1965 urban upheaval in the Watts section of Los Angeles provides historians with a signal event that focused the nation's attention outside the South. Martin Luther King Jr.'s rough reception among Watts's poorest communities in the riot's aftermath, at least according to this narrative, opened his eyes to an unimaginable level of urban misery. King's subsequent activism in Chicago, where machine politics stalled his open housing and slum clearance efforts, are then interpreted as a harbinger of Black Power's growing influence in the urban North. Finally, SNCC's election of Stokely Carmichael in May 1966 and the next month's Meredith March in Mississippi is invoked as the organization's symbolic shift from civil rights to Black Power. The years of 1965 and 1966 seem to offer a perfect storm of rage and new tactics that derailed the civil rights movement just at its peak.

But there is another way to read these events. Years before Watts, racial violence gripped cities such as Oxford, Mississippi, Birmingham, Alabama, and Harlem and Rochester, New York. Though not flaring on the scale of Watts's massive destruction, these riots were dismissed as aberrations. But they were not anomalies. Postwar America found itself stripped of racial innocence long before the Watts rebellion.

Because of this popular narrative, however, Martin Luther King Jr.'s supposed transition to Northern civil rights activity remains misunderstood. King's journey to Chicago did not so much move civil rights politics north as publicize preexisting local struggles that continually revised and deepened his already sophisticated conception of racial justice, economic equality, and social progress. Northern militants, on the other hand, led by Malcolm X, viewed their own struggles for racial justice through different eyes. Black Power did not suddenly appear in Northern cities after 1965 as an alternative to civil rights activism. Instead, it existed alongside its more celebrated Southern-based counterpart. Though mutual antagonisms cut off black radicals from white allies and traditional civil rights leaders, on occasions both camps did form powerful—if provisional—alliances.[13]

Far from being evidence of radical change, SNCC's election of Stokely Carmichael as chairman represented the group's long-standing relationship to Black Power. Although SNCC has been rightfully credited as embodying a style of radical democracy that would influence the New Left and for providing intellectual space for burgeoning second-wave black and white feminists, its relationship to Black Power is more ambiguous, at least during its early history. Both Carmichael and SNCC came to adopt Black Power after bruising experiences in the civil rights movement. Though SNCC became Black Power's organizational face and Carmichael its most visible leader in 1966, the movement predated the organization's birth and Carmichael's adoption of the "Black Power" slogan.

Black Power's immediate origins can more accurately be traced back to the 1950s. It was during this time when, just as Southern civil rights struggles were making national headlines, Northern black activists (many of whom had come of political age during the Great Depression and World War II) formed important relationships with Malcolm X, the Nation of Islam's outspoken, controversial, and eloquent national representative. Malcolm had wisely searched outside the confines of the Nation of Islam for political allies. In New York and Detroit, he practiced his own brand of coalition politics through his association with non-Muslim activists such as John Henrik Clarke, John Oliver Killens, Grace and Jimmy Boggs, and Albert Cleage. These local militants stressed racial pride, the connection between civil rights and the Third World, and political self-determination through pugnacious and at times deliberatively provocative protests that laid the groundwork for Black Power.

Early Black Power activists were simultaneously inspired by the civil rights movement's efforts at direct action and repulsed by the racial violence in Southern civil rights struggles. The national press virtually ignored urban militants in the North, who waged their battles for jobs, equal access to education, and open housing far from the media spotlight. The struggle for racial equality in Northern cities evoked passionate spectacles, bursts of violence, and high drama that matched its Southern counterpart's unfolding intensity. Regardless of this similarity, urban America's modern race men and women (as nineteenth-century civil rights activists were often called), with their raw exhortation for political power, boisterous displays of cultural nationalism, and belligerent critique of white supremacy, seemed at odds with the quiet dignity of boycotters in Montgomery, Alabama.[14] Although Americans stayed riveted to television and newspaper coverage of the racial struggles in the South, they largely ignored its Northern counterpart. Apparently racial turmoil in the North's urban cities during the civil rights movement's heroic period represented a dismal picture most Americans didn't want to see.

By the late 1950s, Northern activists had formed a parallel movement with no name, comprised of urban militants who chafed at the growing spectacles of racial violence directed against civil rights groups and were cynical about American democracy's willingness to defend black citizenship. That cynicism was well earned. The sensibilities and political strategies of Northern militants were contoured by scenes such as Paul Robeson's ongoing and very public humiliations that stripped him of his passport and ability to make a living, W. E. B. Du Bois's arrest and sham trial for his purported ties to left-wing politics during the early 1950s, and memories of the broken American promises made during the buildup to World War II.

As a result, black militants in the United States became increasingly shaped by revolutionary movements that were changing the face of much of the world during that time. A primary example of this is the 1955 Afro-Asian Conference in Bandung, Indonesia, which incited black radicals in the United States. In fact, for much of his career, Malcolm X would invoke Bandung's efforts at Third World solidarity as the kind of "united front" politics required for successful black liberation efforts in America. Additionally, Ghana's formal adoption of independence on March 6, 1957, buoyed American black radicals who linked domestic freedom struggles with African decolonization.[15]

From this, in the 1960s, the influence of international politics on domestic racial struggles began to emerge as direct action. In 1961, after the assassination of Congo prime minister Patrice Lumumba, black militants, including Maya Angelou, Le Roi Jones (later Amiri Baraka), and Mae Mallory, unleashed bedlam at the United Nations' New York headquarters. Writer James Baldwin attributed this activity to growing black rage against Jim Crow and American racism while critics tried with little success to link the outburst to Communist subversion. The following year, radical black college students in Ohio formed the Revolutionary Action Movement (RAM), a group of black nationalists equally committed to socialism as well as armed self-defense. Though black nationalists made up an eager and early wing of Black Power activism, they were by no means its only participants. Civil rights activists committed to integration and racial solidarity, Communists and socialists, black feminists and trade unionists, students and preachers would all play a role in the movement that was expansive enough to reflect the enormous breadth of the black world itself. In California, activists associated with RAM founded *Soulbook*, a cultural magazine whose staff included future Black Panther Bobby Seale. In Motown, Detroit militants organized around the Group on Advanced Leadership (GOAL), who conducted controversial protests against urban renewal plans. Detroit's younger militants started UHURU (Swahili for "freedom"), a militant collective led by Luke Tripp. All of these local forces found a measure of unity and a national leadership in the figure of Malcolm X.

For all his very public provocations, Malcolm X represents nothing less than the civil rights era's invisible man. Malcolm remains offstage in most historical accounts of the era, entering only to dispute King and denounce America as an unapologetically racist and doomed land before he would finally succumb to personal and political trials by fire at the hands of the Nation of Islam—trials that would eventually lead to his assassination.[16]

Nevertheless, Malcolm remains the most important key to understanding the Black Power Movement's gestation. Malcolm is most frequently seen as an icon of racial militancy, a fiery spokesman for urban revolt, and an eloquent critic of white supremacy rather than as a grassroots leader. However, the emphasis on him as prophet of rage, calling out civil rights "Uncle Toms"—most notably Martin Luther King Jr.—unintentionally places Malcolm on the fringes of civil rights activism.

These misunderstandings partly result from Malcolm's legendary aura, which has been reinvigorated in more recent representations. In the late 1980s the rap group Public Enemy further boosted Malcolm's reemergence in black popular culture. Then, director Spike Lee's 1992 motion picture reintroduced the icon—if not the man—to a new generation. This phenomenon garnered street credibility for Malcolm as an icon through the brisk sales of "X" baseball caps, academic credentials via a reissue of *The Autobiography of Malcolm X*, and surprising mainstream acceptability through an official U.S. postage stamp.[17]

However, the Malcolm popularized by the autobiography and, to a lesser extent, Lee's movie, is both inaccurate and pervasive. Additionally, historians have, for the most part, mirrored the autobiography and film versions of Malcolm's life by largely ignoring his organizing during the 1950s, when he emerged as Harlem's most important grassroots political leader. Instead, the standard view of Malcolm finds him belatedly entering history only in 1959 via a sensational and nationally publicized documentary exposé on the Nation of Islam.

Malcolm, however, had been active long before this moment of public attention. When he arrived in Harlem in 1954, it still laid claim to its rich political and social legacy. During the first World War, New Negroes emerged and had helped reshape black America with a politics of cultural pride, racial dignity, and strategic organizing, embodied by the dynamic presence of Marcus Mosiah Garvey. Then, the Harlem Renaissance in the 1920s drew strength and energy from this radical movement by turning intellectual and artistic interest in black culture into a political sword and literary commodity. Consequently, residents of New York's black city-within-a-city still held onto a defiant dignity, one that the Nation of Islam's most creative and imaginative local organizer—the twenty-nine-year-old Malcolm X—tapped into.

If Muslim Mosque No. 7's West 116th Street address stood out as Malcolm's most visible organizational base, the streets of Harlem comprised a larger terrain for building dense political and social networks. Malcolm's efforts to build political connections in Harlem led him to Carlos Cooks and

Lewis Michaux. These men were stalwart black nationalists who kept the burning embers of Garveyism—the philosophy of political self-determination and racial solidarity made famous by Marcus Garvey—alive long past its heyday. Beyond Harlem's fertile terrain of black consciousness resided blacks who considered themselves independent radicals—and Malcolm courted these groups aggressively. Members of the Harlem Writers Guild, including John Henrik Clarke and John Oliver Killens, looked to Malcolm for renewed faith in radical politics. These were activists who had come of age during the war years, when a seemingly clear path toward revolution, proposed by a variety of left-wing groups (most notably the Communist Party), was thwarted by internal sectarianism and the intolerance of a national culture that vowed to preserve democracy at the expense of civil liberties. None of these individuals joined the Nation of Islam, and it's doubtful that Malcolm ever tried to recruit them. From his earliest entrée into Harlem, Malcolm deftly separated aspects of his religious and organizational commitments to the Nation of Islam from his larger ambition to institutionalize a revolutionary politics that went beyond the NOI's religious limitations, political restrictions, and creative imagination.

Malcolm's appeal went beyond the Nation of Islam to touch leading intellectuals and activists who would shape early Black Power struggles. For instance, journalist William Worthy was one of Malcolm's most important political allies during the early Black Power era. A pacifist jailed for his refusal to serve in World War II, Worthy traveled between some of the Cold War's hottest spots and the equally dangerous domestic civil rights terrain of the 1950s, including Montgomery, Alabama, during the 1955–1956 bus boycott. In 1957, he visited China, thereby defying State Department travel restrictions and promptly stirring up an international incident. Then, in the aftermath of the Cuban Revolution, Worthy frequently visited the island, writing a series of articles for the newspaper the *Afro-American*, documenting the revolution that was unfolding before his eyes. By the early 1960s, Worthy's call for a foreign policy guided by a human rights agenda became the cornerstone of his domestic Black Power activism.

Malcolm's interaction with influential black radicals like Worthy showcased both a cosmopolitan political outlook and pragmatic awareness. His outreach extended to leading cultural, intellectual, and artistic figures such as actors Ossie Davis and Ruby Dee, writers James Baldwin, Julian Mayfield, and John Killens, poet Le Roi Jones, and photojournalist Gordon Parks. All became political colleagues, acquaintances, or supporters of Malcolm, being impressed by his intellect, comforted by his humor, and surprised by his compassion.

Outside of New York City, Detroit played the most important role in Malcolm X's political development. Like Harlem, Detroit housed eclectic, seemingly incongruous, radical political tendencies that nonetheless managed to work together in creative tension. Central Congregation Baptist Church minister Albert Cleage Jr. became the face of the city's black militants during the early Black Power period. A black nationalist street speaker disguised as a Baptist preacher, Cleage's powerful sermons drew the dignified and the damned to his citywide pulpit. His key allies included Grace and Jimmy Boggs—grassroots activists, onetime allies of the legendary socialist C. L. R. James, and mentors to an entire generation of young militants, including RAM field chairman Max Stanford (later Muhammad Ahmed). Malcolm's ties to the city were both personal and professional. His brother Wilfred X served as Detroit's leading Muslim minister, a position Malcolm had helped to arrange. Local activist Milton Henry, who owned his own media company, would establish an especially close relationship with Malcolm and help broker an alliance with America's most powerful black radical.

The myth that radical black activism began around 1965 is undermined by a network of writers and artists who played major roles in the growing energy of the movement. For instance, James Baldwin's fierce artistic and literary independence allowed him to comfortably travel back and forth between the social and political worlds of both Malcolm X and Martin Luther King Jr. Baldwin's most famous book, 1963's *The Fire Next Time*, featured an essay (previously published in the *New Yorker* in 1962) that chronicled his dinner with Elijah Muhammad. Baldwin—a religious skeptic, literary maverick, and political cynic—enjoyed a cozy rapprochement with Muhammad, even as he refuted the racial cosmology that the Nation of Islam leader steadfastly preached. Casting himself as a contemporary Jeremiah, Baldwin predicted disaster for America if it failed to live up to its founding ideals of freedom and democracy: "Time catches up with kingdoms and crushes them," he warned. The book's critical and commercial success announced Baldwin as a political heretic unintimidated by the prospect of openly consorting with the NOI and unafraid to confess appreciative relief that the group's very existence forced America to wrestle with its soul. *The Fire Next Time* was a literary breakthrough that penetrated the far reaches of America's political consciousness.

Both Baldwin and writer Lorraine Hansberry navigated a political tightrope that allowed them, for a time at least, to associate with both Malcolm X and Martin Luther King Jr. In fact, Hansberry's political radicalism initially outpaced Baldwin's. The unanticipated success of *A Raisin in the Sun* turned Hansberry into a public intellectual capable of articulating jaw-dropping truths to powerbrokers unaccustomed to such blunt candor. It was this ability to speak truth to power that made her the talk of a well-publicized May 24, 1963, meeting with Attorney General Robert F. Kennedy, which was designed to gauge the pulse of the black community. This meeting was organized by Baldwin at Kennedy's request, and it also featured leading black cultural figures and entertainers such as Harry Belafonte and Lena Horne. However, it quickly turned into a shouting match in which a surprised and increasingly angry Kennedy withstood stinging verbal attacks, including this memorable confrontation with Hansberry: After Kennedy dismissed an angry outburst from a young civil rights worker, Hansberry rose to her feet and expressed feeling sick about the entire affair. Pointing to the young man Kennedy continued to ignore, she chided the Attorney General for his failure to listen.[18]

His unexpected role as Kennedy's uncontrollable emissary raised Baldwin's stature at the Attorney General's expense and earned him a growing list of admirers. Malcolm X counted himself as one of them, famously observing in his denunciation of the March On Washington that Baldwin was denied the right to speak at the event because he was "liable to say anything."[19] Malcolm openly admired Baldwin as a wordsmith capable of leaving white Americans off balance.[20]

If James Baldwin's *The Fire Next Time* and Lorraine Hansberry's *A Raisin in the Sun* represented radical literary manifestos, then Nina Simone's "Mississippi Goddamn," a scalding protest anthem that repudiated America's vigorous self-congratulation in the wake of the March On Washington, became their musical equivalent. Born in the rural South, Simone was a classically trained pianist who took the music world by storm in the early 1960s with a deft combination of blues, jazz, classical, and soul music. With political mentors that included Hansberry, Baldwin, and Langston Hughes, Simone's growing identification with the black freedom struggle's most radical elements placed her in the company of the same activists who participated in the 1961 UN demonstrations.

Following news of Birmingham's 16th Street church bombing in September 1963, Simone's "Mississippi Goddamn" expressed the stark political anger and critical consciousness that was poised on the black movement's outer edges. Judging America to be a "country full of lies," Simone issued grim warnings ("You're all gonna die like flies") more popularly associated with Malcolm X and the Nation of Islam. Headlining SNCC benefit concerts in the South as well as successful European tours, Simone proudly wore African dress, unabashedly proclaimed loyalty to the black movement's most militant sectors, and emerged as a powerful voice among African American radicals.[21]

Simone's criticism of civil rights liberals who preached patience was less a turning point in the civil rights era than a window into a world of radical black art and activism that would fire up the Black Power era.[22] Taken together, the writings and public intellectual activism of Baldwin, Hansberry, and Simone blur the neat demarcations that claim radicalism only occurred after 1965. The truth is that Malcolm's allies traversed easily and aptly between civil rights and Black Power activism, networks, and strategies and tactics.

Stokely Carmichael mirrored Malcolm X's high profile and polarizing public image. Born in Port-au-Spain, Trinidad, and educated at Howard University, Carmichael was elected SNCC chairman in the spring of 1966. He was tall, intellectually agile, handsome, and equal parts angry and gregarious. Whether he was in sharecropper's overalls, business suits, or leather jackets, he carried himself with an air of unadorned dignity and grace that helped turn him into an international icon: Black Power's rock star. His celebrity, rakish charm, and blunt words helped define the in-your-face style of the movement.

More than any other historical figure, Stokely Carmichael bridges and binds the civil rights and Black Power movements. In June 1966, during a late-spring heat wave, hundreds of protesters descended upon Mississippi for a march that was as much about outrage as it was civil rights. The demonstrators, led by Martin Luther King Jr. and Carmichael, had come to the Magnolia State to continue James Meredith's "March Against Fear" after Meredith had been shot on June 6. On Thursday evening, June 16, following his arrest for trespassing, an agitated Carmichael made his first Black Power speech. "This is the twenty-seventh time that I have been arrested," he proclaimed. "What we gonna start saying now is Black Power!"

From this, Carmichael defined Black Power as a movement that would allow blacks to take unfettered control of their personal lives and political destiny. He stated that, "It is a call for black people in this country to unite, to recognize their heritage, to build a sense of community. It is a call for black people to define their own goals, to lead their own organizations." For Carmichael, Black Power would be achieved through a series of political experiments that would bear fruit at the local level. Despite regional variation, Black Power would provide blacks with the basis for a new political identity and relationship to the larger nation.

The national media, however, seized upon Carmichael's declaration as the signpost of a new militancy. Immediately following the Meredith march, *Time* magazine judged the slogan "Black Power" to be "a racist philosophy" that preached segregation in reverse. *Newsweek* called it a "distorted cry" that was deeply frightening to white Americans. The *Saturday Evening Post* editorialized that the phrase would precipitate "a new white backlash," thereby provoking the magazine to starkly confess its own racial prejudices: "We are all, let us face it, Mississippians. We all fervently wish that the Negro problem did not exist, or that, if it must exist, it could be ignored." *U.S. News & World Report* agonized over the term's meaning, looking toward "Negro moderates" to allay fears of reverse discrimination. Almost as soon as it was uttered, a new wave of black aspirations, dreams, and dissent became encapsulated within one powerful slogan that would become as hard to define as it would remain controversial.[23]

Carmichael's call for "Black Power" obscured his own deep ties to civil rights and his long-term commitment to democratic struggles. Between 1960 and 1966, Carmichael belonged to the small fraternity of blacks (aligned at times with white allies) who willingly shed their blood in pursuit of radical democracy. A civil rights militant even when he was a teenager, Carmichael celebrated his twentieth birthday at Mississippi's notorious Parchman Farm prison after serving as a Freedom Rider. After this, his participation in protests would lead to dozens of arrests during the first half of the 1960s. Yet Carmichael's recent past as a local organizer in the Mississippi Delta and Lowndes County, Alabama, would be forgotten in the wake of his 1966 call for Black Power.

Like Malcolm X, Carmichael gained his early political bearings organizing blacks at the local level. In the Mississippi Delta, Carmichael encountered deep poverty, harsh living conditions, and courageous souls. Forever indebted to the example of heroic resilience, dogged perseverance, and fierce dignity of black Mississippians, Carmichael staked his personal future on a quest to politically empower sharecroppers. However, racial progress experienced consistent delays in the form of political assassinations, random violence, and federal indifference.

Informed by his experiences organizing in the South, Carmichael believed that moral persuasion would ultimately prove fruitless: Only raw political power would purchase black freedom. Local people themselves—and not Northern white volunteers, national civil rights leaders, or elected officials—would have to shoulder the costs. By 1965, Carmichael was living and organizing in one of Alabama's remotest regions: Lowndes County. It was there that Carmichael tapped into indigenous political activism to help create a local movement that would seek to elect black officials while bypassing both the Democratic and Republican parties. The Lowndes County Freedom Organization would be nicknamed the Black Panther Party and, over time, come to symbolize the defiant spirit of Black Power.[24]

Carmichael's image at the 1966 march marked Black Power's first moment of public recognition. Carmichael's antiwar activism, punctuated by chants of "hell no, we won't go!" made him the era's most vocal antiwar leader in the months leading up to Martin Luther King Jr.'s famous call for peace at New York's Riverside Church in the spring of 1967. Furthermore, as he became convinced that black Americans' quest for a nation could only be successful if Africa were restored as a world power, a quest for a deeper racial solidarity would, by 1968, find Carmichael embracing pan-Africanism. By the late 1960s, Black Power activists, through antiwar protests, self-defense organizations, and expressions of cultural pride and racial solidarity, fed the growing civil unrest in America as they simultaneously changed its very expression.

Carmichael's civil rights organizing in rural Lowndes County, Alabama, would lead to the formation of the Black Panther Party. The Lowndes County Freedom Organization's quest for radical self-determination through the vote gave the Oakland-based Panthers their name and *raison d'être*.[25] Thus, although the symbol of the panther first appeared in Lowndes County, it would be forever associated with urban militancy out of Oakland. In May 1967, after stepping down as chairman of SNCC, Carmichael vowed to return to grassroots organizing in Washington, D.C., the site of some of his youthful activism as a Howard student. Then, on May 25, Carmichael headlined a fund-raiser for the Black Panther Party for Self-Defense at San Francisco's Fillmore Auditorium.

This Black Panther Party was comprised of loquacious urban militants who lacked the rich experiences that propelled Carmichael's activism. Carmichael's organizing of local sharecroppers in Lowndes County, Alabama, successfully propelled the Black Panther concept to regions outside of the rural South. The Oakland-based Panthers traded bravado for experience, substituting showmanship—complete with shotguns, pistols, and bandoliers— in order to publicize an embryonic antiracist agenda that would soon transform America. In the process, the Black Panthers ignored critical aspects of the political organizing that inspired their very existence. Carmichael's slow, patient, and radical organizing in obscure Lowndes County, Alabama, lent the Bay Area group distinctly Southern roots. In 1968, Carmichael began a short-lived alliance with the Oakland Black Panthers before leaving the United States to settle in Conakry, Guinea (his favorite stop on his global tour), where he lived, in between speaking tours in the United States, until his death in 1998.

In spite of these shortcomings the Black Panthers, with Carmichael's assistance, soon came to represent the face of the new radicalism. They took on the role of modern-day surrealists with the ability to imagine a world not yet in existence, but one that they could will into being. Comprised of reformed troublemakers, college students, and ex-cons, the Panthers brandished guns and law books in an effort—sometimes quixotic—to foment revolution from below.

Their personal lives and limited professional opportunities were shaped by Oakland's impoverished landscape. Perhaps as a result of this they saw themselves organizing the contemporary "Field Negroes" that Malcolm X defined as the black working class. Huey P. Newton, the seventh child of a preacher and a housewife who were transplanted to Oakland from Louisiana, fit this description perfectly. Huddled in the offices of the North Oakland Service Center in October 1966, Newton dictated the party platform while Bobby Seale, his slightly older, equally driven, but more practical friend and cofounder, jotted it down. The Black Panther Party's ten-point manifesto, issued in 1966, called for black self-determination, decent housing, education, and the end to police brutality and exploitation in the ghetto.

For a time it all seemed to work. The party's modest infrastructure did not prevent it from making a splash in Oakland's local political landscape. Organized patrols of Panthers followed police officers during the group's earliest days, earning a reputation for audacious courage. In the winter of 1967, Huey Newton faced off against the cops outside of *Ramparts* magazine's San Francisco offices. The confrontation took place after police were called to the scene and warned the armed Panthers to drop their weapons. After Newton refused, the possibility of a shoot-out seemed imminent until police withdrew. Later, Eldridge Cleaver would trace his membership in the group to this tense moment outside of *Ramparts* when Newton displayed "the courage to kill" for the revolution. Then, on May 2 of that same year, Newton pulled off a dangerous publicity stunt by directing a convoy of thirty Panthers (twenty-four men and six women) to the state capitol in Sacramento. The ensuing commotion propelled the Panthers above the crowded thicket of California's burgeoning Black Power scene. The national attention garnered by the group's Sacramento adventure included fund-raisers headlined by Stokely Carmichael (several Panthers had been incarcerated following the Sacramento incident), major journalistic profiles that helped turn Newton into a revolutionary antihero for a new age, and inquiries from activists eager to start their own chapters.

But the group's greatest impact came, improbably, through the arrest and subsequent murder trial of cofounder Newton. The Panthers rallied around Newton, who was charged with killing an Oakland police officer. In the winter of 1968, Stokely Carmichael headlined two raucous "Free Huey" rallies in Oakland and Los Angles that, over two days, turned Newton and the Panthers into youthful symbols of a revolutionary age.

But the revolution that the Panthers so confidently predicted did not go off as planned. The group's role as a revolutionary party of urban outlaws committed to the violent (if necessary) overthrow of the U.S. government undermined its ambitious community empowerment efforts—which included free breakfast for children, health care, and food giveaways. Legal repression from the criminal justice system would persist long after the group's ability to disrupt, let alone overthrow, the federal government.

By the early 1970s, the Panthers were financially crippled, physically harassed by federal surveillance, and burdened by the descent of once-promising leaders into self-destructive behavior, corruption, and abuse—highlighted by factional splits and Newton's escalating drug abuse. They had retreated back to Oakland as a local group engaged in community organizing (including a stab at local elections as Bobby Seale ran for mayor and Elaine Brown the city council) that seemed far removed from their daringly romantic beginnings.

T hus, the travails of Carmichael and the Black Panthers contributed to Black Power's maturity. It came of age in the early 1970s in the grassroots political organizing of a diverse group of activists. The national black political convention held in Gary, Indiana, over three days in the late winter of 1972 represented the movement's high point. At this event, intellectuals, trade unionists, feminists, students, black nationalists, Marxists, and civil rights leaders across a wide ideological spectrum came to Gary in order to outline a political program that demanded nothing less than radical democracy. Progressive agendas that addressed poverty, failing public schools, crime, urban renewal, and support for African independence movements marked the convention.

Hailing from a wide range of backgrounds that reflected Black Power's generational and political diversity, Gary mayor Richard Hatcher, Michigan congressman Charles Diggs, and black nationalist leader and poet Amiri Baraka served as the convention's coconveners. Elected in 1967, Hatcher served as Gary's first black mayor, and his commitment to progressive politics made him stand out on the far left of even his most liberal congressional colleagues. Diggs's pro-Africa sentiment made him perhaps the leading congressional figure placing pressure on the United States to divest from oppressive regimes in Rhodesia and South Africa. Baraka's political activism dated back to his 1960 tour of Cuba with Robert Williams and his arrest, early the next year, at the UN riot. By 1965, in the aftermath of Malcolm X's assassination (and at that time still named Le Roi Jones), Baraka founded the innovative and short-lived Black Arts Repertory Theater and School in Harlem. By the early 1970s, he had changed both his name and his political outlook. Baraka became an urban activist in Newark, New Jersey, and a national political leader comfortably sharing political stages with elected black officials, charismatic young civil rights activists such as Jesse Jackson, and African revolutionaries ranging from Amilcar Cabral to Julius Nyerere.

These alliances shed light on Black Power's complex relationship to the civil rights movement. Inspired in part by the same legacy that buoyed civil rights activists, Black Power advocates took the notion of righting historical wrongs to a new level. Black Power emerged alongside civil rights activism during a moment of national racial crisis that was pregnant with world historic possibilities. Postwar American prosperity, with its expansive promise of middle-class contentment, home ownership, and educational opportunity, largely excluded the very generation of blacks who helped to enable the nation's dazzling progress.

But African Americans responded in different ways to America's postwar landscape. On the one hand, Southern civil rights activists during the 1950s advocated a brand of social justice that, although dramatically scaled back from the radical politics of the 1930s and 1940s, retained elements of World

War II-era racial militancy. On the other hand, Black Power activists embraced a different radicalism altogether, one that promoted self-reliance, internationalism, and cooperation among blacks. Although some were more effective as political activists and others better at grabbing headlines, Black Power radicals ultimately discovered—just as their civil rights counterparts had—that there were no easy or quick solutions to America's racial crisis. Civil rights activists and Black Power militants both confronted a society unwilling to extend full citizenship to blacks. Rancorous debate over strategies and tactics and differing interpretations over the meaning of freedom and citizenship should not obscure the way in which both movements dialogued and, at times, inspired one another. Activists from one camp just as often shifted to the other, and a dual commitment to both tendencies existed in individual persons and organizations. Both movements dreamed of redefining American democracy but would, instead, settle for exposing rough truths about racial justice, social transformation, and economic equality. Consequently, in spite of the mutually expressed hostilities exchanged between the two movements, there remains a shared poetic symmetry that briefly transcended political differences as it ultimately transformed the very landscape of race relations.

Black Power's demise as a national movement coincided with America's deepening urban crisis that would unfold coast to coast over the next decades. In the 1970s and 1980s, African Americans took political control of metropolitan centers at the very moment that cities were—due to federal neglect, shrinking tax bases, and loss of industries—made most vulnerable to crime, poverty, and failing public schools. Although we will never know how a thriving Black Power movement might have confronted the soaring gang violence, crack epidemic, and poverty that gripped large sectors of the African American community during the late 1970s and 1980s, Black Power activists helped ease the often heartbreaking transition from the hopeful Great Society rhetoric of the 1960s to the conservatism ushered in by the Reagan revolution of the 1980s.

The movement, therefore, was more than a series of shoot-outs, race riots, and provocative sound bites. In fact, beginning with its remaking of black identity, Black Power transformed America's racial, social, and political landscape. In an age when the majority of blacks were still referred to as "Negroes," were ashamed of their natural hair texture, and loathed association with the African continent, Black Power reimagined the possibilities for both black identity as well as American democracy. But if its confrontational posture quickened the pace of racial change, it likewise provoked a visceral reaction in white Americans who, almost overwhelmingly, could more easily identify with civil rights activists than Black Power militants.

More than forty years after the Meredith march, we can now better assess Black Power's impact on American society. For instance, during the late 1980s and early 1990s, a new generation of rap musicians and hip-hop artists deployed Black Power icons as symbols of racially conscious and historically resonant political defiance. In particular, rap group Public Enemy helped introduce the movement's legacy to a new generation with anthems like "Fight the Power!" However, although hip-hop reports a reality from the street in the form of urban violence, drug abuse, and ennui that is neglected by the mainstream media, it also revels in the sexism, commercialization, and materialism that characterized the worst aspects of the Black Power era.

In some spectacular instances, Black Power and hip-hop share bloodlines. Black Panther Afeni Shakur's son, Tupac, became a groundbreaking hip-hop artist and, after his 1996 death, an icon as well. As the child of a Black Panther, Tupac came of age in an era seemingly bereft of the type of political movements that had inspired his mother. But the connections between urban poverty, racism, and economic inequality that gave the Panthers their *raison d'être* likewise became a motif for some of his most poignant, controversial, and successful music.

Thus, Black Power's impact remains powerfully resonant—however fraught and contentious it may be. As a generation of black politicians, artists, and intellectuals have channeled the new black identity it first articulated in diverse and varied ways, the movement's importance for a contemporary generation of black Americans can hardly be overstated. Black Power's unflinching call for self-determination, promotion of black history and culture, pan-African impulses, and radical critique of American democracy remains as timely as ever. Furthermore, echoes of the past continue to abound in present-day issues of mass incarceration of African Americans, an unpopular war overseas, and escalating examples of institutional racism.

Malcolm X, Stokely Carmichael, and the wider Black Power movement have been overshadowed by annual celebrations of martyrs, icons, political legislation, and landmark court cases commonly associated with the civil rights era's heroic period. Although civil rights struggles are rightfully acknowledged as having earned black Americans a historic level of dignity, Black Power accomplished a no less remarkable task, fueling the casually assertive identity and cultural pride that marks African American life today. Yet few Americans of any age, race, and ethnic group have a sense of Black Power's achievements, failures, and continued legacy. This is unfortunate.

Black Power reminds us of democracy's experimental, consistently embattled nature and the high price that blacks and others have paid in efforts to ensure its qualified success. It also brings us closer to understanding the now largely forgotten violence, anger, rage, and mistrust that marked race relations during much of the twentieth century. Black Power not only reveals the depth of the era's despair over poverty, war, and racism, but it also better illustrates the breadth of African American radicalism in the postwar era. Ultimately, Black Power accelerated America's reckoning with its uncomfortable, often ugly racial past. In the process, it spurred a debate over racial progress, citizenship, and democracy that would scandalize as it would also help change America.

Politically, Black Power marked the emergence of militants who, as local powerbrokers, partially helped facilitate the rise of a new generation of black elected officials. The movement's politics included a cultural ethos that redefined black identity by promoting defiantly popular images of racial pride and self-determination. It waged a war of attrition in order to implement Black Studies programs and departments in higher education; establish independent schools, education centers, cultural centers, and think tanks; and become the forerunners to contemporary discussions of diversity and multiculturalism. The new black politics featured alliances between elected officials and black nationalist militants, and a cultural movement that used art to expand black consciousness and help forge an international legacy that viewed African liberation as the crown jewel of a global revolution. In turn, this planted seeds that partially inspired post-Black Power-era anti-apartheid activism. If civil rights worked from the outside-in by paving the way for legal and legislative reforms, Black Power worked in reverse, imbuing the race consciousness and pride within African American communities upon which much of contemporary black identity is based.

Thus, Barack Obama's audacious presidential candidacy, invigorating campaign, and stunning victory reflects the contours of Black Power's contemporary legacy, relationship with civil rights struggles, and enduring impact on America's national racial dialogue. But while Obama invoked the civil rights era throughout his campaign, he largely ignored Black Power (with the exception of one passing reference that chided critics for focusing on identity politics at the expense of larger, more pressing issues). Yet without the Black Power Movement's combatively robust efforts to refashion the politics of citizenship, identity, and democracy, Obama's candidacy, campaign, and election could not have occurred. Black Power allowed American citizens of African descent, perhaps none as notably as Obama, to be rooted in the black community without being narrowly defined by it.

2

MALCOLM X, HARLEM, AND AMERICAN DEMOCRACY

> Whenever a Negro fights for "democracy," he's fighting for something he has not got, never had and never will have.
>
> —MALCOLM X, 1964[1]

"We respect authority, but we are ready to fight and die in defense of our lives," Malcolm X once told reporter Louis Lomax.[2] The resolution behind these words provides insight into the remarkable political journey, personal travails, and intellectual evolution of Malcolm X. For Malcolm, the right to self-defense animated a larger quest for black political self-determination, one that he vigorously pursued in the Nation of Islam. Through the course of his political career that spanned over a decade, Malcolm publicly criticized American democracy as being unable to guarantee black citizenship and protect the lives of civil rights activists.

Malcolm Little was born in Omaha, Nebraska, on May 19, 1925, to a family who would soon be shattered by the death of Malcolm's father, Earl Little. A political activist and part-time preacher, Earl followed the black nationalist teachings of Marcus Garvey, an activity that strained the family's financial resources and personal strength. Though mainly an urban phenomenon, Garvey's advocacy of black self-determination also inspired residents in Southern and rural parts of the United States.[3] Malcolm remembered his father's death as a lynching at the hands of local white terrorists. Malcolm's mother, Louise Little, experienced bouts of mental illness that forced her eight children to lead scattered lives bereft of the safety and security provided by family.

Malcolm's memories of the Little family's spiral into poverty and humiliation would haunt him for the rest of his life. So would images of Earl Little, strong and fierce, passing out pictures of Marcus Garvey at sparsely attended Universal Negro Improvement Association (UNIA) meetings in Lansing, Michigan, that attracted blacks brave enough to listen to taboo discussions of racial pride and black power. The fact that family lore attributed Earl's death to his militant crusading made less of an impression on Malcolm than the swaggering, larger-than-life aura of bravado that his father exuded while alive.[4]

For a time, the big city underworlds of Harlem, Detroit, and Boston served as surrogate homes for the teenaged Malcolm. He was precocious enough to be voted class president in junior high school, yet sensitive enough to feel panic and alienation after a white teacher, with one racial slur, dismissed his dream of becoming a lawyer. The danger that Malcolm encountered during his subsequent descent into a sordid world of urban crime, drugs, and vice approximated—albeit in a decidedly misguided manner—the more political threats that his father had faced. But Malcolm's subsequent incarceration for burglary in 1946 would lead to personal redemption and a political transformation after encountering the teachings of the Nation of Islam (NOI).

While a convict in Massachusetts from 1946 to 1952, Malcolm joined the Nation of Islam. In joining the group, Malcolm was, at least partially, following in his late father's footsteps. The NOI had been organized after the heyday of the Garvey-inspired nationalism of the post-World War I New Negro. As such, it advocated personal dignity, economic self-determination, and organizational discipline in service of an unorthodox interpretation of the Islamic faith as defined by a semiliterate wise man called Elijah Muhammad (nee Elijah Poole).

Thus, Garvey's and the NOI's distinct approaches coincided with each other in ways that would have a profound effect on Malcolm's evolution into a radical activist. While Marcus Garvey advocated the recovery of suppressed historical truths about ancient African kingdoms in order to uplift blacks in America, Muhammad substituted religious prophecy for fact and characterized whites as "devils" created by a renegade black scientist named Yacub. Furthermore, the NOI's rise coincided with Malcolm's growing involvement with the groups in the mid-1950s. Spotting Malcolm's potential, Muhammad became a father figure who allowed his younger protégé creative space to turn the NOI into an international phenomenon. Hierarchical and patriarchal, the NOI demanded strict allegiance from its members who were required to hawk newspapers, pay a numerous array of religious dues, abstain from drugs and alcohol, and regularly attend Mosque. The group's well-trained security force, named the Fruit of Islam (FOI), stood tall and erect at Mosque services and rallies and lent the group's public events an air of military authority. With a relatively tiny stronghold in Detroit (where Muhammad founded the first mosque) and Chicago, the NOI sprouted a limited following in inner cities and small but faithful groups of believers scattered in prisons across America. To the uninitiated, the Nation could be written off as an odd group of religious kooks, a throwback to Depression-era black politics when virtually every community seemed to be bursting with self-proclaimed prophets. However, federal authorities were less dismissive. FBI agents would observe with increasing anxiety the Nation's growth from the margins of black urban life to a central feature of national race relations. By 1957, the Bureau placed Muhammad under state-of-the-art surveillance that included telephone wiretaps and miniature listening devices.

But what the Nation offered for Malcolm was both spiritual nourishment and concrete professional opportunities. In 1952, for the first time in his life, Malcolm found a vocation (as a Muslim minister) that he actually enjoyed. Like many working-class black men of his generation, Malcolm suffered long bouts of unemployment in between a string of unsatisfying menial labor jobs. Prior to his incarceration, from 1941 to 1944, Malcolm was a railroad car porter and waiter in Boston, the Bronx, and New York City.[5] At Charlestown State Prison in Massachusetts and, later, Concord State Reformatory and Norfolk Prison Colony, Malcolm worked in a woodshop, coal warehouse, and machine shop, where he produced license plates.[6] After being paroled on August 7, 1952, Malcolm moved to Inkster, an all-black working-class Detroit suburb, where he lived with his older brother Wilfred and sold furniture in Detroit. In January 1953, Malcolm experienced a brief stint as a line worker at the Ford Wayne Assembly Plant before finding work as a grinder at the Gar Wood furniture factory in Detroit.[7] That fall Malcolm's itinerant laboring continued, this time in Philadelphia's dockyards.

From personal experience, Malcolm now had gained an unvarnished portrait of the black working class. For most of his public career, both critics and supporters marveled at Malcolm's ability to connect with ordinary black men and women. Although many attributed this to personal charisma, in fact Malcolm's life had made him intimately acquainted with the hopes, aspirations, and bitterness of the black working class.[8]

Malcolm then transformed himself from a criminal into a working-class hero. Between 1952, when he was released from prison, up until his untimely assassination on February 21, 1965, at the Audubon Ballroom in New York City, Malcolm X served as a community organizer, national political mobilizer, and an icon of racial justice. Malcolm's years of political activity paralleled extraordinary historical events, ones that he profoundly influenced at the local, national, and later, the international level. Yet the depth, breadth, and scope of Malcolm's impact on America's postwar years remains largely ignored.

During America's heroic civil rights struggles of the 1950s and 1960s, Malcolm X led bold efforts to redefine the tenor and geographical terrain of black politics. In doing so, he invented a new language of political activism whose urgent rhetoric gave voice to the modern movement for Black Power. As Black Power's most powerful spokesperson Malcolm confronted the contradictions, flaws, and shortcomings of American democracy in speeches, lectures, and interviews that represent one of his most important legacies.

As a Muslim minister, Malcolm confronted the contradictions of American democracy in his fiery sermons. Malcolm began to lead Harlem's Muslim Mosque No. 7 in June 1954—one month after the *Brown* desegregation decision. The appointment was a reward for Malcolm's tireless efforts to resuscitate the NOI's faltering Detroit temple and his establishment of Muslim Mosque No. 12 in Philadelphia in March.[9] In his sermons in Philadelphia, Malcolm had tested out the themes of race, democracy, and anticolonialism that would become rhetorical trademarks in subsequent years. Malcolm held up Kenya's Mau Mau rebellion and Vietnamese resistance against French colonialism in Indochina as examples of a growing tide combating white supremacy at the international level. He compared President Eisenhower to an Egyptian pharaoh, foreshadowing a line of attack against sitting American presidents that would one day lead to his departure from the NOI.[10]

For Malcolm, democracy's jagged edges of poverty, police brutality, and squalid living conditions were starkly measured in the racial and class composition of African Americans. In 1955, the Nation's Philadelphia Mosque FBI informants reported that Malcolm "analyzed the word democracy" and judged it to be "the rule of evil" that promoted misery and death in the black community.[11] From this and throughout his career, Malcolm would continue to vociferously argue that nothing short of a black revolution would fundamentally transform a political system he regarded as being intrinsically corrupt.

Furthermore, by the early 1950s Malcolm had developed into a talented and effective community organizer. Between 1954 and 1957, against a national backdrop of school desegregation campaigns, the Emmet Till lynching, the Montgomery, Alabama, bus boycott, and the Little Rock, Arkansas, school crisis, Malcolm X helped to organize NOI strongholds in Detroit; Chicago; Hartford, Connecticut; Washington, D.C.; and Philadelphia.[12] Equally important, Malcolm also forged alliances with secular radicals in all of these cities. Crafting relationships with a wide array of militants helped Malcolm's profile develop beyond the confines of the Muslim world and into the wider arena of African American politics.

When he was named Muhammad's national representative in 1957, Malcolm began serving as the Nation's chief strategist, main recruiter, and organizational architect. That same year, he addressed the Little Rock desegregation crisis from Detroit.[13] In Malcolm's words, "the entire black world" was watching America's civil rights struggles unfold. Recalling his recent visit to the United Nations, he described African diplomats who decried the racist treatment of black Americans. Malcolm connected local black concerns with rapidly unfolding global events. In this way, like a history professor before a large lecture hall, Malcolm challenged his audience to develop a more nuanced appreciation of the racial ramifications of America's Cold War-driven foreign policy.[14] He dissected the legacy of chattel slavery, the impact of racial segregation, and the humiliation of urban poverty with surgical precision, biting wit, and a kind of verbal flair that expertly combined the sacred and the profane. Because of his oratorical command, over time audiences for his speeches grew, stretching from Harlem's 116th Street Muslim Mosque No. 7 to jam-packed university auditoriums and giant outdoor rallies. Impeccably groomed, tastefully dressed, and as well mannered as he was eloquent, Malcolm's imposing personal appearance (he stood six feet, three inches) magnified his growing political stature.

Though Malcolm's primary apprenticeship was with the Nation of Islam, which imparted mental and physical discipline that honed his prodigious mind and untapped skills, Malcolm's second apprenticeship came courtesy of Harlem itself. It was a city within a city, where legendary street speakers such as Carlos Cooks and Lewis Michaux provided insight into black nationalism, political organizing, and institution building. Harlem's political terrain became a lab where Malcolm experimented with organizing methods, collaborated with local activists, and surveyed a national landscape being reconstructed by civil rights insurgency. He applied these lessons first in Harlem, and, over time, across the United States and around the world.

Malcolm X first entered Harlem's consciousness after an act of police brutality against Nation of Islam member Johnson X had left New York City poised on the edge of racial violence.[15] On April 26, 1957, white police officers brutally assaulted Johnson X. James Hicks, managing editor of the *New York Amsterdam News*, contacted Malcolm to mediate sensitive negotiations between law enforcement and Harlem community representatives in hopes of avoiding a riot. On the surface Malcolm X seemed a most unlikely diplomat: an ex-convict barely five years removed from jail who now led the local temple of an unorthodox group of Black Muslims. But through past association with New York City's criminal underworld, Malcolm knew the streets of Harlem like few of his political contemporaries.

Two standoffs took place that evening. The first, outside the 123rd Street police precinct in Harlem, took place between police and a crowd who had been agitated by rumors about Johnson's grave physical condition. It ended only after police agreed to move the imprisoned Muslim to Harlem Hospital. Then, for fifteen blocks, Nation of Islam members marched in formation down one of Harlem's busiest thoroughfares—Lenox Avenue—a sight that inspired an even larger crowd outside of Harlem Hospital, where the second standoff began. After one police official told him to "Get those people out of there," Malcolm declined. He was aware that the Fruit of Islam followed a precise chain of command that frowned upon freelance retribution that an incited crowd might unleash. "I politely told him," recalled Malcolm, "those others were his problem."[16] Malcolm's charismatic presence, along with the disciplined actions of NOI members, helped to avoid further violence. With a few words and a gesture to one of his lieutenants, the Black Muslims dispersed. The crowd quickly followed suit, and a major crisis was averted.

The Johnson case became inextricably attached to Malcolm's growing legend. The black press proved instrumental in this regard, with the *New York Amsterdam News* publicizing the Black Muslims as genuine freedom fighters. This countered white newspapers' depiction of the group as violent and dangerous. Thus, in the story's aftermath, the Black Muslim phenomenon was officially born.[17] "The *Amsterdam News* made the whole story headline news," Malcolm remembered, "and for the first time the black man, woman, and child in the streets were discussing 'those Muslims.'"[18] Malcolm's deft handling of the Johnson X case demonstrated the NOI's growing political strength.

Though it was once an obscure group of religious nationalists founded during the Great Depression, the Nation now fit comfortably into Harlem's eclectic postwar political milieu. Here, Communists, black nationalists, trade unionists, liberals, and socialists all jockeyed for political power. The NOI, however, dismissed overt political action and impugned standard protests of boycotts, pickets, and marches. Instead, they favored an ethos that promoted rugged self-determination—in the form of black entrepreneurship, diligence, and community control—as the key to genuine black empowerment. Because the NOI avoided political activism, Malcolm was unable to directly participate in political demonstrations, and this would impact his political development. As the civil rights struggles swelled and marches and pickets spread across the country, the Nation's ban on participation in conventional politics increasingly seemed especially archaic. Publicly Malcolm presented the Nation's political reticence regarding demonstrations as a symbol of black self-reliance.

On this score, black dignity therefore emanated from within the African American community and would be earned through racial uplift strategies rather than "handouts" from white politicians and powerbrokers. Bootstraps rather than ballots, then, served as the NOI's point of departure for black power in urban centers across the nation. Religious prophecy further fueled this message of personal responsibility. Elijah Muhammad's teachings offered blacks redemption if they were intelligent and disciplined enough to follow. Consequently, as unconventional religious believers and maverick black nationalists, the Nation of Islam positioned itself as a community of fresh faces among a Harlem landscape teeming with militant groups.

The early rumblings of the civil rights movement's heroic years paralleled Malcolm's political organizing in Harlem. In contrast to the Nation of Islam's bleak portrait of black life in the United States, civil rights leaders vigorously extolled the citizenship rights of black Americans. Southern civil rights activists regaled against a system of Jim Crow that was invested in dramatically visible symbols that served to separate blacks from whites in public life. Civil rights activists and black leaders promoting the virtues—indeed the necessity of—racial integration displayed a stubborn faith in the resiliency of American democratic traditions.

However, Northern black activists in Harlem did not share this faith. Harlem's poorest sections featured raw, unfiltered misery that manifested itself in the foreboding shadows of dark alleys, across garbage-strewn sidewalks, and inside tenements. There, random violence, alcoholism, drug addiction, and hunger shaped the lives of thousands of residents. In this way, New York proved to be the ideal city for Malcolm X's political growth and intellectual development. Harlem's aching despair, poignant dignity, and mischievous pride made the neighborhood particularly attractive to the NOI's rugged brand of social reform. Decaying storefronts, trash-strewn alleys, and open vice dotted Harlem street corners. Senseless violence, routine poverty, and creeping apathy stalked the lives of Harlem residents. Out of this, Malcolm X then cast the Nation of Islam and the teachings of Elijah Muhammad as a tangible oasis amid a searing urban wilderness.

As Malcolm searched for inroads among Harlem's most vulnerable communities, Martin Luther King Jr. emerged as the young leader of the successful bus boycott in Montgomery, Alabama. In short order, King's strategy of Gandhian nonviolence became the lynchpin behind a new movement that made deft use of his status as a black preacher. On top of this, his approach gained national recognition for the black church as the headquarters for African American respectability and community. However, long-standing black militancy in the Deep South nonetheless existed in tandem with King's eloquent call for nonviolence, and this reflected a diverse political terrain where the competing rhetoric of King and Malcolm X both found fertile soil in which to take root.[19]

Contemporary media interpretations and subsequent historical narratives would posit King and Malcolm as dueling political leaders waging an epic political struggle for the hearts and minds of black Americans. In this telling, Malcolm argued for black identity as the soul of a worldwide political revolution, and Martin countered with prophetic words that imagined a beloved community where engaged citizenship could transcend racial divisions. Such a reading of the two men misses the way in which Malcolm's and Martin's rhetoric and activism infuriated, antagonized, and yet inspired each other.

Both Malcolm and King played close attention to one another's regions and activities. Civil rights demonstrations bubbling up in the South provided Malcolm with tangible evidence of mass discontent in the black community and offered him poignant examples of black solidarity in service of social and political transformation. Urban unrest in the North revealed to King the depth of black poverty, anger, and despair in ways that helped to shape his evolving political thought and would impact his future organizing.[20]

However, Malcolm was hardly alone in his quest for a revolutionary politics that would transform the black freedom movement. Black radicals in the North combined militant local protests with a pragmatic pursuit of political power that was attuned to national and global developments. These activists found a complex measure of inspiration in racial struggles being waged in the Deep South. By the late 1950s, led by Malcolm X, they had formed an unnamed parallel movement that was cynical about American democracy's willingness to protect black citizens. This movement, with its varied expressions at the local, regional, national, and global levels, was more than just a mélange of black nationalists, civil rights renegades, and iconoclastic radicals. And it was here, within these radical circles, where cynics and optimists intersected in Harlem, Detroit, and elsewhere, that Black Power was forged.

Civil rights and Black Power grew out of postwar freedom surges. In the South, civil rights activists responded to racial segregation by advocating for voting rights and an end to Jim Crow. Black Power activists embraced militant anti-racist protests that included combative demonstrations. In spite of the differences between the two movements, many activists found themselves drawn to, and participating in, both.

Both movements sought to re-imagine the very shape and tenor of American democracy. Ultimately both helped to transform contemporary American race relations. But the failure to acknowledge Black Power's immediate roots in the postwar freedom struggle and its early fermentation under Malcolm X's leadership perpetuates the mythology that the movement represents nothing more than the civil rights era's destructive, violent, and ineffectual sibling—a horrific doppelganger that practiced politics without portfolio and successfully thwarted more promising movements for social and political justice.

Even Malcolm's most ardent admirers tend to characterize him as a man ahead of his time. They see him as a prophet unrecognized in his own country and held political hostage to the period's overwhelming allegiance to nonviolence and gradual racial reform. Most, however, fail to recognize that Malcolm had been more than a charismatic militant. In fact, Malcolm was the leader of a national movement for Black Power that took on new dimensions and a mass public expression—but only after his assassination.

Malcolm X's and the larger Black Power Movement's impact, political importance, and historical legacy remain crucial to understanding the full depth and breadth of African American postwar freedom struggles. From his early political development under the tutelage of some of Harlem's leading nationalists to his deft relationship with the media as well as more enigmatic ties to Adam Clayton Powell Jr., Malcolm proved to be one of the most versatile political leaders black America has ever produced. The national controversy stoked by the Nation of Islam catapulted him to undreamed-of political heights and unprecedented opportunities that helped to satisfy his large intellectual appetite. From his first trip to Africa in 1959 to his final visit there five years later, Malcolm's interest in world affairs grew equal parts radical and pragmatic. Meetings with Fidel Castro, Kwame Nkrumah, and other global figures turned Malcolm into black America's unofficial ambassador. Meanwhile, Harlem would remain as close to a permanent political base (first through Muslim Mosque No. 7's 116th Street headquarters and later the Hotel Theresa and Audubon Ballroom) as he would ever have.

Malcolm's political development, therefore, did not emerge in a simple or linear manner. Instead, it was nurtured by a diverse network of activists and organizations whose efforts paralleled, and at times intersected with, civil rights struggles. Furthermore, Malcolm's radicalism, most often couched as a prelude to the climactic black awakening during the 1960s, took initial shape during the 1950s against the backdrop of Southern civil rights insurgency and global anticolonial movements. Chronicling the Black Power Movement's early origins, activism, and political debates and defeats in Malcolm X's Harlem (a world that shaped and was shaped by civil rights activism as well), then, moves us closer to a more nuanced, complicated, and historically accurate portrait of not simply a man, but the period that shaped his political struggles.

Both before and after the Johnson X incident, Malcolm spent much of his time and energy working as a local organizer in some of Harlem's roughest corners. An uncanny combination of personal brio, rhetorical eloquence, and strategic brilliance provided Malcolm with the organizing edge necessary in order to stand out on Harlem's competitive street corners. Additionally, his political instincts favored broad coalitions to promote racial solidarity that are not often associated with sectarian leaders.

The search for new recruits made Malcolm dig deep for the singular phrase, historical example, or biographical insight that could turn a curiosity seeker into a member of Mosque No. 7. Malcolm saw ordinary citizens, upstanding members of Christian churches, and participants leaving rival black nationalist rallies as fair game. Between 1954 and 1959, he and his envoys patrolled the edges of race-conscious rallies with handbills advancing the Nation of Islam's call for self-determination. This then served as a prelude for "fishing" expeditions at storefront churches whose working-class constituents might prove receptive to aspects of Malcolm's message.[21] "I had learned early one important thing," Malcolm later recalled, "and that was to always teach in terms that people could understand."[22] At times, this meant appealing to the black women who frequently poured out of Harlem's Christian church services. They were greeted by bow-tie wearing Black Muslims, including Malcolm, who extended the NOI's protective shield in an offer of respect and protection for black women.[23]

Malcolm X's self-assured public demeanor and private displays of humor enthralled not only the rank-and-file potential converts but also Harlem's leading figures.[24] Through actor Ossie Davis, he developed important relationships with the city's black intelligentsia. Impressed by Malcolm's brilliance and sharp wit, Davis and his wife, Ruby Dee, introduced him to a group of friends and associates who included writers Lorraine Hansberry and Julian Mayfield.[25] Furthermore, Malcolm purposefully brokered alliances with the infamous: individuals tainted by allegations linking them to Communism and racial and political black extremism. Davis, along with John Killens and Julian Mayfield, approximated the behind-the-scenes support that Martin Luther King Jr. enjoyed in public from movie stars such as Sidney Poitier and Harry Belafonte.[26] Privately, they formed a group of influential advisors who would serve as Malcolm's intellectual inner circle.

Malcolm's personal charms also generated a positive relationship with the press, which led to improving coverage of his activities from a variety of sources. As a result, his high profile propelled him beyond the Nation of Islam into a larger world that introduced him to influential journalists such as William Worthy, Louis Lomax, and Alex Haley. Worthy, a correspondent for the *Baltimore-Washington Afro-American*, frequently covered the Nation of Islam for newspaper and magazine stories marked by their unusual level of depth and complexity. One of the most important black journalists of his generation, Worthy's professional relationship with Malcolm would also turn into a personal friendship.

If Worthy's radical politics made him particularly receptive to Malcolm's charms, however, Lou Lomax would be a tougher project. He would come around only after covering the NOI for several years. Bespectacled, inquisitive, and erudite, Lomax cut his journalistic teeth exposing the Black Muslims before a national television audience in the 1959 Mike Wallace-narrated documentary *The Hate That Hate Produced*. The documentary's scathing portrayal of the NOI and Malcolm X unintentionally produced the first major intraracial civil rights controversy—and in the process it also turned the group and its charismatic spokesman into national celebrities. The public's appetite for information about the once-obscure religious group increased exponentially, as did opportunities for any journalists who had intimate knowledge of the Nation's inner workings. In short order, Lomax became a national expert on the Nation of Islam, and he would even later collaborate with Malcolm X on the 1963 book *When the Word Is Given*.

Alex Haley, whose political sympathies ran considerably to the right of both Worthy and Lomax, would shape Malcolm's legacy in ways unimaginable at the time. Both Worthy and Lomax (and even James Hicks) seemed better suited to write Malcolm's autobiography, at least in terms of sharing Malcolm's radical political sympathies. Primarily organized and edited after Malcolm's death, *The Autobiography of Malcolm X* would indelibly transform Malcolm's legacy for a popular audience, fundamentally casting Malcolm as a lost soul haunted by familial tragedy, a criminal past, and service to a corrupt leader, whose ultimate redemption was found only after acknowledging the potential for interracial brotherhood.[27]

Black newspapers, including the *New York Amsterdam News*, *Pittsburgh Courier*, *Chicago Defender*, *Los Angeles Herald Dispatch*, and *Baltimore-Washington Afro-American*, reported on the growing specter of the Nation of Islam when mainstream journalists ignored the group. Malcolm, for his part, took note, stalking the offices of the *Amsterdam News* and other publications, determined to create a national organ to disseminate the NOI's worldview.

In the December 22, 1956, edition of the *Pittsburgh Courier*, Malcolm published an early essay discussing his religious and political beliefs. The article's title, "We Have Risen From the Dead," succinctly captured Malcolm's unwavering declaration that his life had been transformed, like Paul on the Damascus Road, through his commitment to the Nation of Islam.[28] Arisen from "the grave of ignorance,"[29] Malcolm then embarked on a mission to spread the gospel of black nationalism and political self-determination through some of the era's leading black newspapers.

By 1958, black newspapers such as the *Los Angeles Herald Dispatch* carried Malcolm's column, "God's Angry Men." In an early essay, Malcolm characterized Elijah Muhammad as the heir to Marcus Garvey's global movement for self-determination. According to Malcolm, Garvey's efforts to imbue "a Black nationalist spirit" into the African American community were stalled due to racial treachery. Thus, the NOI represented the living, rather than posthumous, embodiment of Garvey's largest mass black movement in American history.[30]

Malcolm's public image gradually took shape in the year after the Johnson X incident, partially fueled by the popularity of "God's Angry Men." Ultimately, Malcolm's media contacts planted the seeds for one of the Nation's most profitable and important enterprises: *Muhammad Speaks*. In the late 1950s, Malcolm served an ad hoc apprenticeship at the offices of the *Los Angeles Herald Dispatch*, determined to reach the widest possible audience. Trained by the paper's most exacting administrator, he learned the skills that would help him create *Muhammad Speaks*.[31]

In 1957, Malcolm delivered a series of special lectures in Detroit as part of a successful effort to reinvigorate the Motor City's NOI Mosque, which included having Elijah Muhammad appoint Malcolm's brother Wilfred as head minister. During an August meeting, attended by over 4,000 people, Malcolm criticized President Eisenhower for failing to advocate strong civil rights legislation. He then went on to blame ineffectual and weak black leadership's inability to capitalize on black voting power—power that had the potential to turn the tide in national political elections.[32]

As a result, local black militants unaffiliated with the NOI found a kindred spirit in Malcolm. The city's black political culture featured militant Christian ministers, black socialists, youthful revolutionaries, and advocates of self-determination who were unimpressed with the civil rights movement's philosophy of nonviolence. From this, Detroit's leading black radicals would form deep and lasting alliances with Malcolm. Reverend Albert Cleage Jr., minister of the Central Congregation Baptist Church, served as the spokesman for Detroit's "New Guard." A fiery preacher and master orator, Cleage was at once a respected civic leader as well as a rabble-rouser who berated the city's black leadership as too timid to pursue raw political power. Brothers Richard and Milton Henry were local organizers and activists with an entrepreneurial streak. Through Milton's personal friendship with Malcolm, the city's radicals were given direct access to America's leading black militant. Luke Tripp founded the radical group UHURU (Swahili for "freedom") and became the leader of the city's young militants. James and Grace Lee Boggs were practically folk heroes to a generation of young militants. James's job as an auto worker lent gravitas to his theoretical speeches and books about race and class, while his Chinese American wife and political partner held a PhD in philosophy from Bryn Mawr and possessed formidable intellectual and organizing abilities.[33] This national network of informal associations helped to create the movement that would later be known as Black Power.

In the late 1950s, Malcolm was in the process of developing a cosmo-politan worldview that was as expansive as those he would more forcefully enunciate in the year after he left the NOI. In the spring of 1958, during a speech in Los Angeles, Malcolm concluded his address by connecting racial oppression in Mississippi with independence struggles in the Third World.[34] Through this and other similar observations, it is evident that Malcolm's extensive international vision, usually couched as occurring only after his break from the NOI in 1964, actually permeated his entire political career.

However, Malcolm's cosmopolitan perspectives did not preclude sniping at competitors. With the NOI's modest infrastructure, membership, and resources being dwarfed by the black church, Malcolm launched well-orchestrated attacks against African American ministers, characterizing them as charlatans and bottom-feeders who exploited long-standing racial tension and turned Negroes into "satisfied, sanctified beggars."[35] The black press ate it up. The *Pittsburgh Courier* ran headlines stating that, "Malcolm X Blasts Negro Ministers!" after one particularly rough indictment, and the *Miami Times* announced Malcolm's plans to organize Muslims in Florida.[36]

But if newspaper reporters shaped much of the black world for public consumption, powerbrokers, such as Congressman Adam Clayton Powell Jr., ruled it. An old-fashioned politician who rose to become Harlem's most important elected official, Powell was a cunning dealmaker, shrewd legisla-tor, and beloved symbol of national black political power. Reports of Pow-ell's womanizing, drinking, and at times ethically questionable financial dealings made him a kind of folk hero among Harlemites, who reacted to the latest news of his exploits with the glee of witnessing a rakish showman and master entertainer.

Malcolm X and Powell personally bonded over shared reputations as ex-traordinary political showmen, dazzling public speakers, and unapologetic political mavericks. Malcolm spoke at Powell's Abyssinian Baptist Church in Harlem, and the two established an alliance that withstood rumors of dissen-sion over which man wielded more influence over Harlem politics. Mutually providing each other with establishment legitimacy and street credibility, Malcolm and Powell cultivated a pragmatic political alliance.[37]

Malcolm's rapprochement with the Christian Powell represented a dé-tente in his rhetorical war against the black church. Best remembered for his pungent attacks against Martin Luther King Jr. in the early 1960s, Malcolm's skirmishes with black preachers actually dated back to the 1950s. As part of Muhammad's efforts to establish a Muslim stronghold in Los Angeles and the larger West Coast, Malcolm delivered a series of well-attended lectures in Los Angeles in the spring of 1958. These included sharp attacks on black Christian ministers, some of whom walked out of one particularly harsh sermon.[38]

However, Malcolm's growing notoriety also led to elevated scrutiny from the authorities. In 1958, the FBI designated Malcolm a "key figure."[39] NOI plans to establish mosques in the South and throughout the West Coast prompted special concern from Bureau officials.[40] For the rest of his public life, Malcolm's every move would be under strict surveillance by both federal authorities headquartered in Washington, D.C., New York City's Bureau of Special Services (BOSS) unit, and international emissaries from the State Department and other agencies during his trips around the world.

If Harlem was changing during the 1950s, so was much of the wider world. In particular, the 1955 Afro-Asian Conference in Bandung, Indonesia, represented a world historical event. Imagining a world free from the dictates of the United States and the Soviet Union in favor of self-determination by previously colonized nations, Bandung audaciously promoted indigenous self-rule. Calls for Third World solidarity that were unleashed at the Bandung conference would in turn be echoed by Malcolm X (who did not attend the conference) over the course of his career.

Africa represented a key part of the Bandung conference's hopes to reshape the world. Perceived by both American and Soviet interests as a continent vulnerable to Cold War intrigues, Africa plotted its own course of independence through indigenous movements for self-determination that gripped the continent. Then, the arrival of Ghanaian independence in 1957 suggested an African renaissance was well under way. Harlem, with a rich history of black nationalist street-speaking and pan-Africanist organizing that stretched back to the New Negro, greeted African independence with cheers. American officials, however, responded more cautiously. They crafted an imaginative strategy for African diplomacy that both publicized and exaggerated domestic racial progress in hopes of spreading democracy in the region, forestalling Communism, and defending against assertions that Jim Crow practices rendered America unfit to preach democracy to the rest of the world.[41]

Ghana's prime minister, Kwame Nkrumah, made dreams of a revolutionary new Africa seem tantalizingly real. Nkrumah's promise to "show the world" that Africans could take the "lead in justice, tolerance, liberty, individual freedom and social progress" seemed especially encouraging. This was particularly poignant given his singular relationship with black America, having been educated at Lincoln University in Pennsylvania.[42]

Ghana mesmerized black radicals and moderates alike. Radicals viewed Ghana as the potential spark that could move Africa toward a continental-wide insurgency, one that would ultimately trigger a global revolution powerful enough to meaningfully impact American racism. Moderates, on the other hand, adopted a more pragmatic outlook. Instead, they were hopeful that Ghana's newfound stature would pressure the United States into making both symbolic as well as real inroads toward racial progress.

Harlem basked in the reflected glory of Nkrumah's rise. In return, Nkrumah personally invited skilled blacks committed to Africa's restoration to help build a new nation. Around two hundred African Americans would respond to this call, which led to the establishment of an expatriate community in Ghana that included Harlem radicals such as Julian Mayfield and Maya Angelou, as well as the ninety-three-year-old W. E. B. Du Bois. Malcolm would visit Ghana's community of expatriates in May 1964—less than two years before the fall of Nkrumah's political kingdom. Upon his arrival, he was welcomed as a prodigal son returning to Africa.[43]

The black press helped to amplify Harlem—and the rest of black America's—pan-African impulses by meticulously chronicling independence movements surging across Africa. Nkrumah, as well as other prominent African leaders, became instant icons of revolution and self-determination, presented by black radicals and moderates as positive proof of racial progress. Recapping the year's events, the *Amsterdam News* declared 1957 as the "Year Negroes Fought Back" and held up independence celebrations in Accra, Ghana, as one of the year's most important events.[44] Then, Nkrumah's trip to Harlem on Sunday July 27, 1958, served as an unofficial coronation of sorts. Returning to Harlem for the first time since being elected Ghanaian prime minister, a beaming Nkrumah rode in an open car, flanked by New York City mayor Abe Stark, as 25,000 Harlemites lined the streets.[45]

In 1959, Malcolm X and the Nation of Islam became a national phenomenon. *The Hate That Hate Produced*, a five-part *News Beat* documentary broadcast during the week of July 13, ignited the civil rights era's first intraracial controversy.[46] Having been given unprecedented access to the Nation of Islam, black reporter Louis Lomax, along with an all-white camera crew, filmed never-before-seen aspects of the organization.[47]

The documentary pointedly characterized the Nation of Islam as a group of idiosyncratic and potentially violent hate-mongers. America's first glimpse of the NOI featured the foreboding image of thousands of Muslims at a Washington, D.C., rally. In this footage, tens of thousands of members filled Washington's enormous Uline Arena that attested to the NOI's organizational strength. Interviews with Malcolm X and Elijah Muhammad further bolstered narrator Mike Wallace's claims that the "Black Muslims" represented a dangerous, understudied, and increasingly threatening facet of America's racial life. Malcolm X, addressing an "African Freedom Day" rally in Harlem, underscored *News Beat's* chilling claims that the Muslim movement had penetrated the heart of black America.[48]

As *The Hate That Hate Produced* aired, Malcolm was touring Africa for the first time, where he was making arrangements for Elijah Muhammad's planned *hajj*. From the Kandarah Palace Hotel in Saudi Arabia, Malcolm issued dispatches for the black press describing his visit to the Lower Nile Valley in Egypt, Khartoun's Upper Nile, and the Sudan. "The people of Arabia know more about the color problem, and seem even more concerned and angered by the injustice our people receive in America than the so-called Negroes themselves," he wrote.[49]

Though he acknowledged the multicultural nature of racial ethnicity in the Middle East, Malcolm nonetheless discounted the many white Arabs he encountered. He claimed that "none are white" and "99 per cent of them would be jim-crowed in the United States of America."[50] In the service of making an unassailable point about America's racial segregation, however, Malcolm would keep silent about the region's multicultural and multiethnic origins—only to claim a belated discovery of these diverse roots after his second tour five years later. If America once represented the New World, Africa, wrote Malcolm, "is the land of the future," filled with exhilarating possibilities and a fate in which black Americans "are destined to play a key role."[51] In the Sudan, he marveled over the fact that "[r]acial disturbances in faraway New York City, U.S.A., occupied prominent space on the front pages" of African newspapers.[52] The visit to Africa, where he toured the Middle East and met with Egyptian leaders Gamal Abdel Nasser and Anwar Sadat, transformed Malcolm. [53] In Africa, much to his delight, he discovered mutual bonds of trust borne out of shared histories of racial oppression. Furthermore,

Malcolm was acutely aware of America's obsessive quest to maintain a global image of democracy within the context of the Cold War. Because of this, his dispatches from Africa pointedly characterized domestic racism as the Achilles' heel of U.S. foreign policy, one that black activists needed to exploit in their quest for racial justice.

Although Malcolm became an international figure, he still retained close ties to local organizing. In certain instances, in fact, he openly flouted the Nation's dictate of nonparticipation in political demonstrations. In 1959, away from the glare of the national spotlight, Malcolm lent his support to black and Puerto Rican trade unionists of Local 1199. In the midst of an unprecedented 46-day, 7-hospital strike waged by 3,500 workers, he joined the "Committee for Justice to Hospital Workers" that included labor leader A. Philip Randolph and NAACP executive secretary Roy Wilkins.[54] Thus, despite his growing fame, Malcolm maintained a passionate commitment to New York City's local politics.

By the end of the 1950s, Malcolm X's political radicalism was transforming the landscape of black activism. For instance, civil rights activist Robert F. Williams visibly manifested the political rage to which Malcolm gave eloquent voice. Head of the NAACP's Monroe, North Carolina, chapter, Williams confronted the local Ku Klux Klan with militant words and deeds. By leading skirmishes against the Klan with armed civil rights activists, debating the merits of self-defense versus nonviolence, and forging alliances with activists across a wide political and ideological political spectrum, Williams became the South's most controversial civil rights activist.

Tall, broad-shouldered, and confident, the imposing Williams became a national celebrity in 1959 after a violent assault of a black woman in Monroe by a white man. In response, Williams recklessly suggested that he would be "willing to kill if necessary," which led to a six-month suspension and eventual break from the NAACP.[55] Rebuffed as intemperate and ill-advised by civil rights moderates—including Martin Luther King Jr.—Williams turned to Harlem for political support. It was only there that he found kindred spirits.

Activists associated with the Harlem Writers Guild, the Nation of Islam, and others lent Williams their prestige, raised money to support activism in Monroe, and introduced him to new contacts. Harlem activist Mae Mallory helped organize "Crusader Families," who took their name from Williams's mimeographed newsletter, *Crusader*. Designed as an effective means to detail events in Monroe that would be unfiltered through the national press, *Crusader* subsequently became a vehicle that distilled feelings of black nationalism, revolutionary internationalism, and radical democracy. Like Malcolm X, although Williams's political activities were in many ways unique, they were also—at least in certain quarters—quite common.

Previously hidden connections between domestic racial struggles and African independence movements were embodied in the political activism taking place in Harlem and the militancy of certain artists like Lorraine Hansberry. In addition to being a protégé of Paul Robeson—who came of age during the Cold War's early and suffocating infancy—Hansberry came under the tutelage of W. E. B. Du Bois in Harlem. She quickly became a force among the community's cultural workers. Hansberry's *A Raisin in the Sun* was a brilliantly nuanced portrait of black family life on Chicago's south side that mesmerized mainstream audiences and critics alike. The play's bracing verisimilitude made the subjective transcendent, elegantly creating a world that was both fiercely personal and poignantly universal. In Hansberry's prose, Jim Crow's shattering impact on black life existed alongside dreams of self-determination that stretched from Chicago's racially segregated south side all the way to Africa. Furthermore, she claimed ties to Harlem through Paul Robeson's influential, although short-lived, early 1950s periodical *Freedom*.[56] One of the world's most celebrated and respected singers and political activists during the 1940s, Robeson's influence in Harlem, if not corresponding to his national stature, proved resilient against Cold War repression that revoked his passport for close to a decade and smeared him as a traitor. Consequently, through Robeson, Harlem's "University of the Streets" helped teach Hansberry that even luminaries could be ruined. But it also introduced her to activists, such as Harlem Writer Guild stalwart John Oliver Killens, who would help shape her literary and political pursuits.

A Raisin in the Sun plumbed the depths of a style of black cultural nationalism that would become associated with a second generation of Black Power militants.[57] Nationalist themes of robust self-determination and dreams of African independence paralleled the Younger family's efforts to secure the American Dream. These pursuits, for many critics at least, overwhelmed *A Raisin in the Sun's* more radical aspects. A blockbuster analysis of race, democracy, and the very meaning of postwar America, the play elegantly transcended Cold War-era racial myths and social fictions.[58] If Malcolm X served as the avatar for Black Power during the 1950s, Hansberry represented one of the movement's earliest and most eloquent literary voices.[59]

In the summer of 1959, Malcolm X returned to Harlem after visiting Africa. However, he arrived in the middle of the storm of controversy generated by *News Beat*'s Black Muslim documentary. The visit to Africa, where he toured the Middle East, transformed Malcolm. He had met with Egyptian leaders Gamal Abdel Nasser and Anwar Sadat. What Malcolm discovered was that there were "hordes of intelligent Africans" who were unmoved by American propaganda extolling domestic racial progress, therefore penetrating what Malcolm described as a "veil of global diplomatic art."[60]

Although black newspapers had followed Malcolm's tour of Africa with keen interest, the white press had ignored him. Alternately demonized or ignored by white press outlets and lacking editorial control over black coverage, in response Malcolm created the newspaper that would become one of his most important legacies. *Muhammad Speaks* would become the leading black radical weekly newspaper during the early 1960s. Offering coverage of civil rights struggles, labor and rent strikes, and political revolutions raging across much of the Third World, *Muhammad Speaks* would prove to be unconventionally bold and sophisticated in its coverage of insurgent racial unrest around the world. But Muhammad's control over the paper would push its founder, Malcolm, increasingly into the background. Ultimately, *Muhammad Speaks*, with a weekly circulation that exceeded half a million by the mid-1960s, would become a lucrative enterprise that came to help institutionalize the NOI in urban centers across the United States.[61]

Furthermore, in the aftermath of the Mike Wallace documentary, Malcolm spearheaded the NOI's damage-control efforts. He traveled around the country enforcing tight discipline and organizational control over mosques that were seen as shaky. These mosques were conducting numerous radio and television interviews defending Muhammad and the Black Muslim movement, as well as providing handpicked reporters such as William Worthy intimate access to meetings.[62]

Contrary to the documentary's judgment, however, the entire affair proved a financial and public relations boon for Malcolm and the Nation of Islam. Malcolm X's legend, burnished by a prodigious speaking schedule, would soon flourish—as would the organization's entire infrastructure. The *News Beat* documentary successfully characterized the NOI as hate-mongers in the eyes of white America. But blacks viewed the media blitz through different eyes, with a small vocal minority expressing unabashed admiration for the group, while the majority of African Americans offered little more than silent respect.

In the winter of 1960, at the very moment that four black college students ignited the direct action phase of the civil rights movement by sitting in at a lunch counter in Greensboro, North Carolina, Malcolm X escalated his own rhetoric. During the first three months of the year, he engaged in a series of high-profile debates, lectures, and rallies, where he castigated mainstream civil rights leaders and defended the Nation of Islam.[63] At Boston University, Malcolm pointedly discussed the NOI's penchant for using the word "black" instead of "Negro" to describe African Americans. "No matter how light or dark we are," insisted Malcolm, "we call ourselves 'black'—different shades of black, and we don't feel we have to make apologies for it!"[64] During a Yale University debate with NAACP national youth secretary Herbert Wright, Malcolm criticized the "brainwashed, white-minded middle-class minority of Negroes" seeking integration.[65] Malcolm and Wright would continue their debate several months later at City College, where the NAACP activist charged Malcolm with promoting a "bigger and better form of segregation." The Muslim leader countered with a demand for reparations in the form of cash and land. "It'll take more than a cup of tea in a white restaurant," noted Malcolm ruefully, "to make us happy."[66]

Then, in Atlanta, Malcolm confronted Kennedy advisor and Harvard University historian Arthur Schlesinger during a question-and-answer session. After the professor compared Black Muslims to white supremacists, Malcolm, identifying himself only as "a muslim," asked Schlesinger to prove the charges. Schlesinger then cited William Worthy's recent *Esquire* article, "The Angriest Negroes," as evidence. "But sir," replied Malcolm, "how can a man of your intelligence, a professor of history, who knows the value of thorough research, come here from Harvard and attack the Black Muslims, basing your conclusion on one, small article in a monthly magazine?" After Schlesinger asked if he had read the article, Malcolm answered affirmatively, noting that in the article the professor himself blamed the rise of the NOI on white racism. Schlesinger retorted that he still thought the NOI represented a "dead end," but now wished "to change the subject to something other than the Muslims."[67]

If Malcolm's unexpected presence briefly rattled the eminent Harvard historian, he found equal delight in debating with college professors at planned events. A two-and-a-half-hour debate with Morgan State University professor August Meier drew 1,000 students who alternately cheered and booed Malcolm's biting allegations against President Kennedy, white supremacy, and racism. Whites were only trying to help blacks out because "they know their ship is sinking," advised Malcolm. Meier, who would go on to be a pioneering professor of Black Studies who happened to be white, conceded that while Malcolm offered compelling points, Meier still struck fast to his commitment to racial integration.[68]

In 1960, Malcolm grew from being the Nation's intellectual emissary to becoming a diplomatic one as well. On Monday, September 19, 1960, the Cuban Revolution arrived in Harlem. Led by Fidel Castro, the Cuban delegation descended upon the Hotel Theresa's stunned owner and operator, Love B. Woods. But controversy surrounded Castro's unexpected arrival. The midtown hotel originally booked by the Cubans accused the delegation of uncivilized behavior even as Castro leveled charges of racial bigotry.[69] Malcolm then met with Castro while the media speculated that the Cuban leader switched to Harlem's modest but historic Theresa Hotel only to fan local flames of racial discontent.

However, in many ways Harlem had been anticipating Castro's arrival for almost two years. In the aftermath of the January 1, 1959, Cuban Revolution, black radicals in Harlem emerged as some of the island's biggest boosters. Members of the Harlem Writers Guild, including John Oliver Killens and John Henrik Clarke, helped form the Fair Play For Cuba Committee in an effort to provide unbiased media coverage of the revolution. Additionally, Robert F. Williams embarked on two tours of Cuba during the summer of 1960 with a delegation of leading black writers joining his second trip. Thus, connections between Harlem and Havana had been cultivated at the grassroots level long before they became enshrined in legend through a meeting between icons.

Malcolm X and Fidel Castro's meeting positioned Harlem at the center of Cold War intrigue. As they chatted through a Spanish translator, a photographer snapped pictures of the two men sitting at the edge of a bed. The intense conversation included snippets of Malcolm's typically blunt remarks. "I think you will find," he said, "the people in Harlem are not so addicted to the propaganda they put out downtown."[70] Malcolm and Fidel's conversation served as a preparation of sorts for the Cuban leader's upcoming UN speech. Though Malcolm beamed at Castro's remark that "we in Latin America are all African Americans," Castro politely declined Malcolm's invitation to eat at the NOI's Harlem restaurant. The Cuban leader explained that they prefer to "eat all our meals here in the hotel" so as to prevent further media eruptions.[71] All the while, FBI surveillance observed Malcolm and Fidel's meeting with intense interest.

Publicly, Malcolm rejected attempts to connect him to Communism, maintaining that he had the freedom to associate with whomever he pleased.[72] However, the black press reported Malcolm and Castro's meeting as a bombshell political development, while white journalists greeted the entire event as a Communist-orchestrated spectacle.[73] The *New York Times* portrayed Castro's visit as a public relations stunt and characterized Malcolm as "a leader of the so-called Muslim movement among United States Negroes."[74]

Besides Malcolm, Castro received a host of dignitaries at the Theresa, including Egyptian president Gamal Nasser, Soviet premier Nikita Kruschev, and a contingent of black radicals associated with Fair Play. Recognizing America's vulnerability regarding Jim Crow, Castro made race the central focus of his visit. In order to underscore this point, he consorted openly with black Cuban commandante Juan Almeide, who was flown from Cuba only *after* Castro came to Harlem. African American radicals, some of whom had witnessed Cuba's march toward racial equality firsthand, relished the unfolding spectacle.

Followed everywhere by journalists, photographers, and onlookers, the gregarious Castro's wide smile and effusive demeanor charmed Harlem's black community. Describing Harlem as an "oasis in the desert," Castro was celebrated at the Hotel Theresa while President Eisenhower played host to Latin American delegates at the Park Avenue Waldorf Astoria Hotel. Content to mingle with the "poor and humble people of Harlem," Castro enjoyed a reception hosted by Fair Play that featured enthusiastic African American supporters. Journalist William Worthy, who managed to find time to cover both domestic and international racial crises, covered Castro's visit from Havana in defiance of travel restrictions.[75]

Castro's presence in Harlem turned its 125th Street corridor into New York City's most congested area. Harlem residents stood outside the Theresa in hopes of catching a glimpse of him, as did members of the Harlem Writers Guild who led chants of "Viva Castro" amid the blare of Spanish music.[76] Meanwhile, Castro stoked controversy through expressions of admiration for Harlem. "My impression of Harlem is that it's wonderful," he said. "We are very happy here. I think this is a big lesson to people who practice discrimination."[77]

Malcolm X's meeting with Castro was part of his official duties as a member of the 28th Precinct Community Council's Welcoming Committee. This position was held fully independent from his role as NOI spokesman. The committee was designed to prevent embarrassing incidents, such as the booing of local NAACP leaders during a visit by Guinean president Sekou Toure in the fall of 1959. As such, it was tasked to "welcome visiting heads of state to Harlem during the General Assembly Sessions of the United Nations." Despite his success facilitating Castro's visit, though, Malcolm angrily resigned from the position after blasting journalists, the police department, and the *Amsterdam News* for failing to defend the NOI from slanderous accusations that portrayed the group as roving troublemakers.[78] Through this, then, Castro's visit to Harlem provided evidence of Malcolm X's sophisticated involvement in world affairs.

Then, the assassination of Congolese prime minister Patrice Lumumba would further accelerate both Malcolm's and Harlem's political maturation. With the previous year having been designated as the "Year of Africa" by the United Nations, the early winter and spring of 1961 brought grim news of the murder of Patrice Lumumba. Appointed after his release from a dingy jail cell, Lumumba's spectacular rise and fall revealed the hopes and impediments confronting African nation-building. In an international arena unaccustomed to dealing with Africans as equals in foreign affairs, Lumumba's breach of etiquette (reprimanding Belgian officials) triggered political backlash. Lumumba's assassination at the hands of political enemies created the spark that ignited a political love affair that introduced scores of blacks to African independence movements abroad as well as providing many with their first taste of local political organizing.

Primed by trips to Cuba, the increasing profile of Malcolm X, and a resurgence of black nationalist organizing in Harlem, the time proved ripe for resistance. Indeed, writer John Henrik Clarke would mark this event as the birth of a revival of black nationalism not seen since the Garvey movement's heyday.[79] Throughout the second half of the year, the Congo crisis was chronicled in the black press and was a subject of frequent, passionate debates as Congo fever gripped a broad range of the black community. For example, street-corner nationalists in Brooklyn organized a quixotic drive to recruit volunteers to fight in the Congo, but the effort ended in a near-riot.[80] Furthermore, the Harlem Writers Guild cabled President Eisenhower, demanding American intervention in the escalating conflict, while the *Amsterdam News* published a stream of stories and editorials documenting America's inconsistent foreign policy in Africa.[81]

Then, on February 15, 1961, a group of black nationalists took over the United Nations. As over two hundred demonstrators picketed on 42nd Street outside the United Nations' headquarters, dozens of Harlem's most militant activists surreptitiously entered the UN Security Council. Events quickly turned violent. Harlem nationalists helped organize the protest, and its members, both old and new, turned out in full force. Dozens of black protesters infiltrated the UN Security Council meeting to express outrage over Patrice Lumumba's murder. The ensuing disorders, protests, fistfights, and arrests made international headlines, thereby turning Lumumba into an icon of African independence.

In retrospect, the protest that took place inside the UN Security Council represents Black Power's formal arrival on the national political scene. Organized by black nationalists—many of whom came of political age in Harlem—the demonstration quickly turned into a melée that featured fistfights, multiple arrests, and the kind of dramatic political theater that would come to be almost exclusively associated with Black Power groups of the late 1960s such as the Black Panthers. Men and women in black arm-bands and veils formed their own ad hoc funeral procession both inside and outside the United Nations in order to honor and mourn Lumumba's untimely death.[82]

The UN protest featured dozens of radical political activists keenly aware of the unfolding independence struggles in Africa and around the world. Carlos Moore, the young black Cuban, was, as usual, in the thick of the fray. So was Harlem's senior Carlos: the incomparable Carlos Cooks. The young Afro-Cuban had served as interpreter during Castro's Hotel Theresa episode and—until his later disillusionment with Cuba's racial progress—was among the revolution's most ardent supporters. Cooks had also preserved his allegiance to Marcus Garvey's pan-Africanism, even after it fell out of vogue. This distinction once led Kwame Nkrumah himself to personally escort Cooks to a scheduled rally with him after careless organizers snubbed the veteran activist.[83]

Maya Angelou was another of the dozens of black activists who made their way inside the Security Council meeting. Abandoning California to find a new life in the big city, Angelou had found a warm refuge in the Harlem Writers Guild. A single mother whose deep voice matched her tall, elegant frame, she danced, sang, and did whatever else she could to make ends meet. Even the most cynical observer would have envied the sights and sounds of Angelou's New York. Seen through her eyes, Harlem was less of a neighborhood in decline than a community filled with street speakers, food vendors, Black Muslims, nationalists, labor organizers, and children playing stickball in the street.

Although Malcolm X stayed conspicuously absent from the day's protest, his spirit hovered over the entire proceedings. Rumors traced what was now being called a "riot" at the United Nations to an unholy alliance between Black Muslims and Communists. As Malcolm vigorously denied attempts to link the Nation of Islam to the UN protest, he just as strongly resisted efforts to lure him into denouncing the entire affair. "I will permit no one to use me against the nationalists," Malcolm defiantly explained.[84]

Malcolm's decision to remain on the edges of the controversy left it up to writers such as James Baldwin to place the event in a larger historical context. In a scathing *New York Times* editorial, Baldwin characterized the UN demonstration as only "a small echo" of the potentially cataclysmic anger spreading around the world. For Baldwin, American democracy's best hopes lay in confronting the social and political reasons behind the protest—a kind of political maturity the nation had not often been able to show.[85] Lorraine Hansberry then reiterated Baldwin's sentiment in a letter to the *New York Times*. She railed against "the continuation of intrigues against African American Negro freedom" before apologizing to Patrice Lumumba's widow for Ralph Bunche (who had publicly apologized for the behavior of the UN protesters).

Unable to publicly reveal his true feelings about the UN demonstration, privately Malcolm did confess appreciative relief. Although his restraint was rooted in the Nation's public posture against political demonstrations, he privately questioned the viability of such a strategy. He correctly reasoned that this reticence allowed competing organizations to take credit for NOI-cultivated militancy. At the NOI's Shabazz Restaurant in Harlem, Malcolm expressed his support to some of the event's leading organizers. He confided in Maya Angelou, Abbey Lincoln, and Rosa Guy, expressing how proud he was and informing them that he had just finished shooting down rumors of Communist conspiracies.[86] Black women were key organizers in the Lumumba demonstration and, in this instance, organized the kind of direct political engagement that Malcolm could not. Even as they considered the Muslim minister a mentor, these dynamic black women likewise taught Malcolm enduring political lessons about the self-determination and capacity of black women that helped make creeping inroads into the Black Muslims' reflexive misogyny.[87]

In a wide-ranging interview with forty-three black leaders in the aftermath of the UN demonstration, the *New York Times* published a front-page story on black nationalism. Malcolm X was one of a half dozen black activists quoted in a story that traced the Lumumba incident to increasing racial consciousness among African Americans. In these comments, he chided the black middle class for wanting to "live out their lives as carbon copies of the white man," while local nationalist James Lawson warned that "crumbs from the tables of an abundant society" would no longer satisfy the community's aching hunger for freedom.[88] *Amsterdam News* editor James Hicks attributed rising black anger to poverty and rejected Ralph Bunche's efforts to apologize for the UN riot. "If Bunche had spent a little more time in Harlem he wouldn't have apologized for the incident," said Hicks. Dan Watts, a thirty-seven-year-old architect turned full-time activist and founder of the radical *Liberator* magazine, echoed these sentiments. He noted that, despite a good education, "I've never been able to feel that as a Negro I had a valuable heritage." The article then concluded by investigating charges of Communist influence among black nationalists. It surmised that, while they did not control Harlem's militant black forces, Communists eagerly exploited black rage for their own nefarious purposes.[89] It is important to note that, although individual Communists may have attended the Lumumba demonstration, they were not its architects. Any suggestion that they led the protest reflected prevailing stereotypes that simultaneously indicted blacks as too incompetent to pull off such a protest and scapegoated Communists as the invisible agitators behind racial unrest.

The UN demonstration was, in many ways, the culmination of the kind of political organizing that Malcolm had been advocating since he arrived in Harlem as a political activist in 1954. In spirit and practice, the protest reflected the political message of radical self-determination, international awareness, and necessity for self-defense that he had been preaching for close to a decade. But Malcolm's inability to fully participate in an event that his presence and preaching helped facilitate illustrated the paradox of membership in the Nation of Islam. Prevented from taking part in organized boycotts, picket lines, or political demonstrations, he brokered alliances with individuals and organizations who found their métier in the very tactics that the NOI largely disavowed. Despite Malcolm's failure to formally lead protests such as the UN demonstration, activists in Harlem nevertheless looked up to him as a teacher, mentor, and guide. He likewise drew similar inspiration from his deepening political and personal ties in Harlem, relationships that would bolster him as he attempted to turn a sectarian organization into a cosmopolitan one. Thus, although Malcolm is usually thought to have only broadened his horizons in his post-NOI career, his political efforts in 1961 reveal a more complicated story.

For example, Malcolm's participation in the A. Philip Randolph-led Emergency Committee for Unity on Economic and Social Problems found him involved in a coalition effort that included clergymen, labor organizers, black nationalists, and civic leaders. Over 1,000 people showed up for the group's late-summer rally in September 1961. The unity demonstration drew a wide range of New Yorkers who had never heard Malcolm speak. The committee focused on practical issues of unemployment, job discrimination, increasing the minimum wage, and opening up jobs to blacks at Lincoln Center and other restricted work environments. By doing so, they were able to fuse politics and protest in an effort to impact public policy.[90] Ultimately, Malcolm X earned the respect of a wide array of activists, including local militants, civil rights leaders, and labor activists who grew to admire the NOI leader's political instincts, personal integrity, and willingness to work with a broad spectrum of black political leaders.

In 1962, Malcolm further escalated his political rhetoric advocating self-defense as a bulwark against racial violence against blacks. On Sunday, April 22, 2,000 parishioners at Adam Clayton Powell's Abyssinian Baptist Church in Harlem sat in rapt attention as guest minister Malcolm X preached a gospel more focused on a political reckoning than spiritual redemption. "The Muslims and Nationalists are the balance of power everywhere" and were closely observing America's racial politics, he stated. "Because a man doesn't throw a punch," Malcolm insisted, "doesn't mean he can't do so whenever he gets ready."[91] He went on to describe the NOI and black nationalists across the country as a sort of reserve army of political activists ready to engage in an epic battle for racial justice—but only at a time and place of their choosing.

Five days later, the police shooting of twenty-eight-year-old Los Angeles NOI member Ronald Stokes called into question whether Malcolm would make good on the impassioned words he spoke at Abyssinian Baptist Church. Stokes's death placed Malcolm in the precarious position of attempting to elevate an NOI member into the national pantheon of martyrs reserved for civil rights activists, even as he talked up visions of retribution that would lead to race war.[92] But the search for justice for Stokes's death turned into a personal vendetta for Malcolm. Warned by Elijah Muhammad to "play dead on everything," Malcolm dutifully obeyed. Meanwhile, he launched wild verbal broadsides against the police, civil rights leaders, and white racists in lieu of unleashing the NOI's long-promised "War of Armageddon."[93]

Privately, Malcolm fretted over losing face with hard-core Muslims, and he questioned the wisdom of Muhammad's decision. Publicly, however, he toured the country delivering lectures (backed by large photo placards of Stokes) that reviewed the grim details of Stokes's shooting. Sensing prospects for legal justice to be fading, Malcolm took morbid pleasure in a French airplane disaster that left 130 people dead. But if desperation led Malcolm to claim this tragedy as divine justice, it was also calculated political provocation. Unable to deploy teams of Muslims ready to descend upon Los Angeles, Malcolm released verbal pyrotechnics that shocked Los Angeles officials and led Mayor Sam Yorty to ask Attorney General Bobby Kennedy to designate the NOI a subversive group.[94]

Back in New York City, shortly before attending Stokes's funeral, Malcolm joined William Worthy and civil rights leader James Farmer for an evening race-relations forum. Being the last to address the audience, Malcolm described America as a nation steeped in modern-day fascism, with the police playing the role of the Gestapo. For Malcolm, Stokes's death was the final evidence necessary to pronounce America guilty of racial crimes against a broad range of African Americans, from Black Muslims to civil rights workers. Less than two weeks later, a Los Angeles grand jury ruled Stokes's death as justifiable homicide.[95]

The year 1963 signaled a turning point in American race relations. Newspaper headlines reported ongoing civil rights demonstrations and racial violence in Birmingham, Alabama, a spectacle that escalated the civil rights movement into riveting national drama. Martin Luther King Jr. and the Southern Christian Leadership Conference formed an alliance with local leaders, most notably the Reverend Fred Shuttlesworth, in an effort to eliminate Jim Crow in the city of Birmingham. Television cameras and widely circulated photos captured stark images of German Shepherds attacking civil rights demonstrators. By early May, hundreds of elementary school-age children joined the fray, and they, too, were subsequently arrested. This was one of a series of high-profile demonstrations that featured sporadic violence between white and black bystanders, all of whom participated in ongoing events on their own terms. Birmingham would be the site of Martin Luther King Jr.'s stay in jail, where he produced his essay "Letter from a Birmingham Jail," which remains a lasting document of the era. Under pressure from local clergy to slow down his desegregation campaign, King went on the offensive, explaining in pointed and eloquent terms that the denial of black citizenship defamed and distorted American democracy.[96]

Birmingham roused Black Power activists in Detroit who, in June, organized a sympathy demonstration. This event featured Martin Luther King Jr. as the keynote speaker along with the militant Reverend Albert Cleage, one of Malcolm's most loyal allies. Furthermore, the assassination of NAACP leader Medgar Evers in Mississippi in the late spring offered poignant notice of the price of freedom in America, even as the March On Washington offered hope that such sacrifices might pay dividends in the near future.

However, death seemed to outpace hope in the march's aftermath. The church bombing in Birmingham, which cost the lives of Cynthia Wesley, Addie Mae Collins, Carole Robertson, and Denise McNair, attested to this shift. John Kennedy's November 22 assassination in Dallas, Texas, then served as a shocking bookend to the year's domestic violence, which was surprising only to those naive enough to think that elected officials could remain immune to political violence.

The year 1963 marked Malcolm's final time in the Nation of Islam. Throughout the year, Malcolm continued to break new ground politically even as organizational restrictions against arranging pickets, demonstrations, and boycotts partially circumvented his efforts to make the Black Muslims fuller participants in national civil rights struggles. In February, Malcolm led five hundred demonstrators through Rockefeller Center in protest against police treatment of Black Muslims in Rochester, New York.

A city dubbed by one local activist as "the Mississippi of New York state," in the aftermath of an altercation with police and Black Muslims at a local mosque in early January, Rochester seethed with racial tension. The arrests of over a dozen NOI members on riot and assault charges provoked accusations of racism and novel displays of solidarity. The local NAACP and black civic groups offered full-throated support for the Nation, but Malcolm X went further. He led a rally of six hundred people in Rochester on February 18 and, the next week, sent a telegram to President Kennedy and other elected officials. Malcolm charged that the police had unlawfully broken into the Rochester Mosque and covered up their mistake by arresting innocent victims. He then pleaded with Kennedy to investigate the case, comparing conditions in the Northern city with embattled areas of the South. "The State of New York has become worse than Mississippi, and the city of Rochester has become worse than Oxford and Jackson, Miss. Combined," Malcolm wrote.[97]

During a speech in North Carolina on April 18, Malcolm hinted that Muslims would consider marching in picket lines, while adding that NOI members "won't turn the other cheek" if attacked.[98] Less than a week later, Malcolm told a capacity crowd that the motives behind contemporary integration efforts were bankrupt. He argued that elected officials were motivated more by America's image abroad than the status of blacks domestically and were therefore devoted to public relations rather than racial justice. "If you have done us wrong," observed Malcolm, "you should stop doing wrong whether someone is looking or not."[99]

In the spring, Malcolm seethed over the sight of blacks in Birmingham routed by dogs and fire hoses. Barred from formal participation in the era's unfolding events, Malcolm lent measured support to Southern civil rights struggles while also scrupulously maintaining the NOI's policy of nonengagement.[100]

Having recently been named head of Muslim Mosque No. 4 located in Washington, D.C., Malcolm addressed the Birmingham crisis from the nation's capital. In interviews inside Washington's Beltway, Malcolm excoriated the federal government and black leaders whom he decried as little more than modern-day "Uncle Toms."[101] Then, in Los Angeles, while attending the trial of fourteen Black Muslims related to the Stokes shooting, Malcolm announced plans to launch a "revival-type program" to rid the ghetto of crime and vice in Washington.[102] The practical basis for this new directive was comprised of a monthlong series of meetings at the NOI's Fourth Street Mosque that were aimed at attracting the district's poorest residents.[103]

On Thursday, May 9, Malcolm held a press conference at the Washington airport and took questions about events in Birmingham, where the sight of dogs attacking civil rights workers had scandalized the civilized world. "If anyone sets a dog on a black man, the black man should kill that dog," Malcolm responded testily, "whether he is a four legged dog or a two legged dog."[104] In another interview, he denounced civil rights leaders in Birmingham for using children as protesters. "Real men don't put their women and children on the firing line."[105]

Thus, Malcolm suggested that the racial violence in Birmingham demonstrated America's two-faced approach to race relations: Because African Americans no longer feared white violence, the kind of pitched battles waged in Birmingham "could happen anywhere in the country today."[106]

Malcolm's comments about Birmingham took on national significance a week later. At a press conference following a meeting with Congresswoman

Edith Green to discuss juvenile delinquency in the nation's capital, Malcolm held court for two hours as Capitol Hill reporters marveled at his pointed remarks against the president. Federal intervention in Birmingham had taken place only after blacks started an uprising—a scenario that, in Malcolm's opinion, proved Kennedy to be both morally and politically bankrupt. Even more, Kennedy's off-the-record comments to newspaper editors in Alabama, in which he stated that civil rights' failure strengthened radical groups like the Black Muslims, struck Malcolm as religiously offensive and politically naive. Denouncing Kennedy because he did not intervene as "dogs were biting black babies" and Martin Luther King for "trying to please white folks," Malcolm placed himself at the center of the nation's civil rights debate.[107] He argued that Kennedy "urged change not because it is right but because the whole world is watching."[108] Malcolm's arrival in Washington electrified the national media, with the story hitting the front page of the *New York Times*.[109] The sight of the nation's leading black militant inside the heart of America's political Beltway touched off simmering racial anxieties.

Malcolm's foray into the national civil rights arena coincided with the 1963 publication of James Baldwin's best seller, *The Fire Next Time*, which offered an invigorating account of his complex relationship to the Black Muslims. Baldwin traced Malcolm's enormous appeal to an uncanny ability to connect with ordinary black people. "He corroborates their reality" explained Baldwin. Perhaps most importantly, Malcolm expertly conveyed a sense of racial pride in being black. In a television interview, Baldwin noted, "That is a very important thing to hear in a country which assures you that you should be ashamed of it."[110]

The *Chicago Defender* editorialized in June that Malcolm and Martin Luther King Jr. represented two ways of confronting what the paper described as "the lingering crisis."[111] The editorial lauded King's nonviolent vision as deeply rooted in historical struggles for racial justice while it also announced that America had arrived at a racial crossroads. "A new Negro has arisen on the scene," warned the *Defender*, one who grew increasingly pessimistic about the promises of American democracy in the face of brutal realities of violence, segregation, and poverty. How long, the *Defender* wondered, could blacks "remain peaceful in the face of police brutality, snarling dogs, mass arrests and manhandling of women and school children?"[112] Both Baldwin and one of the black press's leading newspapers echoed aspects of Malcolm's stinging indictment against racism, though they stopped short of the solutions offered by the NOI.

Malcolm's meditation on Birmingham anticipated international reactions. These responses were especially poignant in Africa, where the All-Africa Summit conference convened in Addis Ababa that June. Reports of racial oppression in Birmingham proved particularly embarrassing for American journalists covering the conference. While there, Nigeria's foreign minister denounced America and South Africa, and newspapers ranging from the *Ethiopian Herald* and *Egyptian Gazette* to Algeria's *Liberation* carried headlines that condemned white authorities in Birmingham as "Sauvages!"[113]

Shortly after Malcolm's press conference, the *New York Herald Tribune* reported that Malcolm was planning to visit Birmingham to sort things out personally. Interviewed about these startling revelations while at the NOI's New York restaurant, Malcolm backpedaled from the story—which was leaked by Jeremiah X from the Nation's Birmingham temple. Instead, he claimed that he had no plans to visit.[114] But Malcolm's comments on Birmingham, in addition to open hints of NOI members joining pickets and Muhammad's statement in the March 18 issue of *Muhammad Speaks* urging blacks to "elect your own candidates," fueled rumors that the Nation of Islam stood poised, at long last, to directly engage in black insurgency movements sweeping the nation.[115] This was not to be.

The NOI's subsequent refusal to enter the civil rights fracas seemed to confirm notions that Malcolm X and the Black Muslims were unwilling or unable to match their tough talk with action. In fact Jackie Robinson leveled these exact charges against Malcolm during the height of the Birmingham crisis. Revered by the black community for breaking baseball's color line in 1947, Robinson's civil rights advocacy in the early 1960s placed him at odds with Malcolm. The two men traded high-profile verbal jabs in the pages of the *New York Amsterdam News*. According to Robinson, Malcolm reserved his sharpest indictments against white supremacy from the safe confines of Harlem, and he refused to venture down South (as Robinson himself did) to aid blacks who risked their lives for freedom. Robinson also questioned Malcolm's failure to attend the funeral of civil rights leader Medgar Evers in Mississippi and cast the black nationalist leader as a false prophet armed with little more than a finely honed rhetorical arsenal.

Robinson's charge remains part of Malcolm's legacy. However, these criticisms largely ignored the depth of Malcolm's political activism. From the moment he arrived in Harlem, Malcolm insisted on turning the NOI into a viable political force at the local, regional, national, and international level. Malcolm's organizing skills proved pivotal to the development or strengthening of dozens of NOI temples across the United States. Successfully recruiting hard cases, ex-cons, and black professionals to the ranks of the Nation comprised only one part of Malcolm's organizing strategy. For every person recruited to the group, there were considerable numbers that declined to join yet nonetheless remained enthralled by Malcolm's personal charisma and expansive political agenda.

New York and Detroit provide perhaps the richest and best-documented examples of Malcolm's ability to create coalitions. In each city, Malcolm aligned himself with civil rights renegades, Christian preachers, black nationalists, socialists, trade unionists, and cultural workers. It was through these networks, more than the NOI, that Malcolm was able to influence civil rights struggles taking place nationally. He did this even as he served as the de facto head of an emerging Black Power movement that paralleled and intersected with mainstream civil rights activism.

It is true that Malcolm never marched in picket lines, but he did stand next to them. He supported the hospital workers of service union 1199 and also stood on the sidelines of various demonstrations that took place in Harlem and elsewhere.[116] Malcolm's fingerprints are all over the February 15, 1961, UN protest that represented Black Power's first foray into the national political arena. The death of Ronald Stokes ratcheted up Malcolm's behind-the-scenes efforts to push the NOI into the thick of the national civil rights insurgency. Although his forceful attempts to thrust the Black Muslims into overt political activism dominated his agenda for much of 1963, this does not diminish that this drive characterized his entire career in the organization.

Malcolm's high-profile lectures supporting Muhammad's call for separation from whites are usually seen as a temporary adherence to a narrow nationalism that he would, after 1964, reject. Yet this misreads Malcolm's robust—indeed tireless—engagement with the secular world. From the beginning, Malcolm defied Muhammad's entreaties to ignore the wider world for safe (and increasingly profitable) religious cloisters. Initially thrilled by Malcolm's ability to attract recruits, raise vast sums of money, and spread the word to far-reaching audiences, Muhammad eventually grew weary of his protégé's unbridled ambition.[117] What is usually characterized as a clash of egos was in fact an organizational battle for the NOI's very soul.

Over time, Muhammad came to recognize that Malcolm's willingness to forcefully engage with the secular world served as an indictment of the NOI's sectarian teachings that predicted America's eventual destruction. Malcolm's insistence that politics mattered precisely because they could alter oppression in advance of prophecy and divine intervention changed the stakes for both men. During his entire time in the Nation, Malcolm attempted to turn a narrow and sectarian organization toward the secular arena. His cosmopolitan political outlook, far more than clashing personal egos, would lead to his expulsion from the NOI.

Its immediate roots sprang from what should have marked a personal and professional high point. In February 1963, Malcolm had presided over the NOI's annual Savior's Day Conference in Chicago. It was a lavish spectacle that brought thousands of the faithful to hear Elijah Muhammad speak. Malcolm chaired the meeting in the absence of the Messenger, who was too ill to attend.[118] Well aware that his appearance seemed to confirm speculation that Malcolm was the dashing prince to Muhammad's aging king, emotions ran high among Muhammad's insecure relatives as well as threatened Chicago officials. Malcolm's commanding presence, authoritative posture around Muhammad's family, and use of the Messenger's prized Cadillac rubbed already-frayed nerves raw. Over the course of the year, Malcolm would be bogged down in a political hornets' nest. Matters of succession that preoccupied Muhammad's family as well as Chicago officials who presided over the Nation's multimillion-dollar empire paled in comparison to substantiated rumors that the Messenger had fathered several illegitimate children. And Malcolm stood at the center of these controversies, an organizational wild card deemed by all sides as too unpredictable to be trusted. On unsteady ground in the Nation, he fought back to secure his future within the organization.[119]

Meanwhile, Malcolm continued to deliver lectures across the country. Five thousand people packed street corners and sat on fire escapes to listen to Malcolm's call for a "moral reformation" at an outdoor Harlem rally on June 29.[120] For over three hours, Malcolm discussed the state of black America, taking time to denounce President Kennedy as a poseur who was more concerned about the image of democracy abroad than racial justice at home. "He complains about the Berlin Wall," Malcolm said, "but he won't do anything about the Alabama wall and the Mississippi wall."[121] The next day, a thousand cheering listeners packed Camden, New Jersey's Convention Hall to hear Malcolm deliver a speech that attacked King and advocated the creation of several all-black states. In addition, he extolled the NOI's staggering growth, which now featured temples in eighty-nine cities in twenty-eight states, many of which Malcolm had personally organized.[122]

Murky relations with the Nation did not affect Malcolm's readiness to draw authorities into a public dispute. The Los Angeles trial of the group of fourteen Black Muslims connected to the Stokes case provoked bitter recriminations between Malcolm and the L.A.P.D. After arriving in Los Angeles from New York at 9:30 p.m., the car carrying Malcolm and NOI member Edward Sherrill was detained by two plainclothes officers who initially refused to identify themselves and "menaced them with a pistol and sawed-off shot gun." Malcolm responded in an open letter to L.A. Mayor Sam Yorty, denouncing the city's authorities as a "Ku Klux Klan police force" that used Gestapo-styled tactics against African Americans. Los Angeles's open contempt for justice had turned it into a city "wherein white Klansmen disguised as police officers feel free to trample upon the human rights of any Negro in this city."[123] Malcolm's words purposefully drew parallels between Stokes's death and the murder of civil rights workers in the South.[124]

One of the most important aspects of Malcolm's open letter to Yorty was his discussion of "human rights." The following year, Malcolm would make human rights the core of his efforts to craft a new political platform. Conventional wisdom and standard historical interpretation demonstrates Malcolm's later talk of human rights to be proof of his political maturity and rejection of Muslim sectarianism. But for Malcolm, this was no new theme. A passionate defense of human rights propelled his entire career in the NOI.

The August 28, 1963, March On Washington remains perhaps the most memorable mass demonstration of the civil rights era. Designed to pressure Congress into passing major civil rights legislation, the march featured Martin Luther King Jr.'s famous "I Have A Dream" speech and has been memorialized as the period's finest example of nonviolent protest. Behind the scenes, Kennedy administration officials, fearing violence, pleaded with march organizers to halt the proceedings. In fact, only after the day's events had gone off as largely scripted did Kennedy (who, along with the rest of the nation, listened to the young preacher from Georgia's full speech for the first time that day) agree to meet with King.

Fifteen days earlier, on August 13, Bayard Rustin, the leading nuts-and-bolts organizer of the March On Washington, announced that Malcolm X was welcome to participate in the upcoming gathering as long as he adhered to nonviolence.[125] Malcolm accepted this invitation. On August 27, the day before the march, he held court in the lobby of the Statler-Hilton Hotel. He was filled with restless energy and good humor as he alternately met with civil rights activists from SNCC, answered questions from reporters, and commented on rumors that some of the march's more militant speeches were being censored.

Although Malcolm acknowledged the march's historic nature with his attendance, his skepticism was eager from the start.[126] In early October, in Boston's Ford Hall, he denounced the march, declaring that White House officials "kept the demonstrators marching between two dead presidents" instead of meeting with the living one. White participation at the march meant that "they didn't integrate it, they infiltrated it" by helping to burnish "the image of President Kennedy as a great liberal."[127]

During a fund-raiser in Los Angeles to aid the eleven Black Muslims recently found guilty in connection with the Stokes case, Malcolm continued his blistering criticism of the March On Washington. He argued that it was a stage-managed spectacle that was designed by "white liberals to stem the real revolution, the black revolution."[128] Originally planned as a massive day of civil disobedience, complete with plans to shut down the nation's capital, the proceedings degenerated into a "farce" on Washington that extolled the moral virtue of a bankrupt society. The crowd of 1,500 in the Embassy Auditorium cheered and applauded as Malcolm held up self-defense as a sacred right in a nation whose government refused to defend black citizens.

Malcolm's explosive comments regarding the March On Washington dovetailed into a larger indictment of American democracy. "All the hell the black man has ever caught," argued Malcolm, "has been in the name of democracy."[129] For Malcolm, democracy functioned at the expense of African American social, political, and economic power. This contrasted with Martin Luther King Jr.'s steadfast faith in America's capacity, if not willingness, for social justice.

On a four-day speaking tour of northern California, Malcolm addressed students at Berkeley on Friday, October 11. This was a school that, two years earlier, had banned his appearance. But on that day, 7,000 attended the massive outdoor rally, where Malcolm proclaimed that blacks had "lost all fear." On the heels of his Berkeley speech, Malcolm conducted radio and television appearances in the Bay Area cities of Oakland and San Francisco. He then met with local civil rights leaders before concluding his brief tour with a speech in Richmond's Memorial Auditorium attended by 2,000 people, with another 800 at an evening banquet.[130]

It is also important to note that Malcolm's visit to the Bay Area encompassed key cities that would serve as headquarters and major recruiting centers for the Black Panther Party. Almost three years to the day from Malcolm's appearance at Berkeley, Huey P. Newton and Bobby Seale founded the Panthers in Oakland. Berkeley facilitated the group's rise, as students there purchased copies of Mao's red book for one dollar in early Panther fund-raising efforts. By the late 1960s, San Francisco State College represented a major source of the BPP's local political power, and the 1967 police shooting of Denzil Dowell in Richmond inspired the group to publish its newspaper, *The Black Panther*.[131]

In November of 1963, from a podium in Detroit, Michigan, Malcolm delivered perhaps his most important speech in terms of expressing his mature political ideas: "Message to the Grassroots." Malcolm's brother, Wilfred X, was the leading minister of Detroit's Muslim Mosque No. 1, and Malcolm's visit to Detroit brought him full circle to a city that had helped start his career in earnest. In 1957, he had toured the city, giving a series of electrifying speeches that announced him as a fresh new voice of militant protest. In the ensuing years, Detroit continued to serve as a political haven in which homegrown activists such as Reverend Albert Cleage, James and Grace Lee Boggs, and Richard and Milton Henry became some of Malcolm's key political allies, confidantes, and advisors. Detroit's mosaic of political organizing incorporated trade unionists, militant Christians, socialists, black nationalists, and open-minded liberals into an ad hoc headquarters for black radicalism that welcomed Malcolm X even as they merely tolerated the less appealing aspects of the Nation of Islam's orthodoxy.

A case in point is Malcolm's political alliances with Detroit activist Albert Cleage. Cleage's leadership of black militants in Detroit did not prevent him from sharing a stage with Martin Luther King Jr. during the June 23, 1963, Walk for Freedom. A footnote in most historical accounts of 1963, Detroit's freedom walk reveals the blurred lines between civil rights and Black Power activism, where a known ally of Malcolm X could co-organize a sympathy march to support civil rights demonstrators in Birmingham. Comfortable enough to appear onstage with King, Cleage was also bold enough to be a key organizer of the Grassroots Leadership Conference where Malcolm delivered his "Message to the Grassroots" speech in 1963.

The "Message to the Grassroots" laid down the blueprint for a national movement for black self-determination. According to Malcolm, this required a strong historical perspective unafraid to admit that radical change required equally radical methods. Malcolm's daring sense of the possible connected domestic racial crises with international revolutions spreading around the world. This speech took place against a backdrop of growing divisions within the civil rights movement, racial unrest in the United States, and increasing cracks along the world's racial fault lines. It distilled four centuries of racial oppression through a rhetorical tour de force that touched upon race and democracy, war and peace, and self-defense and nonviolence. Malcolm's grassroots speech is most often remembered for the biting allegory through which he argued that America's slaveholding past produced two warring black archetypes—"House Negroes" and "Field Negroes." This speech, then, likewise serves as an example of how his rhetorical jabs—in which he chastised civil rights leaders as "Uncle Toms," ridiculed nonviolence as idiotic, and predicted a growing scourge of racial violence—at times obscured the nuanced, practical, and fluid approach to organizing that marked his political activism.

As the keynote speech to the Grassroots Leadership Conference, Malcolm's "Message to the Grassroots" served as a generational manifesto advocating Black Power during the high point of the civil rights era. Some of the leading figures of early Black Power militancy participated in the conference proceedings, including journalist William Worthy, activists James and Grace Lee Boggs, and publisher Dan Watts. In addition, civil rights renegades such as Gloria Richardson also attended the keynote lecture, becoming one of Malcolm's notable allies following his break from the NOI.[132]

Too little attention is paid to the wide-ranging group of secular activists who considered Malcolm a teacher, mentor, leader, and intellectual. Many of these were organizers whose activism straddled civil rights and Black Power. Some, such as Brooklyn school desegregation leader Milton Galamison, balked at Malcolm's talk of violence and, because of this, formed tenuous and ultimately short-lived alliances with him during his post-NOI phase. Others, such as Chester, Pennsylvania, activist Stanley Branche and Harlem rent strike leader Jesse Gray, stood in solidarity with Malcolm both before and after his departure from the Black Muslims.[133]

Detroit activists, most notably Albert Cleage, the Boggses, Richard and Milton Henry, and Luke Tripp, considered Malcolm the de facto leader of a national movement for black political self-determination that paralleled and intersected with civil rights struggles. Younger militants who were comfortable with black nationalism and the politics of class struggle, such as Donald Freeman and Max Stanford of the Revolutionary Action Movement, regarded Malcolm as the leader of a global political revolution. In the aftermath of the Grassroots Leadership Conference, distinguished activists,

local organizers, and regional leaders made plans to spark a national movement for black political power.

Malcolm X's caustic criticism of John F. Kennedy's civil rights record garnered scattered attention when the president was alive, but it would produce
thunderstorms of controversy following the president's death. On Sunday,
December 1 at the Manhattan Center, nine days after the Kennedy assassination, Malcolm gave a speech entitled "God's Judgment of White America."[134] A considerable portion of the talk criticized the late president Kennedy
for transforming the recent March On Washington from a potentially revolutionary day of civil disobedience into "the greatest performance of this century."[135] Kennedy, observed Malcolm, deserved an Academy Award as best
producer of the year while Negro civil rights leaders merited best supporting
Oscars for their participation. In the wake of the march's "circuslike atmosphere,"[136] Malcolm argued that Kennedy had single-handedly orchestrated
one of the biggest sideshows in American race relations history.

Malcolm concluded what amounted to a fairly standard speech with cryp-
tic warnings suggesting that America risked a racial apocalypse unless it re-
pented and atoned for its racial sins. During the question-and-answer session,
he then characterized the president's death as a case of "chickens coming
home to roost." The widely quoted comments suggested that Malcolm—and
by extension the NOI—gleefully reveled in Kennedy's death. Three days
later, Muhammad indefinitely suspended Malcolm from public speaking and
released a statement expressing solidarity with the United States during a time
of national mourning.[137]

In the wake of his comments about John F. Kennedy's assassination, Malcolm's suspension from the NOI capped internal tensions within the group
that had been festering since at least the late 1950s. His aggressive efforts to
turn the Black Muslims into political activists riled high-ranking Muslim officials who feared government repression. Muhammad loyalists viewed Malcolm as self-aggrandizing and reckless, a chameleon who longed for the aging
leader's throne. For them, the loose remarks about the Kennedy assassination
was just another symptom of Malcolm's hunger for power and publicity. The
fear of federal surveillance then added further layers of mistrust, suspicion,
and paranoia to an already tense environment.

In truth, Malcolm had always been one of President Kennedy's staunchest critics, especially during the racial upheavals in Birmingham. In the midst
of his well-publicized—and posthumously iconic—tour of Berlin, Malcolm

characterized Kennedy as a dilettante more interested in foreign affairs than domestic racial crises. Malcolm, along with King and James Baldwin, appeared on separate segments of *The Negro and the American Promise* documentary on June 24, 1963. King expressed carefully calibrated words of encouragement and disappointment toward the administration. Baldwin suggested the Black Muslims thrived against the backdrop of America's poisonous racial atmosphere, an environment rapidly deteriorating due to lack of presidential leadership. Malcolm, however, continued his assault on the president in the documentary, noting that federal troops were sent into Birmingham to protect whites from "erupting Negroes."[138] A few days later, in front of a raucous crowd of 2,000 during a Harlem rally, Malcolm went on to argue that "Kennedy is wrong because his motivation is wrong,"[139] publicly implying that the president's stance on race relations was rooted in a political rather than moral calculus. Kennedy's civil rights policies and acknowledgement of deteriorating race relations struck Malcolm as episodes based on political expediency rather than genuine concern for the citizenship rights of African Americans. Although much of Malcolm's criticism of Kennedy was buried in the back pages of dailies or simply ignored, his subsequent comments following the president's assassination hardly merited his suspension and break from the NOI that followed. Malcolm's "chickens coming home to roost" statement merely provided disgruntled NOI officials the excuse they had been awaiting in order to silence the maverick leader.

On March 8, 1964, Malcolm set out to carve an independent course, the outline of which he had sketched over the previous decade. Malcolm's bombshell departure announcement made the front page of the *New York Times*, and it concluded three months of simmering tension with NOI officials. He read his official departure statement from a prepared text at a hastily organized press conference. He hinted at ideological differences that led to his departure, implying that his position in the group had been jeopardized by his insistence on political action. As stunned reporters listened, Malcolm played up his willingness to participate in civil rights demonstrations in the Deep South and revealed that he would soon aid activists in Louisiana.[140] "It is going to be different now," vowed Malcolm.[141]

In the weeks leading up to his announcement, surrogates for Malcolm and Muhammad waged dueling whispering campaigns filled with veiled threats and recriminations. These reached a breaking point with the news that the New York minister would not attend the Saviour's Day celebration in Chicago.

Black journalists covered the controversy intently, with pro-Malcolm partisans blatantly suggesting that Muhammad forgive his most able lieutenant. Throughout February of 1964, Malcolm remained silent but nonetheless reclaimed the spotlight through a high-profile association with new heavyweight boxing champion Cassius Clay. Reporters followed Malcolm and Clay through tours of Harlem, the United Nations, and the headquarters of the *Amsterdam News*. Images of Malcolm and Clay fueled unfounded rumors that Clay, a Black Muslim, would bankroll Malcolm's departure from the group. At the invitation of two members of the UN press corps, Malcolm and Clay toured the United Nations during the first week of March. They then lunched with representatives from Gambia and the Congo, who told reporters they were friends of Malcolm.[142] But hope that Clay might offer leverage back into the NOI would prove illusory. Elijah Muhammad personally bestowed upon Clay a new Muslim name—Muhammad Ali. In the process, Muhammad ended a budding friendship before it grew too dangerous to his authority.[143]

Malcolm's independent political direction would unfold over the next year. At the local level this meant organizing Harlem radicals toward political goals that would transcend sectarian impulses. Malcolm now endeavored to turn these local energies into a national movement that would rival the influence of more mainstream civil rights struggles.[144] Finally, the local and national thrust of Malcolm's new directions defined the black freedom struggle as part of an international human rights movement.[145]

In his very first statement, Malcolm tested out one of his new themes: the power of the black vote. He claimed that African Americans "still don't understand the power of the ballot in the North." Black voters had the power to reelect Lyndon Johnson or return him "to his Texas cotton patch," but, he said, they refused to recognize this.[146] Malcolm's new political group would set out to organize black insurgency in the North as a powerful alternative to, and potential ally of, Southern civil rights activism.

Then, on Thursday, March 12, Malcolm X announced the formation of Muslim Mosque Inc. at a massive press conference at New York's Park Sheraton Hotel. He described the group as both religious and secular, politically oriented with an all-black membership—although whites could offer financial contributions. In a wide-ranging news conference, he offered bold talk of creating rifle clubs, cagey demurrals regarding his personal plans to run for political office, and parables about his willingness to accept support from Communists.[147] "There will be" Malcolm told reporters, "more violence than ever this year," an assertion that made his new orientation sound bracingly familiar. Attuned to black America's lower frequencies, Malcolm predicted widespread social unrest and racial disorders that would stun whites.[148]

Perhaps the most important and least quoted aspect of Malcolm's declaration concerned its opening paragraph. In this he described his intentions to actively participate in what he characterized as "the American Negro struggle for Human Rights" in the United States. Malcolm chose his words carefully, purposefully elevating civil rights struggles into the international arena in the hopes of attracting global support for his new organization. In an attempt to broker peace with the civil rights leaders and organizations he routinely criticized during his time in the NOI, Malcolm claimed to have "forgotten everything bad that the other leaders have said about me." He hoped that they could do the same. However, anger did flare even through Malcolm's more soothing passages. "We are completely disenchanted with the old, adult, established politicians," he remarked. "We want to see some new faces—more militant faces."[149]

Some of these new faces included local militants across the country who had been aligned with Malcolm since the 1950s. They were now ready to answer his call to arms. Malcolm's declaration that his new organization would focus "upon the youth" obscured the fact that many of his most stalwart allies were veterans of the black freedom struggle who could trace their political awakening back to Marcus Garvey's and Paul Robeson's cultural and political activism. Veteran activists in Chester, Pennsylvania; Washington, D.C.; Harlem; Detroit; Cambridge, Maryland; and San Francisco—a group one national magazine described as "warhawks"[150]—embodied Malcolm's call for a fresh approach to struggles for racial justice.[151] His words attempted to introduce an already existing coalition of early Black Power activists, Northern black militants, and civil rights renegades into America's national political scene.

Black nationalism, argued Malcolm, required social, political, and economic self-determination for the entire African American community, a process that necessitated a secular vision capable of independent thought and action. Free from NOI orthodoxy, Malcolm held up his personal integrity as his primary political claim to leadership. "I am not educated, nor am I an expert in any particular field—but I am sincere, and my sincerity are my credentials."[152] This was too modest, since Malcolm's voracious reading, personal biography, and political experiences provided him with crucial insights into the black community that few civil rights leaders could claim.

Responses to Malcolm's declaration of independence were wide-ranging. Martin Luther King Jr. denounced Malcolm's support for rifle clubs during a March 14 appearance in New York. That same day, Malcolm met with a coterie of black militants in Chester, Pennsylvania, and offered a group of local yet highly regarded organizers his political allegiance.[153] Black leaders carefully observed these developments amid widespread speculation that Malcolm would now attract hordes of the black underclass into a political army that represented a threat to democracy's very existence.

With newspapers predicting the possibility of "a bloody and suicidal race war," journalists gauged black leaders to check the depth of Malcolm's support in the African American community.[154] Among civil rights leaders nationally, Malcolm's willingness to engage the movement offered tantalizing possibilities as well as grave dangers. Bayard Rustin argued that Malcolm's political strength rose and diminished in proportion to the effectiveness of civil rights struggles. Gloria Richardson, the militant leader from Cambridge, Maryland, welcomed Malcolm into the fray as a fresh face who could "offer something that has not been offered before." SNCC executive director James Forman echoed this sentiment, noting that Malcolm's following went beyond the NOI. On the other hand, Whitney M. Young of the Urban League dismissed Malcolm as a media creation whose advocacy of racial separatism found "an unconscious sympathy" in the hearts and minds of white journalists.[155]

Newsweek, however, reduced Malcolm's evolution to a "new Brand X nationalist movement that believes in racial separation, non-nonviolence, and guns." Denouncing Malcolm's statement at the Park Sheraton Hotel as a "chilling prelude to a second long summer of revolt," the magazine explicitly traced the roots of the era's civil disorders back to 1963 and violence in Birmingham.[156] *Life* magazine interpreted Malcolm's new direction as nothing less than an attempt to "try to lead" national civil rights demonstrations during the upcoming summer. The magazine printed a stream of carefully selected quotes from Malcolm in which he advocated that blacks boycott the armed services, withhold paying taxes, and guarantee "reciprocal bleeding" when attacked by whites. The story concluded with one of Malcolm's patented provocations: "This is going to be the hottest summer in history."[157]

Harlem would remain Malcolm's political base even as he spent more time in other countries than in the United States. He set up headquarters at the

Theresa Hotel while aides searched in vain for more permanent offices. Malcolm also made tentative steps to make good on his promise to join picket lines by publicly supporting local school desegregation efforts led by the Reverend Milton Galamison. Although Malcolm's surprise visit to Galamison's Brooklyn church did cause a stir, he still hedged, refusing to join the demonstration for fear of creating a public spectacle.[158] Questioned by reporters about his support for the New York schools boycott, he remained the ultimate contrarian: "I am against segregation; they are against segregation. But I am also against integration."[159] For Malcolm, such words contained no contradictions since segregation represented an act of white supremacy, while integration, in its posture of begging and pleading for inclusion, presumed black political powerlessness.

Free from the confines of the NOI's organizational and religious strictures, Malcolm began bold initiatives to redefine the very parameters of the black freedom struggle. As a grassroots organizer in Harlem, Detroit, and Philadelphia in the early 1950s, he had witnessed the porous boundaries between conventional civil rights activism and the bone-rattling militancy found in the urban North. Malcolm often sought to change the terms of debate that compartmentalized struggles for racial justice, but his reduced organizational status made such efforts particularly acute. Debates over racial separatism versus integration ignored the complexity of these two positions as well as the fact that an individual could advocate both simultaneously. Similarly, the controversy between proponents of nonviolence and those for self-defense failed to consider the way in which civil rights activists often employed both philosophies as a matter of survival.

Malcolm was aware of the complexities and nuances of the civil rights and Black Power movements because he lived them. As a Muslim minister in Harlem, he had long walked a tightrope between the NOI's religious orthodoxy and a more secular vision that included active political organizing. His political ambitions left him open to alliances with civil rights activists across the country, especially local leaders whose militancy often matched his own. The span of Malcolm's growing political influence in the 1950s included political, cultural, journalistic, and diplomatic contacts.

Agreement with Malcolm became the common denominator for a loose coalition of militants—in the urban North, West Coast, Midwest, and Deep South—who sought to reshape the black freedom movement's very contours. Many of these activists found common ground in their pursuit of bread-and-butter issues such as school desegregation, tenants' rights, and ending police brutality. Others looked to the international arena for a way forward at home, galvanizing street demonstrations in support of African independence, decrying American foreign policy as racist against the Third World, and predicting waves of guerrilla warfare across the United States. Collectively, these activists represented distinct branches of the same family tree, one that was rooted in a historic struggle for black liberation.

Malcolm's unique personal and political biography allowed him to serve as a bridge between two generations of black activists: veterans of the Robeson generation and new militants who came of age in the wake of Ghanaian independence, the Cuban Revolution, and the Southern sit-in movement. Malcolm's trips to Africa in 1964 inspired both of these generations in different ways. Langston Hughes, the Harlem Renaissance luminary and radical activist who had personally witnessed the specter of fascism in Spain as a young man, publicly lauded Malcolm's efforts to internationalize the civil rights struggle. Meanwhile, Hughes also gently reminded Malcolm of earlier initiatives to petition the United Nations by long marchers such as W. E. B. Du Bois, the NAACP, and the National Negro Congress.[160] In Africa, youthful SNCC staff encountered the pervasiveness of Malcolm's influence at every turn, and then they found the man himself in Kenya—a bracing reminder that Malcolm's words carried international weight that could not be underestimated.

Political intrigues emanating from within the Nation of Islam harried Malcolm's organizing efforts. On March 21, the *New York Courier* published an exclusive interview with Malcolm in which he claimed to have narrowly escaped an assassination attempt planned by Black Muslims the month before. Malcolm traced his dismissal from the NOI to an orchestrated coup carried out by New York Fruit of Islam Captain Joseph, a powerbroker and former ally who remained steadfastly loyal to Muhammad.[161] Behind the scenes, the Muslim Mosque attempted to attract disgruntled NOI members even as Malcolm publicly declared he had no intention of doing so. From his spartan headquarters on the second floor of the Theresa Hotel, Malcolm skillfully deflected reporters from around the world who were eager to learn of his next move. He dismissed conventional civil rights tactics as outdated as he also remained tightlipped about his efforts to develop an alternative program. He even whipped out a copy of the Constitution to convince one reporter that he abhorred violence and simply promoted the legal right of self-defense. He then told another that guerrilla warfare had already reached America.[162]

Elijah Muhammad, for his part, alternated between graceful resignation over Malcolm's departure and bitter denunciation of what he characterized as a shocking betrayal. Muhammad questioned Malcolm's decision to promote alliances with civil rights leaders, ridiculed his tough talk of rifle clubs, and repeatedly described his former protégé as a traitor.[163] The Black Muslims methodically launched a public relations campaign of repudiation, which included scathing comments by Malcolm's brother, Philbert X, during a Chicago press conference near the end of March. Philbert denounced Malcolm as a master manipulator who spread false accusations against top Muslim officials.[164]

Black newspapers and the white press found rare synergy in covering Malcolm's increasingly bitter antagonism with the NOI. Malcolm's break from the Nation and the subsequent intrigues between his relatively modest group of followers and the Messenger's loyal stronghold of true believers played out as a kind of Greek tragedy.[165] *Muhammad Speaks*, the rapidly expanding newspaper that Malcolm himself founded to spread the Messenger's teachings, enthusiastically denounced him in a series of articles that spring. Old friends and former protégés, most notably Boston's Louis X, reveled in the newfound attention that came with castigating Malcolm. *Newsweek* summed up a strain of white media response to Malcolm's March 12 press conference with a caption, "Charm and guns," that presented him as a dangerously charismatic leader whose eloquence attracted journalists and large crowds.[166]

Relishing his newfound political independence, Malcolm toured strongholds of civil rights militancy and early Black Power activism. At a massive rally at Harlem's Rockland Palace on March 22, he promised to organize a national convention to deliberate on forming a political party. A crowd of over 1,000 turned out to hear Malcolm declare that 1964 would be a racial turning point in American history. "It's going to be a year of ballots or bullets," he proclaimed. "And if ballots won't work, bullets will." Newspaper headlines found the ballots-or-bullets line of Malcolm's speech irresistible, though they virtually ignored his far more tangible call for 1 million new black voters to back a proposed black nationalist political party.[167]

Malcolm carried these political credentials to an unexpected visit to Washington at the end of March, where he observed the Senate debate the pending civil rights bill. Armed with a visitor's pass, a few loyal followers, and his customary rhetorical brio, Malcolm held ad hoc press conferences in which he blasted America's political process, warned of increased racial tension, and exhibited genuine curiosity about the inner workings of government. He characterized the civil rights bill debate as a "con game." He also explained his presence there as an expression of solidarity with sincere, if misguided, members of the black community who still held faith in American politics. "You can't legislate good will," he reasoned, "that comes about only by education."[168]

The trip also produced an exhilarating, albeit brief, meeting with Martin Luther King Jr. The two men spoke briefly during a chance encounter memorialized in photos that showed Malcolm and King smiling amid a handshake for the cameras.[169] Although both Malcolm and King linked racial violence with public policy in their discussion of the civil rights bill, where Malcolm predicted that violence would erupt if the bill passed, King foresaw "a dark night of social disruption" if it didn't.[170]

Memories of witnessing the civil rights debate fueled Malcolm's appearance, two days later, on the Irv Kupnicet television show in Chicago. Malcolm described the entire debate as an unseemly affair that "shouldn't even exist" in a true democracy. He riffed off of his reputation as a racial arsonist by comparing America to a house on fire. "I think it's only fair that when your house is on fire and someone comes and tells you that it's on fire that you don't accuse him of setting it on fire."[171]

For Malcolm, critics who branded him a hate-monger and racial instigator missed a larger point. American democracy bred poverty, racial discrimination, and a justifiable rage that black radicals sought to hone into an organized movement for revolutionary change. Jim Crow segregation in the South exemplified a national disease that Northern liberals ignored in their own backyard. Conventional narratives of America's civil rights years focus on one region, the South, marked by spectacular racial clashes, political assassinations, and climactic demonstrations. However, Malcolm argued that racial oppression was a national problem with subtle regional differences with which he was intimately acquainted. This understanding came from having grown up in the Midwest, as a hustler in urban cities such as Boston, Detroit, and New York, and, as a member of the NOI who helped found or strengthen Muslim Mosques in the West Coast and South. Thus, Malcolm's collective indictment of American democracy found racial segregation in New York's public schools as important as the Little Rock crisis.

Speaking at the Palm Gardens in April, Malcolm characterized democracy as "white nationalism" in a speech in which he recalled listening to politicians filibuster the civil rights bill in Washington. For Malcolm, America's zealous promotion of democracy overseas, "when you have citizens of this country who have to use bullets if they want to cast a ballot," rang hollow.[172] African Americans shared common political dreams of "freedom, justice, equality" even as they pursued different methods to achieve those goals. If civil rights activists embraced democracy and patriotism in pursuit of these goals, then Black Power militants waged an uncompromising battle for power that would be convened on the world stage. At the close of his speech, Malcolm offered an olive branch of sorts. He claimed that a "blood-less revolution" remained possible if black voting rights were recognized, be-cause this power "would change the entire political structure" of America. Through the ballot, Malcolm argued, African Americans could fundamen-tally alter domestic and foreign policy.[173] Then, during the question-and-answer session, he expressed support for the black-led Freedom Now Party, attacked blacks who registered as Democrats or Republicans as traitors, and admitted that "progressive-minded" whites could assist struggles for racial justice.[174]

In Cleveland and Detroit, 2,000 listened as Malcolm delivered versions of one of his most important speeches. The "Ballot or the Bullet" suggested that the civil rights struggle required reaching higher political and moral al-titudes that only a "human rights" movement could hope to grasp. Malcolm mapped some of the next decade's most pressing concerns in a speech whose provocative title helped to obscure its sophisticated treatment of world events.[175] In many ways this speech represented Malcolm's most scathing yet thoughtful critique of American democracy to date. In it, he identified himself as "[o]ne of the 22 million black people who are the victims of de-mocracy, nothing but disguised hypocrisy."[176]

Yet Malcolm's bitter words denouncing democracy as a failure held out hope for the nation if black militants could transform the very meaning of civil rights in America. Black nationalists, argued Malcolm, needed to par-ticipate in civil rights struggles and "give it a new interpretation."[177] Having been denied the legitimacy and stature conferred on mainstream civil rights leaders for much of his political career, Malcolm proposed expanding the movement's ideological boundaries, organizational diversity, and tactical flex-ibility. This included a newfound receptivity to voter registration. In fact, shortly after his March visit to the Senate, Malcolm told 1,000 people at the Audubon Ballroom in New York City that unregistered African Americans "should be moved out of town." He promised "to see that every black face behind every door is registered" and threatened to organize a massive march on Washington, populated with black militants, if the Senate's civil rights bill filibuster continued after May 1.[178]

In the "Ballot or the Bullet" speech as well as his statements afterward, Malcolm X redefined the temper of democratic struggles for racial justice by imagining civil rights efforts as the terrain of black militants, proposing that America's domestic racial crisis be acknowledged as a human rights issue, and recognizing that, without such revolutionary transformations, racial violence would rage across the country. In the month after departing the NOI, Malcolm had sketched out a political program that included the creation of a new secular organization, a pledge to promote voter registration drives, and his support for New York school desegregation leader Milton Galamison and Harlem rent strike leader Jesse Gray.[179] Energized by his new direction but burdened by legal and physical harassment from the NOI, Malcolm made plans to return to Africa.

Malcolm X consistently re-created himself based on political and professional circumstances, and in the spring of 1964 he set out to do so once again. In need of a new origin story, Malcolm carefully updated his personal narrative for public consumption. He embarked on his second tour of Africa—and first visit since 1959—that April. In a series of carefully written letters to friends and professional contacts, Malcolm described his pilgrimage to Mecca and the spiritual *Hajj* taken by orthodox Muslims as a life-altering experience.

In anticipation of his May 21 return to America, newspapers reported Malcolm's political conversion as a bombshell change of heart. "There are Muslims of all colors and ranks here in Mecca from all parts of the world," wrote Malcolm. The *New York Times* turned this complex appeal for racial rapprochement into a front-page story, noting that Malcolm would return home "in two weeks with new positive insights on race relations."[180] The *Washington Post* profiled Dr. Mahmoud Shawarbi, director of New York's Islamic Center, as the man who "tamed" Malcolm X, thereby helping to produce a "complete turnabout" that turned the eloquent hate-monger into an avowed "ex-racist."[181]

In a letter to the *New York Amsterdam News*, Malcolm compared pan-Africanism with Zionism. He noted that although many Jews remained in the United States, "their cultural, philosophical, and psychological ties to Israel" buoyed their domestic political strength. "Pan-Africanism will do for the people of African descent all over the world," wrote Malcolm, "the same that Zionism has done for Jews all over the world."[182]

The sheer range of recipients of Malcolm's letters, who included nationally recognized civil rights activists such as James Farmer and Bayard Rustin as well as local and national newspaper reporters, suggests impulses guided as much by political calculations as genuine personal transformation. In Malcolm's Promethean vision, the Middle East introduced him to a world where politics were not simply shaped by accidents of birth that resulted in shared racial origin, but rather by choices that offered expanded personal and political opportunities.[183]

Press accounts of Malcolm's entreaties to the possibilities of racial harmony ignored his complex history with whites. Malcolm's "new" position differed from his past indictments of white racism only to the extent that he no longer followed or believed in NOI orthodoxy that claimed whites were genetically predisposed to racial oppression. Malcolm's visit to Saudi Arabia in 1959, his meeting with Fidel Castro the next year, and his dialogue with white progressives over the course of his political career attests to his long-standing complicated relationship with whites. In a 1962 debate with CORE (Congress of Racial Equality) leader James Farmer that was published in *Dialogue* magazine, Malcolm characterized unfolding global and national events as inaugurating "an era of great change." Going beyond facile debates between integration and separation, Malcolm instead advocated the best method to promote and ensure "freedom, justice, and equality." Blacks, he argued, longed for "human dignity" in a manner that rendered political labels irrelevant. If integration accelerated the pace toward equality, "then we will integrate." But if this avenue failed, other methods would be deployed.[184]

As the former leading member of the Nation of Islam, a group regarded in mainstream America as antiwhite and violent, Malcolm required a well-publicized epiphany. He needed to convince white opinion-makers and black civil rights leaders that he no longer subscribed to the NOI's racial cosmology. Malcolm himself helped to publicize this story. Muslim mosques distributed his letters to media outlets, and CORE leader James Farmer trumpeted a handwritten postcard as evidence that Malcolm would "join the integration movement when he gets back."[185]

Malcolm arrived in New York from Africa on Thursday, May 21. At the airport, he cut a striking figure in a blue seersucker suit, an African walking stick, and newly grown facial hair. He hoisted his two-year-old daughter, Ilyasah, and accompanied wife, Bettye, and his two older daughters into a six-car caravan heading for Harlem's Hotel Theresa.[186] Outside, a banner that read, "Welcome Back, Brother Malcolm X," draped the Theresa.[187] Inside, Malcolm evaded reporters at a large press conference in the Skyline Room on the eleventh floor. "I haven't had a shave or a haircut since I left the United States five weeks ago," he informed the packed press conference at the Hotel Theresa. Smiling, Malcolm added that he would "keep the beard for a little while."[188]

Malcolm did immediately launch into a discussion of a strategy that linked the political destinies of black Americans and Africa together as part of transnational human rights agenda. He challenged the State Department's efforts to rehabilitate America's image in Africa by promoting images of racial progress. Malcolm proclaimed support from African countries in his quest to bring charges of human rights violations to the United Nations and, in case reporters missed his point, spelled out the logic behind his forward thrust into international politics. "The United States would be compelled to face the same charges as South Africa, Portugal, and Rhodesia," he said, thereby placing America in the embarrassing company of a rogues' gallery of declining colonial powers.[189]

Malcolm offered a simple explanation for the breathless reports that announced his change of political heart: "Travel broadens one's scope and when I visited the Holy City of Mecca I saw people of all colors, carrying themselves as human beings, worshipping," said Malcolm, before suggesting that white Americans should consider converting to Islam.

As he had done during the Kennedy administration, Malcolm also publicly indicted Lyndon Johnson. He questioned why the president claimed segregationist senator Richard Russell as a friend, arguing that Russell's opposition to the impending civil rights bill cast suspicion over LBJ by association. "I am inclined," said Malcolm, "to question Johnson's integrity." In saying this, he cast himself, once again, as a militant statesman courageous enough to question the president's commitment to civil rights and racial justice.[190] In an exclusive interview with the *New York Amsterdam News*, Malcolm chastised civil rights groups for their "narrow approach to the whole race question." He then promised to build a new organization whose goals, strategies, and tactics would move beyond the political stalemate that bogged down black nationalists and integrationists.[191]

Two days after returning from Africa, Malcolm continued to enunciate his already expansive vision of the world in a debate with reporter Louis Lomax in front of an interracial crowd of 1,500 at Chicago's Opera House. "Our people must look beyond international boundaries," he explained.[192] According to Malcolm, hordes of African leaders were willing to lend support to domestic civil rights efforts. Without such intervention, he claimed, racial brushfires in America would escalate into guerrilla warfare that resembled struggles taking places in Vietnam and Laos.[193] In Chicago, Malcolm added complexity to the clichéd debate over whether separation or integration should be the ultimate goal for blacks. These one-dimensional debates ignored deeper truths and were therefore "merely methods toward" larger goals of "respect and recognition" as human beings. Malcolm's nuanced and at times philosophically charged take on the black freedom struggle led Lomax—whose relationship with Malcolm X dated back to the 1959 documentary that introduced the Black Muslims to an unsuspecting American public—to characterize him as a moderate.[194]

Malcolm continued a very public dialogue regarding the very nature of American democracy. In doing so, he challenged Lomax's assertion that an advocacy of racial separatism hindered political progress. Since democracy "allowed or promoted" second-class citizenship, proponents of racial separatism could not be condemned "unless you're also going to condemn that democracy that produces this reaction," countered Malcolm.[195] While Lomax retained steadfast faith in a system meant to safeguard individual rights, Malcolm expressed resigned skepticism. "Well, I don't have too much confidence in the operation of democracy because I haven't seen it yet," he said, adding that America had failed to practice democratic principles since its founding.[196] Malcolm contended that civil rights leaders remained enthralled in their pursuit of "the American dream called democracy" at the expense of crafting substantive solutions to the nation's racial crisis.[197]

That year, Malcolm's confrontation with American democracy continued to grow more nuanced and complex. In dozens of speeches, he decried democracy as an ironic joke that disguised a system based on black oppression. His life experiences had exposed him to the contradictions of a democratic society—ranging from poverty, drug abuse, and prisons—to his redemption in sectarian religious groups protected by the U.S. Constitution. Civil rights activists extolled the virtues of democracy as an unfolding experiment whose ultimate course could be altered through legal and legislative victories. In contrast, Malcolm argued that the necessity of new laws to protect black citizens proved how bankrupt America's system truly was.

Malcolm frequently pointed to the murders of civil rights workers after the passage of the 1964 Civil Rights Act as proof that black liberation in America required a political revolution. "Any time you find someone in the condition that the American so-called Negroes are in, in 1964, and in a country that professes to be a democracy or that professes to be the leader of the free world," he explained during a 1964 debate, "then something is wrong. It's a paradox."[198] Malcolm devoted much of his political career to exploring this paradox. Yet he did so in a manner that made him the black prosecuting attorney of America.

Malcolm defined the black freedom struggle as "actual warfare," and he turned a nuanced critique of American democracy into part of his rhetorical arsenal. By 1964, he unfavorably compared the United States with colonial states such as South Africa and Angola. In doing so, he accused America of a new kind of hypocrisy because these countries lacked any democratic pretensions. The very fact that blacks were engaged in a bitter struggle to promote civil rights while living "in a country that professes to be a democracy" gave Malcolm pause.[199] He argued instead that America's sacred democratic traditions needed to be fundamentally transformed if blacks were to achieve full citizenship.

Politically, Malcolm encouraged new ideas, expanded existing political alliances, and linked the fates of blacks and Africans to a mutual destiny bound by shared oppression and a hunger for freedom. His bold strategy to inject himself into America's civil rights struggle relied on upsetting existing definitions of civil rights, democracy, and citizenship. This included challenging civil rights leaders who viewed him as a Northern militant with no understanding of Southern struggles. In defining black liberation as a human rights struggle, Malcolm went beyond the Cold War-imposed boundaries that framed civil rights as a purely domestic or regional issue. His public rapprochement with civil rights activists who favored racial integration confirmed that divergent political strategies could find common ground in larger efforts to promote racial dignity and equal citizenship.

In interviews and speeches in the spring of 1964, Malcolm presented himself as black America's unofficial prime minister. Media stories recounting Malcolm's racial epiphany in the Middle East overshadowed his equally important visit to Ghana. There, Malcolm pragmatically surveyed the inner workings of a pan-African state. He arrived in Accra from Lagos, Nigeria, where, on Friday, May 8, he lectured at the prestigious University of Ibadan, became an honorary member of the Muslim Students' Society, and was renamed "Omowale," Yoruba for "the child has returned."[200] In print, radio, and television appearances and interviews, he launched sharp broadsides against American foreign policy imperatives in Africa. At one point he even characterized the Peace Corps as "missionaries of old who are paving the way for neocolonialism."[201]

In Ghana, Malcolm conducted interviews, lectured at universities, attended informal and official dinners, conferred with at least fifteen Third

World ambassadors,[202] and briefly met President Kwame Nkrumah. During a May 12 press conference, Malcolm expressed feelings of intense kinship with Africa, claiming that he "felt more at home than I have ever felt in America."[203] Ghana's community of black expatriates welcomed Malcolm, who knew several of them from Harlem, such as Julian Mayfield and Maya Angelou. Five thousand miles from home, in the Ghanaian capital of Accra, he found himself comforted by the knowledge that Africa contained the seeds for a potential global revolution. Candid, late-night discussions with Afro-Americans in Ghana helped to inspire bold political plans that focused on reimagining domestic struggles for racial justice.[204] In Malcolm, Ghanaians saw an unusually high-profile tourist who snapped photos, smiled broadly, and reveled in simple pleasures of a traditional lunch of plantains, yams, and rice with palava sauce served on native earthenware.[205]

On Wednesday, May 13, Malcolm delivered an address entitled, "Will Africa Ignite America's Racial Powder Keg?" at an event in Legon that was sponsored by the Marxist Forum.[206] In this, he recounted the horrors of the transatlantic slave trade in order to highlight connections between Africans and blacks who were Americans "in name but not in reality."[207] The audience sat in awed silence as Malcolm's words cut through cultural and continental divides. His speech tapped into a shared history of oppression that, perhaps, reminded Ghanaians of their country's pivotal role (and former name—the Gold Coast) as a way station to the slave trade. Because of this, Malcolm's appearance in Legon ignited controversy, especially among local Marxists who were offended by the speech's racial tint. Malcolm nevertheless found his share of defenders, most notably in his old friend Julian Mayfield as well as a writer for the *Ghanaian Times* who applauded the talk's candid tone and fierce sense of urgency.[208]

In Ghana, Malcolm criticized U.S. race relations in language that later groups such as the Black Panthers would come to echo. He characterized America as an empire, a "master of imperialism" blazing a destructive path across the globe. He went on to suggest that the Peace Corps be deployed to Mississippi and Alabama instead of Africa. He noted that "while South Africa preaches and practices segregation, the United States preaches integration and practices segregation."[209] Meanwhile, American officials followed Malcolm's every move and optimistically concluded that, despite his eloquence, Malcolm "created less of a stir than the Embassy feared."[210]

Malcolm published a personal account of his spring tour of Africa in the pages of *Liberator* magazine. "We Are All Blood Brothers" provided a sweeping and remarkably precise snapshot of Malcolm's five weeks in Africa, accompanied by four photos of his trip to Ghana. In Malcolm's narrative, a lecture at Beirut's Sudanese Cultural Center proved to be the pivotal moment when he felt "the collective African reaction" to the mistreatment of blacks in America.[211] Over the course of the five weeks when he toured Mecca, Malcolm was granted a personal audience with Saudi Arabia's Prince Faisel, lectured at the University of Beirut, promoted pan-African alliances at the University of Ibadan in Nigeria, spent a day sightseeing in Morocco, and capped off his visit with a brief stay in Algiers.[212] That spring, memories of his African tour fueled his own personal resolve.

African independence movements awakened Malcolm's interest in organizing a parallel pan-African movement back home. Over a banana split at Harlem's 22 Restaurant in June, he told a journalist of his plans to start an explicitly political organization aimed to unite the black community toward the creation of "a strong Pan African movement."[213] Malcolm yearned to fashion a new political organization that could remain steadfast to Islamic principles "in a Western and highly mechanized society," while simultaneously attracting a large base of secular participants. The name of Malcolm's proposed new group, Afro-American Freedom Fighters, drew inspiration from independence movements in Algeria and the larger Third World.[214]

During a secret meeting at the house of actor Sidney Poitier on June 13, 1964, Malcolm pitched his new organization to a group of leading black cultural, political, and intellectual figures. Organizer Clarence Jones (who served as an advisor to King) left the gathering impressed by Malcolm's worldly vision. Old political friends Ossie Davis, Ruby Dee, and writer John Oliver Killens also participated, as did Whitney Young and emissaries representing A. Philip Randolph and CORE. Malcolm's "brain trust" provided moral and political support for the OAAU as they offered intellectual, political, and financial resources that could translate his human rights agenda into a practical political program.[215]

Malcolm X officially launched the Organization of Afro-American Unity at a late-evening rally in Harlem on Sunday, June 28. That same day, Elijah Muhammad returned to New York for the first time in almost four years in a naked effort to upstage his apostate former pupil—who, in the preceding month, had divulged secrets of the Messenger's numerous infidelities and illegitimate children during legal proceedings to oust him from his NOI-owned house in Queens.[216] The OAAU implicitly recognized the flaws of

Malcolm's earlier organization Muslim Mosque Inc., which had been plagued by sectarian infighting and burdened by a name that turned off Malcolm's more secular supporters. His new group, on the other hand, would approach struggles for racial justice from a national perspective. "When we say South," noted Malcolm, "we mean south of the Canadian border. America in its entirety is segregationist and is racist. It's more camouflaged in the north, but it's the same thing."[217] The organization tested the depth and breadth of Malcolm's appeals to seasoned activists eager for an alternative to the civil rights status quo.[218]

Malcolm's speech at the OAAU's founding rally deftly combined new perspectives gleaned from his recent trip to Africa with an old-fashioned appeal to the politics of self-determination and pan-African unity. Remarkably, even as he proclaimed the ambitious objective of culling "everyone in the Western Hemisphere of African descent into one united force," he continued to confront, challenge, and appropriate American democratic traditions.[219] Malcolm read the OAAU's statement of objectives, which proclaimed African Americans' "inalienable right" to determine their "own destiny." This passage borrowed words from the Founding Fathers in order to make audacious new claims toward black political power.[220] He followed this by reading perhaps the most significant part of the OAAU's statement: The UN charter and Universal Declaration of Human Rights coupled with America's Constitution and the Bill of Rights "are principles in which we believe and that these documents if put into practice represent the essence of man-kind's hopes and good intentions."[221] This statement clearly expressed the evolution of Malcolm's star-crossed relationship with American democracy. Yet the complex, subtle sentiment behind these words remains an unexplored part of his legacy. Intent on making America live up to the lofty principles found in its sacred texts, by 1964 Malcolm had ratcheted up his very public, though often ignored, dialogue regarding the idea of American democracy.

Despite support from well-known local activists, a secular political outlook that tied national ambitions to pragmatic local measures, and a modest two-dollar membership fee, the OAAU failed to capture the imagination of Harlem and black militants around the nation. Malcolm's inability to engage in the slow, patient, local organizing that helped propel the NOI in Harlem and around the nation during the 1950s loomed large in this failure. Further, his extensive travels overseas left him struggling to maintain organizational control over the OAAU and close alliances in Harlem. The scattered nature of Malcolm's final year witnessed promising efforts to speak to multiple audiences, groups, and factions, sometimes simultaneously. The breadth of these pursuits made for jarring portraits.

On July 9, Malcolm boarded an evening flight from New York to Cairo via London. His passport listed him under his new name, Hajj Malik El Shabazz, and his one-way ticket signaled that his journey would be open-ended.[222] In London, en route to Cairo, he told reporters that antiblack violence in the South had "reached the point where members of my race will soon react and American will see a blood bath."[223] For Malcolm, the South represented an enduring metaphor for white supremacy that transcended simple geographic boundaries. "As far as I am concerned," Malcolm once remarked, "Mississippi is anywhere south of the Canadian border."[224] Racial violence in Mississippi fueled Malcolm's rage. It was there that SNCC's "Freedom Summer" campaign to register black voters bumped into traditions of white terror that resulted in the murder of three civil rights workers. In Omaha, Nebraska, shortly before he departed the United States, Malcolm threatened to send OAAU members to Mississippi to initiate guerrilla warfare to protect black life there.[225] The latest incidents of Southern racial violence convinced Malcolm that his human rights strategy represented black America's best chance for progress. In Cairo, he tapped into long-simmering pan-African impulses whose modern expression combined New Negro rhetorical effervescence with the kind of practical nation-building that dwarfed even Marcus Garvey's outsized imagination. There, Harlem would remain on Malcolm's mind and at the center of his political agenda, even as his political sojourn took him from its gritty street corners to exotic places its residents could scarcely imagine.

Malcolm's predictions of racial violence came true that summer as Harlem exploded in the aftermath of the Wednesday, July 16, police shooting of a black teenager. Over two hundred arrests, more than one hundred police and civilian injuries, and fifteen confirmed shootings were reported by the following Monday.[226] At the very moment racial violence swept through Harlem, Malcolm was in Cairo observing the Organization of African Unity (OAU) conference. He issued a memorandum to each of the heads of African states highlighting the political and ancestral connections between Africans and American blacks lobbying for recognition of domestic racism as a global human rights crisis.[227] Aboard the yacht *Isis*, he engaged in intense dialogue with representatives of liberation movements raging across the continent. Freedom fighters from Angola, Mozambique, Northern Rhodesia (Zambia), Southern Rhodesia (Zimbabwe), and South Africa captivated Malcolm with details of the "brutal atmosphere" that existed under colonialism.[228]

Malcolm's absence from Harlem during the July urban rebellion afforded him a venue to display pan-African statesmanship from faraway Egypt. In Cairo practicing freelance diplomacy when violence in Harlem erupted, he issued press releases explaining his activities overseas while a host of national figures, including King, provided more visible leadership. Meanwhile, State Department officials and outraged American journalists trailed Malcolm's tour of Africa, fretting that his well-attended lectures and high-profile critiques promoted anti-American sentiment on racial grounds. Assistant Attorney General Walter Yeagley filed internal reports to inquire whether Malcolm's contact with foreign heads of state violated national security.[229]

Malcolm's itinerary touched strategic parts of the continent, taking him from Kuwait to Ethiopia, Zanzibar, and Dar-Es-Salaam at a rapid pace. He addressed university students at virtually every stop, engrossing audiences with grim lectures on the depth of American racism and the shared ancestral bonds that tied Africans and black Americans in the common pursuit of dignity and human rights.[230] In early October, he lectured in Addis Ababa to Ethiopian university students about America's presidential election. He compared the difference between Lyndon Johnson and Barry Goldwater as the choice between "a fox or a wolf." Malcolm confessed that two months in Cairo had transformed him politically. These changes came into bold relief during the question-and-answer session when he insisted that, despite differences with Martin Luther King Jr. and other civil rights leaders, they nonetheless shared basic objectives. "The main difference," he deadpanned, "is that he doesn't mind being beat up and I do."[231]

The next week in Dar-Es-Salaam, Malcolm delivered the "inside story" of American racial oppression to journalists, students, and foreign dignitaries, including a three-hour meeting with Tanganyikan president Julius Nyerere.[232] In Dar, Malcolm's visit captured wide attention. *The Nationalist* carried his picture and accompanying interview on its front page underneath the provocative headline "Malcolm X Raps U.S.A." But Malcolm did more than just provoke.

From his hotel bedroom, Malcolm parleyed with reporters during the second week of October. Alternately hunched over in deep thought and laid back in a more contemplative repose, Malcolm explained his motivations for touring Africa. He claimed that its unfolding revolution promised a new day in the United States. According to Malcolm, American leaders were "more afraid of Africanism" than Communism because the nation proved more hospitable to Communists than Africans.[233] He told reporters that he planned to stay abroad until after the presidential elections for fear that his presence might animate Goldwater supporters. Malcolm argued that black Americans in Africa who were connected to the State Department presented a false image of democracy that contrasted with the searing realities he routinely exposed in his speeches. Africa's great challenge, he noted, would be in distinguishing genuine black leaders from state-sponsored Uncle Toms.[234]

Malcolm arrived in Nairobi on Friday, October 16, from Dar on a plane whose passengers included the prime ministers of Kenya and Uganda. His comment that "providence put us together" downplayed his tenacious efforts to build international political alliances.[235] Although not an official guest of the Kenyan government, Malcolm attended Kenyatta Day festivities and maintained a conspicuous presence at major social events. American aid to Africa, suggested Malcolm during a speech in Nairobi, paled in comparison to the continent's historic contributions to the United States, assistance that came in the form of "human flesh."[236]

Malcolm riveted audiences with grisly stories of how civil rights-related violence flourished in the United States, perhaps most notably the summer murders of three civil rights workers in Philadelphia, Mississippi. During an October 21 television interview, he denounced the recently passed civil rights bill as naked propaganda aimed at convincing Africa and Asia of American sincerity on racial matters. He added that Africa's anticolonial movement inspired domestic civil rights struggles. He then repeated his plans to charge the United States with human rights violations at the United Nations. Malcolm's high-profile criticism unnerved U.S. embassy officials, whom he suspected of discouraging Americans from visiting him in Nairobi.[237]

During a chance meeting with SNCC activists John Lewis and Donald Harris in Kenya, Malcolm found kinship with the young civil rights workers. SNCC's presence in Africa delighted him and reassured him that his dreams of a more worldly approach to racial justice would not fall on deaf ears back home. In Africa, SNCC workers discovered that local leaders gauged their level of political sincerity within the radical framework that Malcolm had left in his wake.[238] Furthermore, his time in Nairobi paid immediate dividends. His firsthand reports of American race relations inspired local political groups, such as the Kanu Parliamentary Backbenchers' Association, to pass a resolution of support for African American freedom and citizenship. Following Malcolm's lead, local newspapers referred to the civil rights movement as a "struggle for basic human rights."[239]

Back in Addis Ababa at the end of October, Malcolm held a press conference trumpeting his plans to take his quest for racial equality to the United Nations. Here, he discussed his recent foray to Nairobi at the Ethiopian Hotel in front of a group of admirers before departing to Lagos (his second visit to Nigeria in five months).[240] According to Malcolm, internal divisions threatened to undermine Africa's rapid political development. "In East Africa it is the African against the Asian," he observed, "and in West Africa it is the Moslem against the Christian and all these are fed by outside forces."[241]

Malcolm arrived in Liberia one week later on the evening of Friday, November 6 for a three-day visit. There he delivered his now-typical human rights stump speech with the elegance and ease of a seasoned politician. Greeted as "a friend and brother" by the mayor of Monrovia at a Saturday luncheon organized in his honor held at the Tropical Hut, Malcolm thrust America's racial domestic crises into the wider arena of global politics.[242] In speeches, luncheons, and interviews, he applauded China's recent nuclear progress as a deterrent against American aggression, suggested that the late Patrice Lumumba deserved the Nobel Prize instead of Martin Luther King Jr., and blasted Lyndon Johnson and John Kennedy as political poseurs. He answered questions from luncheon guests who were impressed by his political passion but also curious about the origins of his simmering rage against racial oppression. While civil rights leaders continued to talk in the language of love, peace, and nonviolence, Malcolm countered that "the only language white people understand" was one of "hurt, pain and blood."[243]

By the end of his second tour of the continent in November of 1964, Malcolm X was a genuine star in Africa. He was capable of having his comments on the need for African unity and a trip to Monrovia to gain support for his UN petition reported in Nigeria's biggest daily as newsworthy.[244]

Malcolm X arrived at New York's Kennedy Airport on Tuesday, November 24 amid a fresh storm of controversy. *Muhammad Speaks* had launched new broadsides, payback for Malcolm characterizing the Messenger as a religious "faker" while abroad. Regardless of this, however, about fifty cheering supporters waving "Welcome Back Brother Malcolm" signs greeted him—although Bettye Shabazz and their three daughters comprised his most important entourage. He told reporters that he intended to travel to Oxford for a debate the next week, and he then went on to jab at Martin Luther

King Jr.'s recent Nobel Prize victory, without mentioning King's name, stating, "You know, I, too am a man of peace, but I never could accept a peace prize in the middle of a war."[245]

Malcolm plunged back into America's domestic race war even as he sidestepped the latest eruption in his increasingly bitter feud with the NOI. Following a brief but exhilarating speech at Oxford University, Malcolm made plans to organize voter registration drives in the Deep South and address HARYOU-ACT trainees, an antipoverty effort in Harlem patterned as a domestic peace corps. On Saturday, December 12, Malcolm addressed three hundred trainees in a talk in which his uncompromising insistence on the right to self-defense evoked memories of his NOI heyday. Despite his strident tone, Malcolm maintained his ongoing commitment to working with civil rights groups on bread-and-butter issues such as education and housing.[246]

The following day, Malcolm spoke at a massive OAAU-sponsored rally in Harlem in support of the Congo. Muhammad Babu, a hero of the Zanzibar Revolution, and comedian Dick Gregory joined Malcolm and a capacity crowd of 1,500 to demand an end to U.S.-backed intervention in the Congo. The audience cheered as Malcolm read a message from Che Guevara, who Malcolm called "a good friend." In it Che expressed regrets for lack of attendance but promised that "united we will win." Malcolm excoriated the white press for colluding with Cold War impulses that propped up African dictators as suitable alternatives to Communist influence. He also praised Harlemites, as he did during his meeting with Castro years earlier, as mature political observers immune to anti-Castro propaganda. "You don't see any anti-Castro Cubans around here," he observed. "We eat them up!" Gregory regaled the crowd with a comedic routine that wrung humor from the Birmingham racial crisis by lampooning the FBI as an arm of the Klan and King as an unflappable mediator. Babu then hailed Malcolm as a bold visionary, praising him for being the only major black leader to visit Africa and educate the continent about the status of black Americans. Babu, who Malcolm introduced to Harlem as an authentic revolutionary, claimed solidarity with African Americans based on shared histories of struggle. "The struggle of the people suffering in Africa and those suffering here is one and the same," he explained.[247]

The OAAU's pro-Congo rally illustrated Malcolm's pragmatic efforts to internationalize the black freedom struggle. In the wake of his extensive trips overseas, some of his closest supporters and confidants were anxious and confused over his evolving political direction. Had their champion abandoned the struggle in America for a jet-setting career as a maverick diplomat? Did African struggles really outweigh the rugged political, social, and economic terrain traveled by Harlem residents? The rally, however, showcased Malcolm's continuing interest and involvement in local politics. Judging by his organizing efforts after his return in November 1964, the answer to these questions was a resounding no.

Instead, Malcolm used the extensive knowledge, contacts, and prestige from his international tour to open up new arenas of struggle domestically. Muhammad Babu's presence introduced rank-and-file black New Yorkers to the politics of Zanzibar, a place most could not pick out on a map. In addition, reading the message from Che Guevara confirmed Malcolm's defiance of Cold War dictates that labeled Cuba and its revolutionary heroes as petty tyrants and subversives.

Later that year, representatives of the Southern civil rights movement met with Malcolm in Harlem five days before Christmas. Fannie Lou Hamer, a sharecropper from Ruleville, Mississippi, turned SNCC organizer, appeared onstage with Malcolm at a rally sponsored by the Freedom Democratic Party committee. "We don't only need a change in Mississippi," Hamer reminded the people of Harlem. "We need a change in this nation."[248] Hamer's presence, along with SNCC Freedom Singers and Kenyan vice president Oginga Odinga offered eye-opening examples of the pan-African solidarity Malcolm now preached. "America is Mississippi," he remarked, in his latest rhetorical effort to erase geographical boundaries that separated Southern and Northern black freedom struggles.[249]

Malcolm's efforts to expansively redefine civil rights struggles reverberated from Africa to Washington. As a result, State Department officials fretted over the long-term implications of Malcolm's efforts to bring human rights charges against America before the United Nations. In response, conservative journalists linked his international exploits back to a global Communist conspiracy.[250] Furthermore, the Nation of Islam ridiculed Malcolm as a globe-trotting "international hobo,"[251] while NAACP executive director Roy Wilkins marveled that anyone was paying any attention to him at all.[252] But many continued to pay attention. In Philadelphia, in late December, Malcolm launched a drive to reorganize the city's Muslims, a task on which he had first embarked a decade earlier. At that time, Malcolm had been Muhammad's eager young lieutenant. Now, however, seventy-five police officers guarded Malcolm when he spoke on a local radio program for two hours under the threat of death from NOI enforcers.[253]

At the beginning of the New Year, seven hundred stalwart supporters braved frigid Harlem temperatures to attend the OAAU's Sunday-evening rally. There Malcolm played film clips that documented his recent tours of Africa. The striking footage of Malcolm in Ethiopia, Kenya, and Egypt, resplendent in color film, allowed African Americans a tantalizing taste of what might be possible.[254]

Over the next seven weeks, Malcolm made good on a promise to join in civil rights struggles taking place down South. At the Tuskegee Institute in Alabama, Malcolm lectured to a standing-room-only audience, a visit that would thrust him into the maelstrom of the Southern civil rights movement. In Alabama, he received an invitation to speak to civil rights workers in Selma, the site of a voting rights campaign spearheaded by Martin Luther King Jr. Before three hundred students, many of whom were in high school, Malcolm reiterated that black voting rights would be won "by whatever means is necessary," while nervous local civil rights leaders held their breath. The audience responded to his wide-ranging remarks with sustained applause, and the Reverend Fred Shuttlesworth followed Malcolm's rhetorical vigor with more soothing tones of reconciliation.[255]

It is fitting, then, that Malcolm X made his last public appearance in Harlem on February 21, 1965. Late-arriving speakers added to the stress of an unusually disorganized Sunday-afternoon OAAU rally. Backstage, Malcolm paced the floor in anger and disappointment over the organization's still-unfinished platform, and he dismissed supporters from his dressing room. After a warm-up speech by one of his lieutenants, he approached the stage to loud applause. After he dispensed with the traditional Muslim greeting ("A Salaam Alakium"), a smoke bomb went off and eyes riveted toward the commotion. Over Malcolm's call to "Hold it! Hold it!" three gunmen crept toward the stage with one shotgun-toting assassin delivering the fatal blast to his chest. The premeditated diversion turned the Audubon Ballroom into a jumbled scene of frightening confusion, scattering assassins, and panicked supporters that concluded with Malcolm's bullet-riddled corpse being rushed to Columbia Presbyterian Hospital.[256]

Hailed by black militants in Harlem and the rest of the nation as a bold prophet cut down in his prime, Malcolm would, in death, become an even bigger icon than he had been while alive. King, who had remained aloof to Malcolm's public overtures of rapprochement, sent a statement of remorse from Atlanta, stating, "I am deeply saddened and appalled to learn of the brutal assassination of Malcolm X."[257] Outside the United States, demonstrations of grief proved widespread. In Jakarta, Indonesia, five hundred banner-waving protestors stormed the home of the American ambassador in a demonstration against Malcolm's assassination.[258] Ghanaian president Kwame Nkrumah, who responded coolly to Malcolm's presence in Accra a year earlier, issued a statement of grief that characterized the slain leader as exemplifying a "life of dedication for human dignity" on behalf of blacks all over the world.[259] Headlines in African newspapers memorializing Malcolm as a champion of racial justice counteracted the American media's depiction of the slain black leader as a prophet of rage cut down by his own violent rhetoric.[260] From London, the Council of African Organizations assailed Malcolm's assassination as a "brutal and cowardly" example of American imperialism. In Dar-Es-Salaam, revolutionary organizations in exile—including South Africa's African National Congress—responded to Malcolm's death with expressions of grief and outrage.[261] But perhaps the most personal expression of grief emanating from the African continent came from Ghana, courtesy of Julian Mayfield, who considered Malcolm a personal friend and hailed him as a global leader whose death would not end the black struggle for freedom.[262]

In the popular imagination and most historical narratives of the era, Malcolm X serves as Martin Luther King Jr.'s most well-known counterpart. Whereas King is celebrated as the national leader of the civil rights era, Malcolm's leadership is largely regarded as an enduring symbol of African American rage and anger. King's efforts to desegregate public accommodations in the South, his historic March On Washington speech, and his influence over the successful passage of the 1964 Civil Rights Act and 1965 Voting Rights Act have the cumulative effect of making him the leader of a movement. Meanwhile, Malcolm remains only the fiery expression of a political mood. Such a perspective separates Malcolm from the social and political context in which he lived, operated, and died in.

This approach is as unfair to King as it is to Malcolm. King served as a national political mobilizer who inspired far-flung local movements, organizations, and individuals toward the civil rights movement's goals of racial reform, which included desegregation, equal protection under the law, and voting rights. King's eloquence, creativity, and global stature accelerated civil rights victories and, over time, would resonate around the world. However, King's political mobilizing would have been impossible without local groups, organizers, activists, and everyday people, all of whom bled for American democracy during the civil rights era.

Malcolm X served as more than just a symbolic leader of racial militancy. In Harlem, Detroit, Los Angeles, and other cities, he organized coalitions of early Black Power activists who championed political self-determination as the key to a revolutionary politics that would transform American race relations. At the same time, he also cultivated a wide range of secular radicals who included civil rights renegades, socialists, intellectuals, artists, and independent organizers. Such activists confronted unemployment, police brutality, crime, and drug abuse through local organizing that took place outside bookstores and bars, public schools and police precincts.

Black radicals who unleashed bedlam at the United Nations in 1961 were only a small part of the constellation of activists who looked to Malcolm for leadership. Both seasoned veterans as well as youthful militants found inspiration in him. In contrast to King, years before Malcolm rose to national prominence he participated in grassroots organizing in some of urban America's toughest neighborhoods. It was there that the quest to convey political ideas played out as a kind of trench warfare where combatants included the police, criminals, rival political sects, and apathy.

Malcolm's formidable status as an icon of Black Power militancy continues to obscure the practical political organizing that he conducted for over a decade. Conventional interpretations characterize Malcolm's time in the NOI as a period of unrealized potential. In contrast, his last year is held up as a daring rejection of his misguided past, tragically cut short by his premature death. The publication of Malcolm's best-selling autobiography, complete with an epilogue by Alex Haley, cemented this narrative in historical memory and popular discourse.

But Malcolm's time in the NOI proved more painful and complex than his autobiography suggests. From the moment he arrived in Harlem in June 1954 to the day of his death on February 21, 1965, Malcolm X forcefully confronted American democracy's jagged edges. In Harlem, he embarked on a mission of recruiting converts to Temple No. 7. In doing so, he successfully turned the tiny storefront operation into a political headquarters whose strength, prestige, and financial resources rivaled NOI strongholds in Chicago and even Elijah Muhammad's personal kingdom in Arizona. Moreover, Malcolm reached out to the secular world that Muhammad and the NOI dismissed as doomed by religious prophecy.

Over the course of his long professional association with the Nation, Malcolm explored the fundamentals of his own developing political thought.

His intense interest in foreign affairs naturally drew him to Africa, where independence movements—both peaceful and violent—swept the continent and the larger Third World. In the process of founding or solidifying Muslim mosques around the nation in the 1950s, he established formal and informal networks of contacts who included trade unionists, elected officials, journalists, civic and business leaders, intellectuals, as well as ordinary citizens.

In Northern cities, Malcolm's influence extended into the secular world of black militants who toiled in the Southern civil rights movement's long shadow. While racial turmoil in the Deep South captured headlines, Northern black freedom struggles encountered an equally hostile reception to efforts to secure jobs, decent housing, and to end police brutality. Organizers of bruising school boycotts in New York and Chicago, rent strikes in Harlem, and desegregation campaigns in Chester, Pennsylvania, and Cambridge, Maryland, looked to Malcolm X as a national symbol of black political power. His closest allies ranged from teenaged revolutionaries in Detroit, Harlem, and Philadelphia to the more seasoned veterans of the Robeson generation. They helped organize an early Black Power movement that advocated African American political self-determination, linked anticolonial struggles abroad with domestic civil rights campaigns, and attempted to redefine black citizenship and American democracy. What is evident from both travels, political activities, and speeches is that Malcolm viewed struggles for racial justice holistically.

After leaving the NOI, Malcolm attempted to use his extensive knowledge of organizing, sizable reputation, and global network to form a secular organization capable of uniting the far-flung political and ideological tendencies that formed the black world. However, his organizing efforts took place against a backdrop of sectarian violence between his relatively small band of followers and the much larger Black Muslims. FBI agents and local police agencies documented the increasingly brazen attempts by the NOI to harass, threaten, and kill Malcolm, but did little to prevent the conflict from resolving itself tragically. Shadowed by death threats, plagued by fears for his family's safety, and undermined in his organizing efforts by the NOI, FBI, and a hostile white press, Malcolm turned to the international arena. There, he engaged in rounds of freelance diplomacy with representatives of African states, including Cairo, Zanzibar, Kenya, Ghana, and Ethiopia.

Domestically, Malcolm's "Ballots or Bullets" speech broke new ground in its provocative synthesis of civil rights activists' unyielding quest for the vote and Black Power militants' promotion of racial justice by any means necessary. Moreover, the speech also highlighted Malcolm's optimism. "If you take this warning, perhaps you can still save yourself," he remarked in a 1964 television documentary. "But if you ignore it or ridicule it, well, death is already at your doorstep."[263]

During Malcolm's last year, he pursued both personal and political redemption. Personally, he embarked on a religious and spiritual quest that culminated in his acceptance of orthodox Islam after successfully completing his *Hajj* pilgrimage in the Middle East. Spiritual redemption fueled more politically minded plans to expose the NOI and his former religious leader, Elijah Muhammad, as unworthy of the mantle of trust and devotion that Malcolm had helped to instill in thousands of true believers.

Malcolm's legacy is often defined as much by his speaking style and public image as his political accomplishments. Immediately following his assassination, dozens of Black Power activists and organizations invoked Malcolm as a patron saint, mentor, teacher, and enduring icon. But many never adequately absorbed his political thought, investigated the contours of his domestic and global activism, or comprehended his complex relationship with civil rights and American democracy.

Malcolm was more than simply an eloquent though ultimately ineffectual rabble-rouser who attacked civil rights from Harlem's safe streets while young activists—both black and white—risked life and limb in the heroic pursuit of democracy and citizenship. Malcolm pursued the same goals as his civil rights counterparts, first as a Nation of Islam activist, and later as an independent political organizer and mobilizer.

Malcolm's political, cultural, and intellectual leadership transformed postwar America. As an activist, intellectual, organizer, and icon, he sought to reimagine the very meaning of American democracy. He redefined it on his own terms and in tough language that intimidated, frightened, and disgusted critics who, even in their denunciations, admitted the power of Malcolm's rhetorical eloquence. Ironically, his genius for language, gift of connecting with ordinary African Americans, and penchant for the outrageous sound bite have overwhelmed Malcolm's impact as a historical figure. There is still no definitive biography of this important historical figure, and scholars too often rely on his speeches as a means to explain his impact rather than actively seeking to reconstruct the breadth and depth of his political activism. Malcolm's twelve years as an NOI minister are easily dismissed, even as his final twelve months are extolled for providing the glimpse of a brilliant work in progress cut down in his prime.

This is as unfortunate as it is shortsighted. As a Black Muslim minister, Malcolm participated in the front lines of struggles for racial justice even as he conformed to the NOI's dictates to refrain from overt political activity. In Harlem, his power base rivaled that of the legendary congressman Adam Clayton Powell Jr., and in urban cities he led a coalition of black militants who engaged in both local civil rights organizing as well as the spectacular displays of militancy associated with Black Power insurgency. Furthermore, Malcolm's political presence was not limited to the urban North. In the 1950s, as the NOI's roving national organizer, he helped to facilitate and strengthen temples in Miami, Birmingham, and Atlanta.

By the early 1960s, then, Malcolm was a powerbroker. His sprawling influence extended beyond NOI enclaves through his prodigious speaking schedule and the success of *Muhammad Speaks*, perhaps the most important black radical periodical of the era. The newspaper found its voice and secular appeal through its meticulous documentation of the global nature of civil rights struggles and generous coverage of black militants both in the United States as well as African independence movements abroad.

Malcolm's threat to the existing civil rights establishment and America's elected officials lay less in his provocative predictions of a coming race war than in his efforts to redefine the terms of a debate that guided America's civil rights struggles. Using the NOI's infrastructure to inject himself into national controversies surrounding Birmingham, Alabama, he turned into a militant statesman by the early 1960s. The same year as the March On Washington, his allies helped organize a massive demonstration in Detroit that featured Martin Luther King Jr. as the keynote speaker.

The breadth of Malcolm's influence was such that black nationalists in Harlem, black preachers in Detroit, and even civil rights activists in the Deep South all debated the merits of his critiques regarding the very nature of American democracy. Rallies in Harlem in December of 1964 and a trip to Tuskegee and Selma, Alabama, in February 1965 offer glimpses of his evolving worldview. All of these events featured jarring alliances between black nationalists, Southern civil rights activists, and African revolutionaries. He found strength in these juxtapositions by acknowledging that political distances once thought to be insurmountable could be bridged through robust debate.

Malcolm's revolutionary posture also hid a surprisingly pragmatic political side. For a time, the NOI offered Malcolm an organizational vehicle to promote spiritual redemption and political activism, the latter primarily through his association with black militants around the country. Paradoxically, his successful foray into the secular arena through college lectures and speaking tours in the early 1960s doomed his standing in the NOI even as it helped turn the once-modest organization into a financial colossus. The NOI remained aloof from political protest initially. It did so in order to hide its irrelevance on the national stage and, later, as a form of self-preservation against a phalanx of threatening government authorities including the IRS, which could potentially revoke the group's tax-exempt status. Malcolm, however, contrasted this caution through a passionate engagement with local, national, and international politics. As the NOI's national representative, Malcolm served as the de facto leader of a national movement for black political power that paralleled, and at time intersected with, conventional civil rights struggles.

During his year of political independence, Malcolm attempted to confront the very institutions of democracy that he spent his entire career challenging—but on his own terms. His biggest successes combined his credibility on the world stage with street knowledge of America's gritty inner cities. When he left the NOI, Malcolm attempted a number of different organizational strategies, including an effort to recruit disgruntled Black Muslims into his newly created Muslim Mosque, Inc., an attempt to develop a working alliance with civil rights leaders, and lobbying African leaders to petition the United Nations on behalf of black Americans.

Malcolm took three tours of African between 1959 and 1964. A member of the NOI during his brief first visit, by 1964 he toured Africa as an independent political activist and budding pan-Africanist. Malcolm's presence in Africa reverberated from the global cities of Lagos, Nigeria, and Dar-Es-Salaam, Tanganyika, all the way to western citadels of power in Washington, D.C.

For Africans unaware of the complex dynamics of American race relations, Malcolm offered a crash course in the politics behind the civil rights struggle and his own efforts to expand the movement's goals, strategies, and tactics. Like a politician engaged in an endless campaign, he held dozens of press conferences, conducted numerous interviews, spoke at countless lunches and dinners, and attended soirees in an effort to convince Africans of their shared political destiny with black Americans. In Cairo, Addis Ababa, Nairobi, Accra, and other African cities, Malcolm spoke with local activists, national leaders, and diplomats. However, his evolving political dreams would bear partial fruit only after his death, as a generation of Black Power activists crafted a political agenda inspired in part by his political thought and activism. But Black Power activists also encountered the limitations inherent in efforts to forge pan-African alliances that transcended history and geography. Postcolonial visions expressed by new African states would, in too many instances, buckle underneath the combined weight of ethnic and regional tensions, political corruption, environmental and natural disasters, and financial and diplomatic pressure from the West.

Ultimately, Malcolm X exposed the gulf between America's democratic rhetoric and practice at home and abroad. In doing so, he critically participated in a conversation about race, democracy, and citizenship that was local, national, and global. But Malcolm did more than simply react to proliferating instances of racial injustice during the civil rights era's heroic years. He also advanced a constructive and radical political dialogue about black people's future in America and around the world. Part of this national conversation included a critical engagement with democracy. His legacy opened up new avenues of political expression as well as intellectual and cultural understanding of American race relations. Only by finally coming to terms with Malcolm X the activist and organizer and placing him within the larger historical context in which he lived, worked, and died can we come to a more complex and sophisticated understanding of the era he indelibly shaped.[264]

3

STOKELY CARMICHAEL
AND AMERICA IN THE 1960s

Stokely Carmichael is one of the most important political leaders of the postwar era, and yet he also remains one of the most obscure. A civil rights militant turned Black Power revolutionary, Carmichael's call for "Black Power" in Greenwood, Mississippi, during a late spring heat wave in 1966 sent shockwaves throughout the United States and beyond.[1] Carmichael identified with the political struggles of poor blacks in the rural South through personal experience as a civil rights organizer. Furthermore, trips to Europe, Africa, Asia, Latin America, and the Caribbean allowed him to imagine the world as a global stage wherein political leaders—no less than black sharecroppers—could play pivotal roles that would determine the course of history.

A panoramic view of postwar freedom struggles can be found in Carmichael's unusual biography. He was a Caribbean-born, Bronx-raised, and Howard University-educated activist who worked to register black sharecroppers down South, only to unexpectedly emerge as a national leader, world traveler, and international icon. He embraced black America's rural and urban folkways. Unglamorous everyday people—ranging from men and women, teenagers, schoolchildren, and trade unionists—participated alongside preachers and street speakers, politicians and political leaders, intellectuals and artists. The resulting movement ranged from gritty Harlem neighborhoods and industrial-shop floors in Detroit to Dixie's cradle, Birmingham, Alabama, and even out West to postwar boomtowns like Oakland, California. These local political struggles helped shape a movement for social and political justice that couched specific goals in universal themes.

Carmichael's call for Black Power would scandalize American society. In response, the national media quickly turned the slogan into a national Rorschach test. For blacks, Black Power was a righteous exhortation. Whites, however, interpreted the term to be filled with violent foreboding. Newspapers brooded over Carmichael's words, quickly forming a consensus that judged the slogan to be at best intemperate and, at worst, a blatant call for antiwhite violence and reverse racism. For the next decade, Black Power would reverberate around the world. It would galvanize blacks, outrage whites, and inspire a large and varied group of ethnic and racial minorities.

Despite his critical influence over much of the 1960s, Carmichael's life remains shrouded in mystery. A civil rights militant turned Black Power radical, by 1969 Carmichael abandoned the United States for Conakry, Guinea, and claimed pan-Africanism as the highest stage of black political radicalism. For the next thirty years—until his death from terminal cancer on November 15, 1998—Carmichael (who renamed himself Kwame Ture after his move to Guinea) remained a diligent political activist, a throwback to the heady years of the 1960s who remained defiant in his belief that a worldwide revolution was still possible. Yet his image obscures as much as it reveals. Carmichael's role as an advocate of radical democracy and as a tireless civil rights organizer during the 1960s remains too often buried beneath the celebrity that would engulf him by the summer of 1966.

Carmichael's life proves that the goals of civil rights and Black Power activists were never mutually exclusive. He advocated both black nationalism as well as democratic pluralism in justifying his dual commitment to Black Power and democracy. Carmichael endured physical beatings, unjust arrests, and prolonged weeks in jail in pursuit of his vision of the American Dream.

For Carmichael, Black Power represented a means to provide poor African Americans in the rural South and urban North with the political power necessary to control their own destiny. As an organizer, he attempted to put theory into practice in Lowndes County, where Black Power militancy and civil rights activism existed side by side. The nickname of the independent political group he helped organize between 1965 and 1966 in Lowndes County—the Black Panther Party—would reverberate around the world.

Yet Carmichael was also an alumnus of the civil rights movement. He belonged to the small fraternity who literally bled for American democracy during the early 1960s. As a young student activist at Howard University, he helped transform American democracy by fighting on the front lines of social and political upheavals during the civil rights movement's *heroic* years.[2] By

Carmichael's own recollection, between June 1961 and June 1966, he was arrested twenty-seven times while participating in civil rights activities. For him, the decision to endure physical violence, personal discomfort, and economic uncertainty was part of a disciplined commitment to radical democracy in service of racial equality, economic justice, and black community empowerment.

In Carmichael's experience organizing, the dream of self-determination was stymied by traditions of white supremacy, random violence, and economic retribution. He worked with poor, unlettered blacks from Cambridge, Maryland, to Washington, D.C., and from Mississippi's Delta region to the backwoods of Lowndes County, Alabama. Through these efforts, Carmichael increasingly realized that political power, rather than legal redress or moral suasion, held the key to racial justice in America. This led him to preach a politics of Black Power that, in his mind, reflected democracy's best face and last hope.

This point cannot be overstated: Carmichael's political activism as a local organizer in the Deep South, border state of Maryland, and in the nation's capital of Washington, D.C., represented a commitment to transforming American democracy fundamentally. From modestly built churches to decaying sharecroppers' shacks to hastily constructed tent cities, he helped organize meetings, register black voters, and lead citizenship classes that promoted civil and human rights.

Carmichael's path to national prominence would prove arduous. Under constant surveillance from authorities and local vigilantes, he faced illegal arrests, punishing violence, and routine intimidation that left him with an ulcer when he was still a young man. But by 1966, he would emerge as a national leader of an insurgent Black Power Movement that would help inspire the creation of militant groups such as the Black Panthers—for whom Carmichael would serve as honorary prime minister for a little over one year. An icon to a generation of young people who hailed him as a new Malcolm X, he searched for common ground with Martin Luther King Jr., experienced harassment at the hands of federal authorities, and enjoyed the company of international revolutionaries.[3]

However, over time Carmichael became overwhelmed by his celebrity in the States and burned out from years of service on the front lines of civil rights and Black Power struggles. Because of this, he departed for Africa at the height of civil unrest in the United States. Beginning in 1969, Carmichael made Conakry, Guinea, his permanent home. By 1979, he had changed his name to Kwame Ture, in homage to two West African revolutionaries,

Ghana's Kwame Nkrumah and Guinea's Sekou Toure. These men had mentored him upon his arrival to Africa in 1967. Up until his untimely death from prostate cancer in 1998, Ture remained, in his own inimitable phrase, "ready for revolution."

Carmichael's political activism during the 1960s provides a unique prism through which to view issues of race, war, and democracy in the United States at the local, national, and international level. Tall, handsome, and charismatic, when Carmichael burst onto the American political scene in 1966, he was the leading proponent of Black Power radicalism. A Renaissance man equally comfortable in sharecropper's overalls, business suits, and dashikis, he projected the passionate temper of a street speaker, the contemplative demeanor of an academic, and the gregariousness of a Baptist preacher—all traits that helped turn him into an international icon.

The political equivalent of a rock star during the late 1960s, Carmichael's historical significance receded over time. In contrast to Malcolm X, Carmichael's political exploits remain both less documented and revered.[4] He represents arguably the most important bridge between civil rights and Black Power activism: a grassroots organizer equally comfortable among sharecroppers in the Mississippi Delta and urban militants in Los Angeles and the Bay Area; bold enough to trek through Cuba's *Sierra Maestra* with Fidel Castro and denounce Lyndon Johnson as a warmonger; yet compassionate enough to share unscripted moments of friendship with Martin Luther King Jr. He was all of these things, but in the end Carmichael represents perhaps the most important individual key to unearthing the buried intimacies between the civil rights and Black Power eras.

B orn on June 29, 1941, in Port of Spain, Trinidad, Stokely Carmichael immigrated to New York City in 1952. A precocious student enrolled at the prestigious Bronx High School of Science, he spent his adolescence shuttling between the upscale homes of liberal classmates, attending outdoor lectures on Harlem's famed 125th Street corridor, and committing acts of juvenile delinquency as part of a local—predominantly white—street gang. In 1960, Carmichael enrolled as a freshman at Howard University in Washington and quickly joined the civil rights movement.

In June 1961, one month after completing final exams for spring classes at Howard University, the nineteen-year-old Carmichael flew from Washington to New Orleans to join an integrated group of Freedom Riders traveling from Louisiana to Mississippi. That spring, groups of interracial volunteers embarked on an experiment in democracy that placed political principle ahead of personal safety by challenging restrictions that barred blacks and whites from interstate travel. Originally conceived of by CORE (Congress of Racial Equality) in 1947, the group resuscitated the concept early in 1961 after being inspired by the wave of sit-ins that were unleashed the previous year. From May 4 to December 10, 436 Freedom Riders embarked on over 50 separate trips. After violent clashes with white vigilantes in Alabama and other parts of the South, this campaign was able to turn the subject of racial segregation in interstate travel into a national priority.[5]

When Carmichael arrived in New Orleans at 3 a.m. on June 8, he was met by a nervous escort. They were hopeful that their early-morning rendezvous would mask the trip's political intentions as part of the seventeenth deployment of Freedom Riders that spring. The sight of strange trees glittering with Spanish moss evoked ominous images of a gothic South teeming with lynch mobs, and indeed, a large white mob met the group outside the New Orleans train station. They forced Carmichael and his fellow Freedom Riders onto the train headed for Jackson. The Freedom Riders' relief at having survived the blur of concentrated violence left them too exhilarated to dwell on the cuts and bruises they sustained during the frantic boarding.[6]

Their short-lived Freedom Ride ended almost as quickly as it began. On June 8, Carmichael and the Freedom Riders entered a white waiting room in Jackson, Mississippi. There, they were quickly arrested and, after a short stint in Hinds County jail, sent on a two-hour drive to Mississippi's Parchman Penitentiary. The inmates were welcomed to Parchman Farm with the sight of cattle prods pressing against the naked flesh of prisoners. Ringed by barbed-wire fences and defended by shotgun-toting sentries, Parchman's warden threatened that the Freedom Riders' punishment would come from the "bad niggers"—death row inmates with a predilection for random violence.[7]

The Freedom Riders kept their composure under pressure. The Riders in Parchman, who now included Congress of Racial Equality leader James Farmer as well as a yarmulke-wearing young preacher named James Bevel, responded to escalating brutality with prayers, freedom songs, and a hunger strike. Carmichael celebrated his twentieth birthday, June 29, in Parchman Farm. He eventually spent more than five weeks in this prison before his release on July 19.[8] He would cherish this memory as a rite of passage and preparation for dozens of future arrests.[9]

May Carmichael would spend a tense evening listening to the radio before learning of her son's fate. Stokely had prepared May for his probable incarceration before heading to Mississippi. He gently told her that she shouldn't worry, that he was going to jail and that she should be proud, not ashamed. Responding to neighbors who asked, "Is that your boy Stokely they've got down there?" she responded as her son had instructed. "Yes, that's my boy and I'm so proud of him I don't know what to do!" Adolph Carmichael, on the other hand, frowned on his son's activism. Nevertheless, he took Stokely at his word that he would earn a college degree before devoting his life to the movement.

May and Adolph Carmichael were immigrants from Port of Spain, Trinidad, who had transplanted to the Bronx. They learned early on that they couldn't tell their son what to do. Instead, they resolved to compromise with Stokely, who seemed more willful, mischievous, and political than his two sisters. If May identified with her son's independent streak, Adolph retained a stubborn faith in God and hard work. Adolph's hope in the promise of America's immigrant roots contrasted with Stokely's ingrained skepticism. After his father's premature death in 1962, Stokely would come to view the American Dream as a cruel joke played at the expense of honest men like his father, who worked himself to an early grave believing in that myth.[10]

The forty-nine days Stokely Carmichael spent in Parchman Farm transformed him in ways that could hardly be expected. In the same Mississippi where others saw poverty, he saw a landscape teeming with beauty. The Mississippi Delta's wide spaces were punctuated by flatlands and dotted with decrepit shacks, simple one-story churches, and historic plantations. Carmichael saw the area as an impoverished yet distinctive landscape that most Americans chose to ignore. He marveled at the surreal physical environment comprised of dense black soil, dark wetlands, and huge plantations.

Mississippi exposed the young Carmichael to the "pain and joy of struggle" that bound together citizens in a "brotherhood of shared danger within bonds of loyalty."[11] The delta hid untold potential in the faces of obsidian-eyed sharecroppers who toiled in anonymity, many whose birth, life, and death would never be officially recorded. He saw that these same sharecroppers held the power to alter the course of American history through an individual act of self-determination—the vote. This act could express the collective will of black communities in the South who bore no visible chains yet still lived in bondage. Black sharecroppers in Mississippi distilled the very meaning of citizenship in their resilient, patient, and courageous folkways, and their example earned Carmichael's respect for the inhabitants of the rural delta.

However, Carmichael held more than just admiration for sharecroppers in the Mississippi Delta. He loved them, developing a lifelong sensitivity to the rhythms, customs, and folkways of rural Southern blacks, a compassion that made him a staggeringly effective organizer. Older residents viewed him with respect and admiration, and, in return, he fiercely guarded their trust.[12]

Carmichael's prison experiences in Parchman and his political organizing in Mississippi shaped the development of his adult identity. He was keenly sensitive, but this virtue could cut both ways. He could be temperamental, brash, and arrogant: a know-it-all whose easy smile masked a nervous energy that left him saddled with an ulcer by the age of twenty-two. Furthermore, a larger-than-life personality meant, at times, an outsized ego. His ability to make split-second, life-saving decisions in the field could, in other settings, come off as impetuous, intemperate, and reckless. Regardless, in the face of dangers both seen and unseen, Carmichael—by turns bold and compassionate, belligerent and contemplative—inspired hope and confidence among fellow activists in the field who looked to him as a leader among equals. If Carmichael's aura of uncompromising certitude attracted scores of admirers in the movement, making him a sort of minor celebrity among veteran activists, it would, however, likewise serve as a major repellent once it was amplified by media projection that cast him as a dangerously charismatic heir to Malcolm X.[13]

Besides a landscape and people that Carmichael adored, Mississippi also housed the grotesque. Mississippi's level of racial violence during the 1950s and early 1960s approached the surreal. Following World War II, racial tensions in the state grew as returning black veterans lobbied in vain for voting rights. Remnants of this militancy persisted in the 1950s via the NAACP's proudly effective organizer Medgar Evers, and it only increased after his June 1963 assassination. In 1964, three years after his first trip to the delta, Carmichael served as project director of Mississippi's Second Congressional District during the Student Non-Violent Coordinating Committee (SNCC)-led summer project. In the midst of what would come to be known as Freedom Summer, Carmichael plotted strategy, coordinated the deployment of resources, and tried to stay alive. SNCC's Sojourner motor fleet featured modified cars designed to help civil rights workers outrun local vigilantes, Klansmen, and law enforcement officials. Carmichael's skills behind the wheel earned him the nickname the "Delta Devil."[14]

The next year, Carmichael rode the wave of Martin Luther King Jr.'s Selma-based voting rights campaign into clandestine organizing in the rural woods of Lowndes County, Alabama. In the late winter of 1965, he roamed the wilderness on mules trying to attract rural people who were daring enough to talk to civil rights activists—and some who were brave enough to provide shelter. Inspired by his experiences in Parchman, his work as a campus organizer at Howard University, and his experience in roiling demonstrations alongside Gloria Richardson in Cambridge, Maryland, Carmichael would pour all of his organizing energies into one of Alabama's obscurest regions.

In a 1966 letter to Lorna D. Smith, a white SNCC supporter, Carmichael wrote, "We are trying to build democracy, and we have dedicated our lives to that task." Carmichael's letter discussed SNCC's recent opposition to the Vietnam War, his organizing efforts in Lowndes County, Alabama, and his personal dedication to transforming society. Sacrifice, expressed in the shared willingness of civil rights workers to bleed for democratic principles, animated Carmichael's political activism. However, the deaths of colleagues—both black and white—made him impatient for enduring justice that transcended legal and legislative boundaries. "Our commitment is to man not to a plot of earth or even our country," Carmichael explained, confessing appreciative relief for Smith's support in the face of both Carmichael and SNCC being dismissed by critics as "beatniks or communists." Carmichael resurrected hope through language that found kinship with Martin Luther King Jr.'s notion of political transformation through the heroic witness against historic miseries. "It is the human contact that we make," Carmichael wrote, "while suffering that will make the difference."[15]

In January, Carmichael published an essay in the *New Republic* in which he tested out a theory of radical democracy based on his personal experiences as an organizer. He held up African Americans as a metaphorical battering ram, capable of denting the conscience of a nation that was too often content to look the other way. Substituting the painful details of organizing in Alabama with passing references to anonymous martyrs, Carmichael directed his gaze toward an impoverished American political landscape. For him, this poverty stemmed from a naive belief that democracy's restorative powers were equally available to rich and poor, black and white. "The majority view is a lie," he wrote, "based on the premise of upward mobility which doesn't exist for most Americans."

Carmichael's blunt criticism gave way to a roll call of grief, an indictment of Lyndon Johnson's Great Society as "preposterous," and then, finally, a hard-earned faith that poor, unlettered sharecroppers represented democracy's best hope and example. Legislative and legalistic racial breakthroughs inspired hope even as they magnified the tragedy of white supremacy's stubborn refusal to regard blacks as fellow citizens. The disenfranchised, he declared, would "redefine what the Great Society is," thereby imparting meaning that would soar above Johnson's rhetoric. Carmichael wrote, "I place my own hope for the United States" in the ability of black sharecroppers who showed through their quiet determination that "they can articulate and be responsible and hold power."[16]

In the winter and spring of 1966, Carmichael discussed issues of race, power, and democracy in a wide-ranging series of interviews published in *The Movement*, SNCC's monthly magazine. Having spent almost a solid year organizing sharecroppers in Lowndes County, Alabama, he claimed that political power, rather than morality, was the key to racial and economic justice. SNCC's efforts to organize within the Democratic Party through the Mississippi Freedom Democratic Party (MFDP) had also provided tough lessons about American democracy. After successfully unseating the segregated state delegation to the 1964 Democratic National Convention in Atlantic City, MFDP activists—most notably former sharecropper Fannie Lou Hamer—watched in disappointed shock as the official powerbrokers rejected their legal victory in favor of a political compromise that refused to seat their delegation.[17]

Carmichael responded to the Democratic Party's political betrayal by organizing. "We thought we could take over the Democratic Party in Mississippi," he confessed, "and that's a farce." According to him, independent black political power at the local level would ensure that blacks would control "the law, the taxes," as well as the bread-and-butter issues that comprised actual political power. Months before his famous Black Power speech in Mississippi, Carmichael calmly made plans "to take over Lowndes County."

In February 1966, Carmichael characterized his organizing efforts in Lowndes as a sort of civic experiment. He recalled the lessons he had learned from political science classes at Howard University—that voting power promised better roads, street lights, and housing. "I don't know that for a fact. And that's what I have been telling the people of Alabama," he explained. "We are about to find out."[18]

Carmichael's first task as an organizer was to combat the poverty that stifled dreams, thereby turning the American myth of upward mobility into reality for illiterate black sharecroppers. These workers, who toiled from "sunup to sundown" for $2 a day, resided on the other side of the American Dream. But a revolutionary application of democracy threatened to change the old order by ushering in a new class of black leaders, powerbrokers, and educated citizens. Acknowledging that "Negroes in this country have come a long way" since SNCC's founding in 1960, Carmichael warned that "it would be silly to throw it all away" by swearing blind allegiance to either major political party.[19] Instead, African Americans needed to demand and receive tangible benefits from the existing political system. But this act would be interpreted as audacious by white powerbrokers who continued to rule over black labor via an almost feudal system—complete with plantations—that remained remarkably unchanged since the antebellum era.

Carmichael's approach to organizing in Alabama followed SNCC's disciplined focus on developing local leadership and empowering ordinary citizens through education. On this score, local activist John Hulett served as chairman of the LCFO (Lowndes County Freedom Organization) while candidates for tax collector, sheriff, and the school board were drawn from the ordinary people of Lowndes County. However, the process of convincing African Americans who had never voted before that they were qualified to run for political office was not easy. As a result, Carmichael and Hulett ended up organizing weekend bus trips to Atlanta for workshops conducted by SNCC's Research Department.[20] These workshops focused on general principles of citizenship and the intricacies of local offices, such as sherriff.

Black citizenship, Carmichael argued, would stretch the boundaries of American democracy beyond the imagination of the Constitution's framers. "Lowndes County is going to be very interesting," he puckishly noted, "as indicative of what could happen across the country when propertyless people" acquire political power. This was both a declaration of hard-fought independence and a warning against efforts to halt this rising movement for black political power.

According to Carmichael, Lowndes represented a microcosm of a national movement that was under way to redefine and reimagine American democracy. This included deciding where and how the nation's resources and wealth would be spent and distributed. Furthermore, blacks would have to "confront the question of Vietnam." If Vietnam redirected energy and resources that could be better spent in Alabama overseas, Carmichael argued, "it's going to be in our interest to stop the war. Not even on a moral issue but a very practical issue."[21]

Thus, several months before the start of the June 5 Meredith March, Carmichael had already offered an extensive blueprint for what he would come to define as Black Power. He had demonstrated a strategy of promoting African Americans in pursuit of radical democracy at the local level, and doing so even at the cost of turning tradition on its head and outraging white Americans. Clearly aware of the audacious aspect of his efforts before they had even come to fruition, Carmichael acknowledged that the results of Lowndes County's political experiment would reverberate—for good or ill—nationally.

Carmichael's faith in local people's ability to govern themselves was justified on May 3, 1966. On this day, nine hundred blacks in Lowndes County attended a nominating convention at the First Baptist Church of Hayneville, a half mile from the county courthouse. Carmichael watched with unabashed pride as Lowndes County's African Americans voted to make the Black Panther a third party for the upcoming November election. This victory inspired both black hope and white anxiety. Over time, it would even come to be seen as a symbol of revolution recognized around the world.[22]

Five days after Lowndes County's convention, Carmichael was elected chairman of SNCC. As chairman, he sparked immediate controversy by publicly describing integration as "an insidious subterfuge for white supremacy." His remarks elicited swift rebuke from Martin Luther King Jr., who regretted SNCC's overt flirtation with black nationalism.

King's criticism belied what would become an enduring personal friendship. In fact, shortly after his election, King called Carmichael to offer congratulatory words and advice. Meanwhile, in tense meetings with SNCC staff, Carmichael candidly admitted that he was losing faith in American politics. The optimistic—but by now apparently mistaken—assumption that America "is really a democracy" left Carmichael and SNCC reeling, anxious, and unprepared for the violent resistance that met each step toward racial progress.[23]

Then, in May 1966, SNCC announced its new political direction with a pointed rejection of an invitation to attend a civil rights conference sponsored by the White House. Carmichael characterized President Johnson as a man who "flagrantly violates the human rights of colored people in Vietnam."[24] "Political and economic power," he went on to say, "is what the black people have to have."[25] Beyond the issue of Vietnam, SNCC rejected the White House Conference's plans to focus on the "Negro family" as a diversion from the roots of black oppression—namely white racism. Because President Johnson had proven himself unable or unwilling to enforce civil rights legislation in the Deep South, SNCC refused to attend a conference designed, at least in part, to buoy American prestige around the world. Instead, SNCC called for blacks around the country to "begin building independent political, economic and cultural institutions" for the purpose of fundamentally transforming American democracy.[26]

In 1966, black freedom struggles reached a critical apex in America. SNCC's call for the creation of a new political framework stemmed from Carmichael's practical experiences in both Democratic Party politics as well as his awareness of the quotidian struggles of black citizens in places like Lowndes County. By the spring of 1966, he and the organization embarked on a quest to acquire political power outside the channels of interracial coalitions and a Democratic Party that had once been SNCC's ally during their early years. As a result, the call for self-determination in pursuit of black political power threatened the civil rights movement's status quo, and this would take on new dimensions in Mississippi.

However, that June, an almost three-week civil rights march forged an enduring personal friendship between Carmichael and King, even as it highlighted their political differences. The shooting of James Meredith during his one-man "March Against Fear" attracted major civil rights leaders to Mississippi. The first Negro to graduate from Ole Miss in 1963, Meredith had returned to the state to embark on this one-man march that symbolized his defiance of what he called "white supremacy" in the Magnolia State. Although his initial march attracted little attention from the media or civil rights workers, this changed when he was shot on his second day. Then, from June 7 through June 26, civil rights demonstrators walked from the state's upper northern region toward the capital of Jackson. Marching side by side, Carmichael and King were opposites both physically and in temperament. Tall, lanky, and restless, Carmichael laconically informed reporters that he held no personal commitment to nonviolence and that he saw it as little more than a political tactic. Meanwhile, the disciplined and diminutive King politely disagreed, maintaining an outward appearance of self-control that had been honed over a decade in the national spotlight.

Behind closed doors, the two men enjoyed an easy familiarity and bantered like old friends. Just thirty-seven, King admired the almost twenty-five-year-old Carmichael's commitment to struggle. In return, Carmichael appreciated King's unassuming demeanor and earthy sense of humor. The march allowed Carmichael to see a different, less formal side of King. "During those sweltering days Dr. King became to many of us no longer a symbol or an icon," he remembered, "but a warm, funny, likeable, unpretentious human being who shared many of our values." But this march also exposed a new side of Carmichael to civil rights activists. During a planning session with NAACP leader Roy Wilkins, Carmichael pressed for a radical march manifesto that was critical of the Johnson administration. He remained adamant that the Johnson administration be held accountable for its failure to protect the lives of civil rights workers. Hearing this, Wilkins, who had written an article describing SNCC's new politics as a form of "black racism," bolted from the proceedings, convinced that Carmichael and SNCC were determined to undermine racial progress.[27]

For the next two and a half weeks, the Meredith March made its way through Mississippi, veering purposefully into large swathes of the delta left untouched by modernity. With King flying back and forth to Chicago in order to pursue intense efforts at open housing and slum clearance, Carmichael became the march's de facto leader. With this authority, on Friday, June 10, to crowds of local people in Batesville, Mississippi, Carmichael preached a message of political self-determination. "If you want to change this state, you're going to have to do it yourself," he said. "You're going to have to register. You have to have power."[28] During a lunch break, he then rang an ancient plantation bell housed on a church ground that, in another era, summoned enslaved Africans from cotton fields. Now, however, the crowd chanted "freedom" every time it tolled.[29]

Journalists contrasted the belligerent demeanor on display in Mississippi with the more soothing portrait of 1965's Selma-to-Montgomery voting rights demonstration. Traveling through "virgin territory" untouched by civil rights protests, Carmichael exemplified the kind of "truculence never shown in the Alabama demonstration." After noting that Carmichael had called for "black power," one reporter from the mainstream press presented a story that warned of growing dissension among the ranks of march leaders.[30]

As the march progressed, so did Carmichael's confidence. SNCC workers took the increasing attention that the march generated in stride. They made plans to unveil a new slogan that the inimitable Willie Ricks had been testing out among sharecroppers with promising results. "This is the twenty-seventh time that I've been arrested," Carmichael informed a large crowd in Greenwood on the evening of Thursday, June 16, 1966. "I ain't going to jail no more. The only way we gonna stop them white men from whuppin' us is to take over. What we gonna start sayin' now is Black Power!" King arrived the next day just in time for a demonstration at Greenwood's Leflore County Courthouse. "We are here because we are tired of being beaten, tired of being murdered," said King. Speaking from the steps of the courthouse,

King defined power as the "ability to make the power structure say yes even when it wants to say no"—a development that the *Los Angeles Times* suggested made Carmichael and King appear as speaking "with almost one voice."[31]

Carmichael and King were among 2,000 demonstrators who experienced what one headline called "TEAR GAS TERROR." In Canton, early in the day of Thursday, June 23, Carmichael and King led two columns of marchers to Canton's courthouse as shotgun-wielding sheriff's deputies stalked the lawn grounds beneath magnolias. Then, that evening, twenty-five miles outside of Jackson, protesters were confronted with Mississippi's mercurial racial politics after being denied permission to camp on the grounds of a local black school. Troopers who had originally been dispatched to protect demonstrators now reversed course under orders from Mississippi's governor, firing tear gas and indiscriminately pummeling marchers who were in the process of setting up an evening camp.

March leaders restored order to a chaotic scene as crowds scurried away from the school grounds.[32] Some groups found safety in the bowels of Canton's local black community, while more than 1,000 found refuge alongside King at Asbury Methodist Church. For Carmichael, the violence unleashed against peaceful demonstrators exemplified the need for black political power as it simultaneously exposed sordid connections between the nation's domestic and foreign policy. "While our black brothers are fighting in Vietnam," he explained shortly after the incident, "we're getting gassed for trying to vote in Canton, Miss."[33]

The Meredith March concluded on Sunday, June 26 with an enormous rally at the Mississippi State Capitol in Jackson. Hundreds of blue-and-green helmeted state troopers armed with riot gear formed a ring around the capitol that kept demonstrators seventy-five yards away. In so doing, Governor Paul Johnson drew not only a figurative but also a literal line in the sand regarding the prospects for racial justice in the state.

A "CBS News Special Report: The March in Mississippi" hosted by Harry Reasoner carried live coverage of speeches interspersed with correspondent John Hart's on-camera interviews from the capitol. As helicopters swirled above, march leaders spoke on an outdoor platform under the gaze of an oppressive sun. They did not mince words. Andrew Young introduced a local minister to read scripture and asked news helicopters to back away from the stage because of the interference they caused. Thousands of American flags waved by the predominantly black crowd in attendance marked the final rally. James Meredith recalled his graduation from Ole Miss and, despite his shooting, expressed a stubborn faith in his father's belief in the innate decency of white folks. A "system of white supremacy," he said—using a term that would become popular as the 1960s progressed—imprisoned both blacks and whites in a world ruled by fear. Lawrence Guyot, head of the MFDP who sparred with Carmichael over the use of electoral politics in Mississippi, spoke of self-determination and was the first speaker to mention Black Power. It was at that time that CBS broke away from Guyot's speech to reassure viewers that the police had the situation under control.

The live broadcast hour did not carry Carmichael or King's speeches. Carmichael promised King that he would not use the Black Power slogan at the final speech—a pledge he kept. Regardless, the term's omission from Carmichael's speech did little to quell the roiling controversy surrounding its meaning. Without ever voicing the phrase, Carmichael nevertheless sounded Black Power themes by announcing that "if a black man is shot in the state of Mississippi, we will move to disrupt this country."[34] In King's speech, he predicted that the Meredith March would "go down in history as the greatest demonstration of freedom in Mississippi." He noted that local people in Mississippi were "no longer afraid." King marveled over the fact that "thousands and thousands of Negroes have straightened their backs up. They realize that a man can't ride your back unless it is bent."[35]

After the Jackson rally, Carmichael—and not King—had become the most talked-about figure of America's civil rights movement.[36] Three days after giving a rousing, combative speech in Jackson, Mississippi, that cemented his status as the new spokesman of black militancy, Carmichael celebrated his twenty-fifth birthday.

An *Ebony* feature story on the heels of the Meredith March opened with an appropriately cinematic scene that described Carmichael in hot pursuit of white toughs who were fresh from screaming racial epithets at a busload of black SNCC workers. Carmichael's high-speed chase of anonymous white thugs served as a metaphor for the way in which Black Power was being interpreted around the country: The hunted had now become the hunters. Historian Lerone Bennett's profile cast Carmichael as the avatar of a new movement—a handsome, brilliant, cosmopolitan who unnamed SNCC compatriots had dubbed "the Magnificent Barbarian" in homage to his ability to inspire everyday people and alienate powerful figures in equal proportion. Civil rights lawyer Len Holt compared Carmichael to a "statue of a Nubian god," just as Bennett suggested a resemblance to contemporary movie stars Harry Belafonte and Sidney Poitier.

However, beyond Carmichael's glamour, good looks, and personal charisma lay intellectual depth and sensitivity. Nevertheless, Carmichael's substance was at times overshadowed by a brazen confidence and naked candor that, as one anonymous civil rights leader admitted, "terrifies me and exalts me at the same time."[37] Invoking self-defense as a personal right beyond political debate, Carmichael offered Black Power as a strategy for self-determination not seen in the black community since Reconstruction. On its face, given the individuals and organizations who had courageously protested against Jim Crow's expanding breadth in the preceding century, this seemed to be an exaggerated claim. But in Carmichael's view, such heroic resistance remained hidden beneath a more acquiescent public face. White backlash against Black Power only revealed the persistence of racial fault lines that had existed since time immemorial. Ultimately, Bennett concluded, Black Power would take the lead in society's transformation through the at-times unsettling figure of Carmichael, a forward-thinking visionary who represented the "most advanced social and democratic interests in America."[38]

Thus, Carmichael showcased an uncanny ability to impress the unlettered as well as the elite. In front of a group of Harlem teenagers, he presented himself as a dashing man about town, donning a fashionable blue suit, Italian boots, and striped tie to deliver a speech that played up the soft remnant of his Trinidadian accent. Later, before a more mature, harder-edged crowd in Newark, New Jersey, that included LeRoi Jones (later Amiri Baraka), Carmichael disarmed participants with homespun wisdom packaged in a slightly exaggerated Southern drawl—"Is it okay if ah take of mah jacket?" he asked at one point. Then, from Newark, Carmichael traveled to Glen Falls, Vermont, for a leadership institute where he starred as the young sage before an interracial group of middle-aged clergy, seasoned activists, and youthful hippies.[39]

Carmichael's notoriety as a Black Power advocate and King's well-known commitment to nonviolence would seem to place both men on a collision course that would mimic King's earlier combative relationship with Malcolm X. Though mutual respect and personal friendship prevented this from happening, King nevertheless made clear his distaste for the slogan of Black Power, if not the substance behind its meaning. Even as Carmichael argued that the Black Power controversy provided a necessary "forum" for blacks, King characterized the slogan itself as a distraction from raw "evils of Mississippi and the need for the 1966 Civil Rights Act."[40]

Black Power soared into the maelstrom of American political discourse following the Meredith March. In a matter of months, the twenty-five-year-old Stokely Carmichael had been elevated to an icon and generational touchstone, even as some reviled his militancy and denounced him. Mainstream newspapers charged that Carmichael's term was a destructive harbinger of violence and racial separatism. White journalists who had reported racial politics in the South during the movement's early days forecast ideological and generational splits that placed King and Carmichael at the center of a battle over the movement's future direction.[41]

Carmichael's high profile continued after the Meredith March. His appearance at a June 30 press conference, where three young infantrymen announced their refusal to fight in Vietnam on moral grounds, suggested the complexity behind his blunt-spoken manner.[42] In doing so, he became the first activist to combine themes of Black Power, civil rights, and antiwar protest as intertwining strands of a singular issue. Almost a year before King's famous antiwar speech at New York's Riverside Church, Carmichael emerged as the nation's most visible and charismatic opponent of the Vietnam War. The next day, he met with reporters in Washington's Mount Bethel Baptist Church during a press conference announcing SNCC's position on the impending civil rights bill. He described the proposed civil rights act as "totally useless and totally unnecessary" because vigorous enforcement of existing law rendered much of its substance irrelevant. However, he refused to respond to questions about SNCC's political differences with other civil rights groups in the wake of the Black Power controversy, and several reporters responded by walking out. Regardless, Carmichael remained defiant. "The press in this country will not decide what our press conferences will be," he said. "The press may or may not come."[43]

Carmichael's subsequent appearance at the CORE Convention in Baltimore provided reassurance for journalists disappointed by the SNCC leader's recent restraint. Because his antiwar rhetoric and appeals to resist the draft smacked too much of nonviolence, they muddled the story for reporters in search of a more straightforward and digestible narrative in order to cast the young SNCC chairman as Malcolm X's Caribbean heir. With King absent from the convention for fear of its nationalist overtones, Carmichael continued his relentless efforts to link civil rights with the Vietnam War, insisting that American violence overseas made domestic debates over nonviolence moot.[44]

In July 1966, Roy Wilkins countered the enthusiasm of *Ebony*'s flattering profile of Carmichael with unfettered criticism of Black Power that made national headlines. In Los Angeles at the NAACP's annual convention, Wilkins described Black Power as racism in reverse that could potentially lead to "black death." Wilkins's attack followed up Vice President Hubert Humphrey's comments the night before that deplored hate speech—without mentioning Black Power directly. The Congress of Racial Equality's recent commitment to Black Power and SNCC's activities during the Meredith March fueled Wilkins's remarks. Because of this, by the convention's last day, the NAACP passed a resolution to reassess its relationship with other civil rights groups, signaling in no uncertain terms to SNCC and CORE that their shared struggle no longer guaranteed future financial support.[45]

Undaunted by the controversy, throughout June and July of 1966 Carmichael amplified his call for Black Power while adding new shades to its meaning. During a plenary discussion at Spelman College in Atlanta, he defined Black Power as black unity in the service of elected political power. He went on to state that media hysteria served to obscure this simple truth by attaching white fears to a quest for black self-determination. Carmichael envisioned Black Power as a movement to transform American political culture by placing the needs of the country's most desperate group at the center of political discourse. Because of this radical need, conventional black politics would no longer suffice under this formula. Instead, Black Power called for—indeed mandated—a new political ethos that would seek the eradication of poverty, violence, war, and despair. In this, Carmichael shared King's concern over humankind's very fate.[46]

The question of what kind of leader Carmichael would turn out to be continued to gain national attention over the summer. During a tour of Chicago in July, Carmichael publicly solicited a summit meeting with Elijah Muhammad even as he rejected the notion that talk of Black Power meant that SNCC had embraced racial separatism.[47] After Chicago, Carmichael appeared in Detroit, where he addressed a rally of over five hundred with a speech denouncing black participation in Vietnam and promoting racial unity.[48] On August 3, amid national reports of civil disturbances in Cleveland, Omaha, and Chicago, Carmichael was accused of instigating a near-riot in Atlanta after police officers stopped a car carrying three SNCC workers. Reports that Carmichael led an angry crowd in chants of "Black Power!" thereby forcing the authorities to withdraw with no arrests, portrayed SNCC and its young leader as daredevil agitators with a slogan capable of harnessing the pent-up rage swirling in the black ghetto.[49]

The New York Times profiled Carmichael in early August under the headline "Black Power Prophet." Recounting Carmichael's early childhood in the Caribbean, the article traced his dissatisfaction with America's system of racial segregation to his coming of age in the majority-minority port city of Port of Spain. Comfortable in predominantly black environments, Carmichael had to acclimate himself to being one of the few Negroes in the overwhelming Italian American Morris Heights section of the Bronx and one of the handful of black faces at Bronx Science High School. His subsequent experiences in the Bronx, Harlem, Washington, and Mississippi crystallized a worldview that was remarkable in its ability to adapt to local vernacular, custom, and culture. Carmichael's personality and political ambitions reflected the part of the black community—whether the rural South or urban North—in which he currently resided.

Alongside new revelations about Carmichael's personal biography, the *Times* published SNCC's Black Power position paper, which would be used as evidence that the group's new trajectory had been planned since long before June 1966. The position paper argued that the movement for racial justice required black leadership. Its philosophy of racial separatism emanated not from the genetic proscriptions of the Nation of Islam but rather from political considerations. These viewed white patronage of a black movement as paralyzing the development of black consciousness, sapping the communities' political energies, and paralyzing potential leaders. The chronology that the *Times* proposed suggested that Carmichael was influential in formulating the paper and, hence, the intensified rhetoric of SNCC. Although this made good copy, it also made poor history.

In truth, the paper's authors were SNCC dissidents from Atlanta's Vine City project. Their Black Power position paper had disrupted the organization early in 1966. The ensuing controversy found Carmichael defending white SNCC workers from criticism that he regarded as narrowly ideological. It also resulted in the eventual dismissal, accompanied by mutual recriminations, of several Atlanta staffers. The position paper's advocacy of racial separatism placed it at odds with Carmichael, whose views on interracial organizing remained complicated. This complexity was due in part to the murder of his white friend and seminarian Jon Daniels in Lowndes County in 1965. After that incident, Carmichael came to view the cost of interracial organizing as outweighing its potential benefits. Nonetheless, he remained adamant that white SNCC workers who displayed past service to the organization had the right to remain a part of the group. In the aftermath of the Meredith March, Carmichael's public statements seemed to support the sentiment expressed by Atlanta staffers but with subtle differences, including the advocacy of pragmatic interracial coalitions.[50] The collectively written paper, authored by apostates driven out of SNCC, nevertheless became a lasting artifact of transformation, forever linked to Carmichael's and Black Power's dramatic arrival on the national stage.[51]

Coverage in the *Times* was part of a media blitz that also saw Carmichael appearing on the *Today Show* and *Meet the Press* as well as in numerous, mostly negative, editorials around the country. The *Wall Street Journal*'s warning that blacks needed "the white man far more than the other way around" punctuated a mainstream sentiment that ran overwhelmingly against Black Power.[52] Carmichael soon became blamed for the "riot mood" that was gripping the nation.[53] Less frequently mentioned by the press and Carmichael, however, were the years he had spent as a grassroots organizer in the Deep South pursuing citizenship in the face of terror. As one perceptive reporter suggested, the Carmichael who believed in democracy's powers to heal the South's racial wounds remained permanently scarred by the little-cited murder of his friend Jonathan Daniels, a white organizer gunned down in Lowndes County in 1965. "Daniels' death and acquittal of his slayer by an all-white jury," wrote Jack Nelson, a veteran civil rights reporter, "seemed to be a traumatic experience for Carmichael."[54]

An important part of Carmichael's new strategy revolved around developing a working alliance between the Nation of Islam and SNCC. Carmichael met with Elijah Muhammad on Sunday, August 7 at the Messenger's large home on South Woodlawn Avenue, Chicago. Carmichael's recent parley with Harlem congressman Adam Clayton Powell had produced an agreement for Powell to host a Black Power conference in Washington that would include the participation of black militants and moderates in a national display of unity. Powell matched Muhammad's messianic visions with actual political power. Powell viewed Black Power as potential leverage for his own recently rocky political fortunes and proposed a Labor Day conference to discuss the new movement. *Muhammad Speaks'* post-Meredith March coverage of Carmichael frequently held up the young SNCC chairman as a breath of fresh air in the stale arena of black leadership, highlighting quotes from his speeches expressing admiration for Muhammad and the Black Muslims. This was exemplified by a picture of a beaming Carmichael and Muhammad, flanked by heavyweight champion Muhammad Ali and SNCC activist Cleveland Sellers, that was prominently featured in *Muhammad Speaks* shortly after the meeting. However, although the cordial discussion produced mutual expressions of respect, no actual formal alliance was forged between the two men, each of whom remained stubbornly convinced that he held the key to the black community's political future.[55]

Although he never managed to captivate the old guard of the NOI, Carmichael's glamorous image did help Black Power appeal to a new generation of activists. Addressing standing-room-only audiences in Chicago, Detroit, and Harlem, Carmichael made Black Power the cornerstone of an intricate critique of American democracy. He assailed the Vietnam War, applauded resurgent expressions of black pride, and challenged whites to acknowledge racism's broad and deep impact on society with action rather than denial.[56]

In Boston, during a joint appearance with Nation of Islam minister and former Malcolm X protégé Louis Farrakhan, Carmichael called for black unity in a series of meetings that energized New England militants.[57] Farrakhan introduced Carmichael, calling him "one of us." In the process, he sent FBI agents scrambling to decipher whether the SNCC chairman had joined the Black Muslims.[58] Agents pursued other wild goose chases as well, including erroneous reports that Carmichael had attended the eighteenth National Convention of the CPUSA (Communist Party of the United States of America).[59]

While in Boston, Carmichael played the fire-eating black nationalist to great effect. During an appearance on *Meet the Press*, he slipped into the role of the intellectual. In a widely publicized August 21 appearance, he debated with both civil rights leaders as well as the show's moderators, all the while defending Black Power and offering incisive criticism of the Vietnam War.[60] Carmichael proclaimed that the biggest question confronting the movement would be the question of whether or not America would answer pleas for racial justice peacefully, or if violence would remain the only consistent spur for national action.[61]

The *Meet the Press* dialogue echoed the thoughts of black activists nationwide. From Chicago, where he was leading open-housing demonstrations, King deplored the "tragic gulf between promise and fulfillment" that was threatening to undermine racial progress, while Wilkins smoothed over talk of ideological divisions by noting that the courtroom remained the final arbiter of those seeking racial justice.[62] That same day, at a Free D.C. Movement rally, Carmichael struck an even more combative pose, telling Washington residents that they would achieve political representation the instant they recognized their power to "burn down this city" if their demands were not met.[63]

During this time, the FBI was documenting Carmichael's rhetorical out-
bursts, collecting background evidence of his past arrests as part of a thick
surveillance dossier. Preliminary reports gleaned information from newspapers, informants, and New York City's Bureau of Special Services. These
accounts chronicled a pattern of political activities that inevitably ended in
arrests in Mississippi, Baltimore, and New York. A recommendation for a
Howard University "senior class humanity award" for "enduring many hard-
ships for his people" balanced out Carmichael's string of confrontations with
law enforcement, which suggested a dissident streak guided by compassion
as much as outrage.[64]

Increasingly, Carmichael's public appearances thrust him in the role of
Black Power's national political mobilizer. Unable to engage in the kind of
long-term organizing that had made his efforts in Lowndes County so successful, he remade himself as a roving national ambassador. Trailed by adoring
crowds of young people wherever he went, he visited churches, community
centers, and housing projects in order to spread the gospel of Black Power.
Like an itinerant evangelist setting up ad hoc revivals across the country,
Carmichael's message of Black Power attracted both the dignified and the
damned. On any given day, he could meet with gang members in Chicago,
jump on top of a car outside a housing project in Newark's Central Ward, or
attend a star-studded fund-raiser with Harry Belafonte.

However, Carmichael's rhetoric inspired almost universal disdain from
editorial page writers across the nation. The *Chicago Tribune* openly questioned whether his political statements spread further racial tensions, and the
Washington Post compared him to American Nazi Party leader George Lincoln Rockwell.[65] Meanwhile, SNCC's efforts to organize Black Power in inner cities collided with local authorities in Philadelphia. This produced lurid
headlines and an imagined "dynamite plot" that cast both the group and
Carmichael as the architects behind proliferating waves of urban violence.[66]

Regardless of this negative press, Carmichael continued to find creative
ways to publicize his political agenda. On Friday, October 28, he underwent
a well-publicized reevaluation of his draft status. At a military hospital in
New York City, he received a preinduction mental and physical exam. Although his vociferous antiwar speeches placed his 1-Y exemption under official scrutiny, he refused to back down. "I'd rather go to Leavenworth," he
told reporters, insisting that he would refuse to serve "on the grounds of my
own conscience."[67]

At Berkeley the next day, Carmichael offered a purposeful and contemplative message about the paradox of American democracy. This speech was

punctuated by eye-opening sound bites that mesmerized the white students in attendance even as it excoriated their parents' generation as unapologetic racists. Over 10,000 people packed Berkeley's Greek Theater to listen to Carmichael's address, which capped off a daylong conference organized by the Students for a Democratic Society (SDS). The paradox of delivering a Black Power speech before a predominantly white audience gave Carmichael pause, especially after black militants questioned SDS's motives. The largely white audiences that made up Carmichael's itinerary in northern California upset SNCC activists, who felt the chairman should speak primarily to black communities. Ultimately, however, the opportunity offered an irresistible platform for Carmichael to clearly articulate the meaning behind an increasingly controversial slogan.[68]

Carmichael's meditation on Black Power's relationship to larger failures of American democracy soared into new heights of eloquence even as it plumbed the racial and historical depths of black life. The main contradiction of the civil rights movement, Carmichael noted, was that although whites were "the majority" and thus accountable for "making democracy work," blacks inevitably bore the brunt of this responsibility. Blacks faced death on America's racial front lines of the South even as most whites remained comfortably on the sidelines. "The question," according to Carmichael was, "how can white society move to see black people as human beings?"[69]

In hundreds of speeches over the next year, Carmichael would develop this theme into a dazzling stump speech that imagined novel connections between race and war as it also found intimate kinship between Black Power and American democracy.[70] He implored those in attendance to use their individual will to form a collective barrier against an escalating war. "There is a higher law than the law of a racist named McNamara, a higher law than the law of a tool named Rusk, a higher law than the law of a buffoon named Johnson—it is the higher law of each of us," said Carmichael. Waves of applause overtook this last line as thousands stood up and cheered.[71]

A deluge of editorial denouncements followed Carmichael's Berkeley speech, with politicians trailing the media in lock step. California governor Pat Brown and his conservative challenger, Ronald Reagan, decried Carmichael's appearance, although both men knew that it boded well for Reagan, who was already riding a wave of popularity buoyed by resentment over black militancy.[72] In Washington, Attorney General Ramsey Clark received a fresh batch of requests from Congressmen to prosecute Carmichael for antiwar speeches that promoted defiance of the draft.[73] Mississippi senator and arch-segregationist James Eastland telegrammed Clark in his capacity as chairman of the Senate Judiciary Committee, stating that Carmichael's "reckless and inflammatory speeches" promoted "acts bordering on treason."[74] Meanwhile, after school administrators canceled his scheduled appearance at Spelman College in Atlanta, Carmichael delivered an extemporaneous address standing on top of a car on Halloween evening, in which he reiterated his vow to never fight in "Lyndon Johnson's war."[75]

On Wednesday, November 2, four days after Carmichael's Berkeley appearance, a Justice Department spokesman responded to the growing controversy. He confirmed that an investigation was under way focusing on the SNCC leader's public statements regarding the Vietnam War. Spurred by congressional outrage, the Justice Department maintained an outward appearance of dispassionate legal interest while acutely aware that Carmichael's statements stirred galvanic passions among politicians and ordinary citizens alike. "We are keenly aware of the allegations and the factual background," said the spokesman. "When and if the facts warrant it, under the law as determined by the courts, the department will take prompt action."[76]

Despite Carmichael's national celebrity, he remained keenly attuned to political developments in Lowndes County. Throughout the summer and fall, he kept in contact with SNCC staff there and, when able, made occasional visits. On Saturday, November 5, three days before Lowndes County's local elections, Carmichael was arrested in Selma, Alabama, on charges of inciting a riot. His attempts to organize an ad hoc protest at the local jail following the arrest of two SNCC workers led to this latest stay in jail. After a weekend being incarcerated, Carmichael posted bail in time to join almost seven hundred people at Monday night's meeting at Mount Moriah Baptist Church.

Carmichael's activities in Lowndes County defy the conventional split between civil rights and Black Power. The young SNCC leader spoke in churches, bonded with local children and the elderly, and maintained his commitment to interracial coalitions even while organizing an all-black political party. Threatened by white vigilantes, local activists kept themselves armed in case of attack. On November 7, 1966, the eve of the election in Lowndes County, Carmichael delivered a passionate speech at Mount Moriah Baptist Church, in which he cited Old Testament prophets, held hands with congregation members, and sang gospel hymns.[77] The gathering combined the procedural and organizational details of a workshop with the energy of a political rally. Carmichael would remember that night as "magnificent," also noting that Lowndes County political leaders such as John Hulett discussed making the next day a "model of democracy."[78] "These people did not have to argue Black Power," Carmichael would later recall, "they understood Black Power."[79] In a speech that paired typical intensity with folk wisdom, he stated, "[W]e have been beaten, killed and forced out of our homes." When he said that, "Lowndes County used to be called the Devil's Backyard. Now its God's Little Acre," Carmichael captured the raw emotion underneath the evening's high drama. "Tonight is our night," he proclaimed. "Tomorrow is our day."

In his speech, Carmichael heralded progress in language that drew from the black community's spiritual and moral reserves. Democratic breakthroughs, proclaimed Carmichael, required "the will, the courage and love in our hearts." For him, the next day's vote offered a reckoning that would deliver Lowndes County residents to a new promised land. Playing to the religious sensibilities all around him, Carmichael reminded locals that "[w]hen Moses crossed the Red Sea he left some people behind. We are going to leave some Uncle Toms behind." Blacks in Lowndes County would, at long last, be able to "say goodbye to shacks, dirt roads, poor schools."[80]

The moment's power, Carmichael noted later, defied those journalistic accounts that depicted Black Power as brash, angry, and void of genuine political goals, strategies, and tactics. "All the uninformed editorial writers throughout the country, all the panic-stricken whites in insulated suburbs across this land should have been there that night," Carmichael would recall.[81] His words offered precisely the kind of nuanced description of Black Power that critics claimed the slogan lacked. With a flash of humor on the eve of the election, he instantly relayed the way in which future chroniclers would interpret tensions between civil rights and Black Power: "When you mention Selma, people say—There's some mean white folks down there. But when you mention Lowndes County, they say—There's some mean niggers down there!"[82] Indeed, Black Power's origins, at least in Lowndes County, mimicked the slow, patient, institution-building commonly associated with civil rights organizations such as SNCC. This story would prove, in the short run at least, too unruly, as symbols of snarling black panthers overwhelmed the more complicated images that remained at the heart of the Black Power era—such as Carmichael locking arms at Mount Moriah singing "We Shall Overcome" before hugging and kissing streams of supporters leaving the church.[83]

On Tuesday, November 8, hundreds of Lowndes County's blacks quietly and unapologetically voted for the Black Panther political party that Carmichael had helped to organize. Drivers heading west on U.S. Highway 80 were greeted by a large sign emblazoned with a picture of a black panther, perched just between Montgomery and Selma, in Lowndes County: "PULL THE LEVER FOR THE BLACK PANTHER AND GO ON HOME!"[84]

By prearranged signal, Black Panther supporters waved pieces of white paper to signal transport vehicles to taxi voters and supporters to safety. However, reports of election irregularities spread instantly and SNCC staff raced to combat a wide range of violations. Black voters received marked ballots in certain precincts, were accompanied by whites in others, and faced widespread harassment and intimidation. On a Fort Deposit roadside, vigilantes fired gunshots as Carmichael left a filling station.[85] At least one supporter endured a savage beating, and a plantation owner evicted a family of eleven for its support of the LCFO.[86]

In an election plagued by voter fraud that was authored by plantation owners, all seven candidates represented by the Black Panther Party lost. Regardless, important precedents ruled the day. White supremacy in Lowndes was doomed and the drive for self-determination through the ballot would spread throughout the country.

The results of the Lowndes County election most likely contributed to Carmichael's increasingly confrontational style. During the second week of November, he toured the Bay Area making public speeches, conducting television and radio interviews, and attending private receptions. At a forum sponsored by San Francisco State College's trailblazing Black Student Union, Carmichael attacked institutional racism and the Vietnam War. During closed-door meetings with Black Power groups, he stressed the need for a kind of racial unity that would transcend personal and political differences. In front of predominantly white audiences, Carmichael read from his recent *Massachusetts Review* essay and gave an impassioned, lucid defense of Black Power that, journalists reported, "disappointed" audience members eager for the "expected fireworks."[87]

In Los Angeles, the prospect of Carmichael's appearance at a rally in Watts provoked a storm of controversy. City officials balked at his planned visit. Los Angeles County supervisors, who characterized Carmichael as an advocate of "racial hate and violence" that threatened a "repeat" of the Watts riots, voted unanimously to deny rally sponsors the required permits. The Black Congress—a group of Los Angeles militants sponsoring Carmichael's appearance—denounced the decision as a freedom of speech violation.[88] However, Governor-elect Ronald Reagan praised the ruling as "wise" just as the *Los Angeles Times* defended Carmichael's freedom of speech and a superior court judge ruled that Carmichael could speak with or without a permit.[89] Carmichael traced official response to his impending speech back to SNCC's "militant stand on Vietnam."[90] "The fight today," he suggested, "is for black people to define their futures without interference from white people." Having been turned by media projection into the living embodiment of black anger and a figure proliferating racial strife, Carmichael struggled to separate his volatile personality from the larger social and historical roots of urban unrest. "I'm not responsible for the black ghettos like Watts," he said.[91]

On Saturday, November 26, two days after Thanksgiving, Carmichael addressed an estimated crowd of 6,500 people at Will Rogers Park in the Watts neighborhood of Los Angeles. Dressed in a suit and tie, he stood perched on top of a pickup truck bed. He spoke through a makeshift loudspeaker set up by organizers after park officials denied him the use of the public address system. Shouts of "Tell them how it is!" and "That's right!" greeted Carmichael's discussion of Vietnam, racism, and American race relations. He implored blacks in the audience to be proud of their unique beauty and condemned Western culture as bankrupt.[92]

Local militants carrying two-way radios ordered white reporters and cameramen to the rear of the crowd. Plainclothes detectives milled about, but fears of violence proved unfounded. "There is a new breed of black people in the country today," explained Carmichael. "My mother scrubbed floors so I could have black power." For forty minutes, he electrified the assemblage with talk of renewal born out of bitter despair. His two raised fists thrust high into the air marked the end of the speech as waves of cheers and applause filled the park's open spaces.[93]

Three days later, Carmichael appeared in a magistrate's court in Selma to defend himself against rioting charges stemming from his arrest earlier in the month. Acting as his own attorney, he strolled up and down the courtroom in blue jeans and army boots, presenting a defense that exhibited "a flair for the dramatic." At one point, he called Selma mayor Joe T. Smitherman to the stand, and the two men verbally sparred as stunned onlookers, including undercover FBI agents, watched the proceedings.[94] Carmichael, as FBI agents noted, "plainly dominated the scene," particularly relishing the chance to display "his forensic skill." The court found him guilty and sentenced him to sixty days hard labor and a $100 fine. Undaunted, Carmichael quickly appealed his conviction.[95]

In 1967, after a year in which he achieved unprecedented national attention, Carmichael would embark on a domestic and international tour that made him a global icon. Black Power hovered over American politics that year, connecting a generation through expressions of combative resistance against war, racism, and poverty.

During a whirlwind speaking tour of historically black colleges in the South, Carmichael tested out twin themes: He extolled the virtues of Black Power and denounced the Vietnam War in rapid-fire lectures that roused student bodies ranging from Mississippi to Louisiana. Like a political candidate in an election year, he made his way to both prestigious and obscure black college campuses alike. For him, higher education's black belt represented an untapped base of power with resources and skills that could transform living conditions in some of America's poorest communities. SNCC's plans called for banning mandatory ROTC at black colleges, encouraging student autonomy over outside speakers, and imposing curricula reforms so as to include black history and culture. "If we don't get that," said Carmichael during one speech, "we gonna disrupt the schools."[96]At elite white universities and private colleges, however, he adopted a more professorial mien. He gave polished and at times purposefully subdued seminars that combined world history and political philosophy as part of a larger dissection of American democracy.

The lecture circuit comprised a broad effort to unify local groups who were committed to Black Power. Experience as a local organizer made Carmichael aware of the tendency of popular leaders to view politics from on high while barely touching the sacred ground of everyday struggles. Conversely, six months as national political leader made him peculiarly attentive to the telescopic vision of grassroots activists as well as the heavy burdens of instant celebrity. The philosopher in him regarded Black Power as capable of bridging the gap between black people's local needs and national ambitions. Because of this, Carmichael attempted to use his speaking tours as a vehicle to organize local colleges and communities and to spread a national message of Black Power through newspaper and television coverage of his exploits.

On January 29, Carmichael headlined a Black Power conference in San Francisco that helped to unite a group of militants whose influence would prove enduring.[97] His speech explored the conference's theme of "black survival" by discussing the urgent need for a new national politics that would be attuned to global events. "We must begin to think international politics and alliances" in order to "align ourselves with people of color around the world who are also oppressed." According to Carmichael, "[t]he enemy around the world is the same." If Carmichael's early activism had made him into an eloquent proponent of radical democracy, his new political orientation resisted conventional notions of American prosperity. "We are determined to tear up the pie," he said, "because to get a piece of that pie one has to be anti-black. SNCC says and is determined to be successful and black."[98]

Among the conference's most promising militants was a young intellectual name Maulana Karenga. The bald-headed, loquacious, and creative Karenga headed the Los Angeles-based Organization Us and served as the area's leading representative of Black Power's cultural thrust.[99] Karenga's group showcased a love for African culture, and they ritualized expressions of racial solidarity by adopting Afrocentric names, dress, and rituals. The group patterned themselves after both Malcolm X and the Nation of Islam, replete with a paramilitary security force, separate women's auxiliaries, and a cult of personality surrounding its leader. Karenga's obvious intelligence, puckish sense of humor, and sartorial flair seemed ready-made for mass consumption. Even so, iconic fame would allude him, if not his ideas. Overshadowed by—and later in deadly conflict with—the leather-jacketed allure of the Black Panthers, Organization Us would endure through invented traditions (most notably the African American holiday Kwanzaa, which still serves as an Afrocentric alternative to Christmas) that would be adopted by generations of black Americans.

Huey P. Newton and Bobby G. Seale, young militants who were inspired by Malcolm X's legacy and impressed with Carmichael's Black Power rhetoric, were among the conference's most enthusiastic participants. Itinerant college students, street hustlers, and part-time activists, Newton and Seale had organized about a dozen Oakland militants and formed the Black Panther Party for Self-Defense in the fall of 1966. As Carmichael recounted his recent visit to Puerto Rico and made plans for a national federation of Black Power militants, Newton and Seale envisioned something no less ambitious. Their fledgling group sought nothing less than to transform the living conditions for poor blacks in Oakland via a ten-point program that called for land, peace, bread, and justice. After Carmichael's visit, the Black Panther leaders immediately made preparations for a Malcolm X commemoration day that would coincide with the second anniversary of the assassination of their patron saint.[100]

Eldridge Cleaver observed the Bay Area's burgeoning political radicalism with a cautious intensity. Still just weeks out of San Quentin prison, Cleaver was a staff writer for the radical periodical *Ramparts*, a position that he secured with the help of his lawyer Beverly Axelrod. Cleaver's biography included long prison stretches, which is where he discovered hidden literary talents. Cleaver joined the Nation of Islam while he was in prison and followed Malcolm into apostasy. By the winter of 1967, he was both a participant and observer in Black Power politics. His *Ramparts* salary and other connections allowed him to maintain a relatively secure lifestyle while also providing eager white radicals an entrée into black militancy. On this score, the tiny Black Panther Party for Self-Defense attracted both *Ramparts* and Cleaver, for different reasons. The Malcolm X memorial in February, planned by Newton and Seale, featured a contingent of armed Panthers escorting Malcolm's widow, Bettye Shabazz, to *Ramparts'* San Francisco offices. Pandemonium followed as police officers and Panthers briefly stood on the edge of a near shoot-out, one that gave Cleaver newfound respect for a group of militants who had previously asked him to join their fledgling group.

If the Black Panthers appealed to Cleaver's sense of danger, Carmichael inspired more intellectual ambitions. This is especially so as Cleaver trailed after Carmichael from the Bay Area to Chicago as part of an assignment for *Ramparts*. Cleaver's description of SNCC's decrepit Chicago offices gave a Bohemian edge to the ragged conditions where young civil rights workers organized to the blaring sounds of John Coltrane. The fleeting presence of Cleaver's father, who briefly accompanied him to SNCC's offices in search of Carmichael, served as the article's opening riff. The title, "My Father and Stokely Carmichael," announced the young SNCC chairman as the symbol of a new era, one that stood in sharp contrast to the embarrassing accommodation of a previous generation, represented by Cleaver's own father. In the middle of a freezing Chicago winter, Cleaver watched Carmichael conduct television interviews, dialogue with local militants, and speak before a predominantly white audience at the University of Chicago.

In the resulting article, Cleaver positioned Carmichael as the latest in a black nationalist pantheon that included Malcolm X, Elijah Muhammad, and Marcus Garvey. "Stokely Carmichael," Cleaver wrote, "is the first of his stature to finish a college degree." He praised Carmichael's six years of service down South as a courageous tour of duty in service of a larger revolutionary war. For Cleaver, the combination of Carmichael's intellectual agility and mass appeal presented black America with historic opportunities. Cleaver exhibited Carmichael's plans to tour Africa, his antiwar activism, and his recent trip to Puerto Rico as part of a necessary cosmopolitanism that soared above the Nation of Islam's racialist cosmology and the at-times narrow separatism adopted by black militants. Cleaver would take Carmichael's dictum of establishing "specific alliances on specific issues" as potent collateral against whispers that questioned his close interracial personal and professional contacts.[101]

Carmichael's youthful vitality, intellectual agility, and ability to evoke fear and admiration in intimate and large settings alike made a lasting impression on Cleaver. Barely three months out of prison and with a full three years left on his parole, Cleaver requested permission to accompany his new hero on a tour of Africa. The request pivoted on Cleaver's status as a journalist for *Ramparts* magazine. If granted, it would take him to exotic locales, including Egypt, Liberia, Guinea, Ethiopia, and Ghana, that were far removed from the California prison system that had, for so long, been home. Citing his "short time on parole" and past parole violations, Cleaver's request was denied.[102]

In a series of public speeches at the beginning of the year, Carmichael escalated the tone and temper of his Black Power advocacy and his criticism against the Vietnam War before impassioned audiences. Carmichael's public speaking tours increasingly served as ad hoc organizing sessions for local militants and grassroots activists. They showcased his uncanny ability to tailor his message to specific audiences. For instance, at predominantly white Portland State University, Carmichael invoked Frederick Douglass's famous maxim that power "conceded nothing without demand" and described the black freedom struggle as a quest to civilize America by raising "hard questions." He then settled into a prepared lecture (as he often did in front of white audiences), "Black Power: Its Needs and Substance," culled from an earlier essay that appeared in the *New York Review of Books*.[103] On February 17, near the end of "Negro History Week," an audience of 7,000 Berkeley students listened in rapt attention as Carmichael gave an account of his years as a local civil rights organizer. After five years of nonviolent direct action, Carmichael explained, white authorities would no longer be able to brutalize him without fear of retaliation. "If he touches me, I'm going to try and kill him."[104] From the steps of Sproul Hall, Carmichael challenged Berkeley's white students and the larger New Left to become radical missionaries in an effort to cleanse America's racist soul.[105] In Long Beach that evening, the verbal pyrotechnics continued, and Carmichael addressed welfare recipients who were protesting the impending closing of a local antipoverty center. Long Beach police officers seethed as Carmichael accused George Washington of selling a "black woman for a barrel of molasses" and went on to describe blacks as modern-day slaves.[106]

After leaving Los Angeles, Carmichael attended an East Coast Malcolm X memorial at the site of his death. New York City's Malcolm X memorial service took place on February 22, as two hundred supporters marched in a procession that concluded at the Audubon Ballroom in Washington Heights.[107] Carmichael's frequent appearance as a keynote speaker at these commemorations served as a living example of the way in which supporters increasingly viewed him as the one activist capable of inheriting Malcolm's legacy. Meanwhile, Carmichael also conducted a brief speaking tour of leading Canadian universities.

In Montreal's prestigious McGill University, white students sat enthralled as Carmichael delivered his standard Black Power speech in front of an audience who found his combination of physical appeal and intellectual provocation irresistible. The next day, Cedric Lewis Robinson James, a popular Marxist, joined dozens of blacks, among a sea of white students, who attended Carmichael's February 24 lecture at Sir George Williams University during the same tour. Over 1,000 students filled an auditorium designed for 750, leaving Carmichael and SNCC stunned by the crowd's unexpected size and enthusiasm. The standing ovation that followed Carmichael's presentation rivaled the wild cheers and large crowds that greeted his appearance, the same day, at the Université de Montreal.[108]

Carmichael's speech, demeanor, and charisma impressed James. A Trinidadian-born, onetime Trotskyist, and lifelong Marxist, James's prodigiously eclectic writings on Haiti, class struggle, and cricket made him an intellectual hero among radicals drawn to his idiosyncratic blend of intellectual theory and revolutionary politics. Deported to England in the early 1950s, his influence extended to black radicals in Detroit, Caribbean revolutionaries turned statesmen, and newly elected African rulers. At sixty-six, James was old enough to be Carmichael's grandfather, but he nevertheless regarded Black Power as the culmination of mass political energies harnessed by Caribbean figures, including Marcus Garvey, George Padmore, and Frantz Fanon.[109] Carmichael's ability to impress one of the eminent black radical scholar-activists attested to his growing international profile.

In frigid Chicago, Carmichael urged community activists to duplicate the political experiment that had been launched in Lowndes County by running independent political candidates.[110] After a speaking engagement in Elmhurst, Illinois, he traveled by car to the 28th Ward Headquarters on Chicago's west side in order to support Curtis Foster's independent candidacy for alderman. He then capped the day's events by appearing at a political rally at the Senate Theater. That event also doubled as a memorial for George Jennings, a black man who had been shot and killed by the police. Two thousand participants, including representatives from some of Chicago's most militant civil rights organizations, attended Carmichael's address. This speech helped to serve as political fuel for the next day's primary elections, which featured a slate of independent candidates looking to succeed where those in Lowndes County had fallen short. The ballot, it seemed, would bring Black Power to neighborhoods where African American political clout remained overwhelmed by ward heelers, corrupt politicians, and urban political machines.[111]

On February 28, Carmichael arrived on the campus of Cornell University as the star attraction of "Soul of Blackness Week." In Ithaca, he led a government seminar, where he offered revisionist interpretations of the Civil War—he called Lincoln a racist—before giving a keynote speech on "Soul and Black Power" attended by 2,000 students. The next day, resplendent in a yellow sweatshirt bearing a picture of Malcolm X, Carmichael discussed the intricacies of Black Power at a panel discussion before leaving for Pittsburgh.[112]

Around this time, Los Angeles's Special Agent in Charge sent FBI director Herbert Hoover an Airtel (an internal bureau communications measure characterizing a memo to be typed and mailed the same day) explaining that, despite the bureau's fears and Carmichael's inflammatory speeches, "the racial situation" in both Los Angeles and Long Beach were back to normal.[113] Meanwhile, Carmichael's punishing schedule continued with a swing through western Pennsylvania that included two universities and a church in Pittsburgh followed by a speech at St. Vincent College in Latrobe.[114] But after Carmichael's trail went cold after Pittsburgh, panicked FBI agents made surreptitious telephone calls to New York's SNCC offices. Bad intelligence and sloppy policing made Bureau officials nervous. By March 3, reports concerning Carmichael's plans to return to San Juan for an extended day proved false, as did rumors that he was back in Chicago.[115]

Carmichael had in fact returned to SNCC's Atlanta headquarters for a few days. While in Georgia, he lent support to members of NOI Muslim Mosque No. 15 who had engaged in a violent altercation with the local police. After a short trip to Bimini, Bahamas, to confer with Adam Clayton Powell, "my congressman-in-exile," Carmichael then embarked on a tour to "radicalize the black college campus."[116] Following a speech in Lynchburg, Virginia, he gave what would have been a standard stump speech on March 14 decrying American involvement in Vietnam. Then, his appearance at

Lafayette College in Eaton, Pennsylvania, came the day after his local draft board changed his classification from 1-Y to 4-F, thereby virtually exempting him from military service.[117] With the threat of induction behind him, Carmichael continued to launch nationally publicized attacks against Vietnam and Lyndon Johnson.[118]

As Carmichael toured the United States making antiwar and Black Power speeches, the FBI's Research-Satellite Section released a report, "Stokely Carmichael—Advocate of Black Power." This information was disseminated to the White House, the Attorney General, Secret Service, Bureau of Intelligence and Research, State Department, and all military intelligence agencies. Twenty-one pages long and supported by seventy-eight endnotes (that included references to Carmichael's secret bureau records), the report characterized Black Power as a racial Pandora's Box that frightened "white and Negro alike" through "the threat of violence and reverse racism."[119] Inspired by Frantz Fanon's revolutionary handbook for colonial independence by any means necessary, *The Wretched of the Earth*, it noted that Carmichael ridiculed the president as a "buffoon," criticized Secretary of State Dean Rusk as a "fool," and called Secretary of Defense Robert McNamara a "racist." Ad hominem attacks against individual government leaders had evolved into a totalizing depiction of the Vietnam conflict as "illegal" and "immoral," one in which young people should refuse to take part.[120] The report marked Carmichael as an enemy of the Bureau and national security. It paid particular attention to Carmichael's antiwar criticism and identified him as an activist capable of single-handedly stirring civil unrest.

Over the course of almost one year in the national spotlight, Carmichael exhibited unmatched youth and energy and a charisma equal to that of Martin Luther King Jr. Thus, the FBI took him as seriously as they took King. A deft public speaker who spoke of Black Power in provocative and intellectual terms, Carmichael, according the bureau's secret report, was a changeling capable of pushing emotionally charged audiences over the edge and into the abyss of violence.[121] A catalogue of both Carmichael's grueling speaking schedule as well as his eclectic political influences and associations, the report mixed rumor and fact, innuendo and documentary evidence. His meetings with supporters of Malcolm X and members of the Nation of Islam fueled speculation that he coveted the slain Muslim leader's mantle. Imaginary links to Communists and more tangible ties to black revolutionaries implied that sinister forces were merely using the young leader. Carmichael's trip to Puerto Rico, where he donned a straw hat and marched with local nationalists and antiwar activists, along with his well-received lectures in Canada foreshadowed an international appeal that could be potentially damaging to American foreign interests. The bureau's paranoia notwithstanding, however, a measure of begrudging admiration crept into the official record, with an admission that "Carmichael has a flair for the dramatic."[122]

The public's appetite for high drama made Carmichael a sought-after speaker after the Meredith March and subsequent controversies. A flexible schedule in his position at SNCC allowed him "to appear anywhere in the country at any time." This, more often than not, meant prestigious colleges and universities eager to host (at a fee between $1,000 and $1,300) Black Power's most dangerously charismatic icon. The FBI's report concluded by stating that major civil rights leaders disagreed with Carmichael's advocacy of Black Power and then pointing out the harmful effects of his antiwar rhetoric. Ultimately, Carmichael's contempt for law and order, advocacy of Black Power, and pungent antiwar speeches made him a sort of walking purveyor of chaos, capable of upsetting domestic race relations, undermining national foreign policy, and spreading general disorder and unrest that had been disguised as peace and freedom.[123] Although there were kernels of truth in such fears, in large part this assessment projected the bureau's most fulsome nightmares more than Carmichael's actual ability to start a one-man revolution.

The correlation between Carmichael's speaking appearances and civil unrest did raise eyebrows that spring. Speaking engagements over consecutive days during the first week of April at Fisk University and Tennessee State, culminating with an appearance at predominantly white Vanderbilt, would be followed by three days of rioting. Nashville officials linked these to Carmichael, SNCC, and Black Power. His anticipated lecture at Vanderbilt had sent the Tennessee legislature into a fit of censure that ended in a resolution to withdraw the invitation. Local black activists decried the successful efforts to repress Carmichael's lecture. Then, after proponents of academic freedom won a provisional victory, local newspapers whipped local fears of violence into full-blown hysteria by suggesting that white citizens form vigilante squads. A single arrest of a black student in Nashville sparked days of unrest that officials linked to Carmichael and Black Power agitators, but whose actual roots lay in tense police community relations.[124]

The national press response conformed with a now-mainstream narrative that cast Carmichael as the nation's most dangerous black man. The *New York Times* judged Carmichael to be "a romantic young man" with the peculiar ability to mesmerize white audiences with irresponsible rhetoric that helped to instigate violence. *U.S. News and World Report* went further, charging Carmichael with stirring Nashville's civil disturbance before cryptically announcing that the SNCC chairman was scouring the South "before head-ing north again."[125] Carmichael responded to these charges with cool aplomb. He resumed his speaking tour by leading six hundred undergraduates at Mis-sissippi's Tougaloo College in antiwar chants of "Hell No, we ain't going!" sporting sunglasses and a resplendent African dashiki in a federal court in Selma, Alabama, and forthrightly affirming his belief in self-defense in a Nashville court five weeks after the city's riots.[126]

Perhaps the individual most affected by Carmichael's passionate Vietnam deliberations was Martin Luther King Jr. In the spring of 1967, King ele-gantly amplified Carmichael's seasoned antiwar rhetoric in a measured yet resolute speech that sent shockwaves across the nation. King's April 4 address at New York's Riverside Church lent international stature and moral clarity to the antiwar speeches that Carmichael had been steadfastly delivering for almost a year. At Riverside, King contrasted Carmichael's bitterness toward the failed promises of American democracy with weary hope. "The world now demands," pleaded King, "a maturity of America that we may not be able to achieve."[127]

Although King's words now resound with an authority that would, over time, swell, shortly after his Riverside speech he found himself in the un-comfortable position of "having to fight suggestions at every stop that his Vietnam stance merely echoed the vanguard buzz of Stokely Carmichael."[128] In retrospect, he needn't have worried. In time, historians came to highlight King's peace advocacy as a daring rejection of the status quo, just as Carmi-chael's stridently eloquent antiwar position would, in the long term, be muf-fled by association with Black Power. More comfortable with Carmichael as a youthful saber-rattler than a thoughtful antiwar activist, journalists and future scholars would virtually ignore the SNCC chairman's meticulous criticism of American involvement in Vietnam as an example of the larger failure of the nation's democratic experiment.[129]

Only twenty-five years old, Carmichael's complex identity was already be-ginning to take hold. This was felt not only through his public appear-ances and personal interactions with diverse communities of activists and ordinary citizens, but also—and perhaps most importantly—in the world of African American arts and letters as well as among the writers who shaped public opinion within and beyond the black world. Carmichael's casual man-ner struck a chord with *Life* magazine photojournalist Gordon Parks. Parks (an equally adept writer, memoirist, and raconteur) and Carmichael bonded over shared reputations as mavericks. "Stokely gives the impression," Parks impishly observed, that he could "stroll through Dixie in broad daylight using the Confederate flag for a handkerchief."[130] Four months of traveling with SNCC's young chairman made Parks appreciate the nuances of Carmichael's personality that were both outsized and earthy. In Parks's *Life* magazine narrative, Carmichael ("complex, sensitive, and angry") popped off the page as a "spokesman not so much of a movement as a mood," one that stood in contrast with the presumed passiveness of earlier generations.

Parks marveled at Carmichael's "ability to adjust in any environment." Tracking Carmichael on university campuses, with hard-core inner-city militants, and with rural blacks in Alabama, Parks lauded the young revolutionary as a new kind of Renaissance man, one who was at ease among sharecroppers, intellectuals, and urban militants alike.[131] Flashes of humor over childhood memories (the white kids at Bronx Science High School considered Carmichael, a self-proclaimed bad dancer, "their chocolate Fred Astaire") turned to grim recognition of his mother's long days as a maid and his father's premature death due to backbreaking labor.

Perceptively, Parks described King's current antiwar stance as following on the heels of Carmichael's, whose rage against Vietnam, the draft, and Lyndon Johnson marked his standard stump speech.[132] Carmichael's unshakable antiwar position evoked conflicting feelings in Parks, whose son served as a tank gunner in Southeast Asia. This led Parks to wonder which of the two young men's fight was more just. Finding "no immediate answer," he concluded that Carmichael's passion for justice gave physical risk a clear political purpose that the Vietnam crisis lacked. For, "in the face of death, which was so possible for the both of them, I think Stokely would surely be more certain of why he was about to die."[133] Stokely Carmichael had become, for Parks as well as millions of other black Americans, a surrogate son.

On May 1, Carmichael accompanied SNCC program secretary Cleveland Sellers to Sellers's army induction ceremonies in Atlanta, Georgia. Colleagues since Howard University and friends and confidantes soon after, Carmichael and the twenty-two-year-old Sellers complemented each other well. The charismatic Carmichael and the even-tempered Sellers admired the other's contrasting personality traits. Just as Carmichael masked an imposing intellect with explosive oratory, the deceptively fierce Sellers hid a quiet rage behind a placid—at times even blank—exterior.

Arriving early at the induction center, Sellers remained in place when he was told to step forward. Because of this, he made national news with his refusal to serve in the army. Carmichael stated the fact that sixteen key

SNCC workers had suddenly been called up by local selective service. Being suspicious of this surge of SNCC conscription, he told reporters that none of them, including Sellers, would serve.[134] For Carmichael, Vietnam exposed America's racial hypocrisy even as it cast a spotlight on the country's growing list of international atrocities. "They are drafting Negroes to commit genocide against their race," he declared.[135]

Carmichael's bold stance on Vietnam reverberated to the upper echelons of American politics. On the Friday after Cleve Sellers refused induction into the military, members of the House Armed Services Committee pelted Assistant Attorney General Fred Vinson with questions, demanding to know why Carmichael had yet to be prosecuted for sedition. Vinson defensively admitted that Carmichael's "outrageous" anti-Vietnam talk failed to meet the legal threshold, which was met with skepticism and anger. At one point, Louisiana representative Edward Hebert suggested forgetting "the First Amendment" to "show the American people that the Justice Department and Congress were trying to clean up this rat-infested area."[136] After pointing out the Constitution's inherent protections of dissident speech, the Assistant Attorney General was asked by another committee member for his personal opinion of Carmichael's now famous "Hell no, we ain't going" catchphrase. "I think it is an outrageous statement that is under the protection of the 1st Amendment in the circumstances he made it."[137] After much hand-wringing, Justice Department officials decided against prosecuting Carmichael.

Amid calls at the national level for his imprisonment and worse, Carmichael looked forward to a return to local organizing. With his tenure as SNCC chairman coming to an end on May 12, he made plans to resume local organizing. "This is sort of my last speaking engagement," he told an audience at a Sunday-evening dance that capped off "Stokely Carmichael Day" in Chicago, "'cause after this I got two more to go to, and then I'm going to D.C., and we're going to sure enough take over that city and it's going to be ours, lock, stock, and barrel."[138]

Carmichael's status as a national leader complicated his projected return to grassroots organizing. Events in California would soon make it altogether impossible. On May 2, 1967, the Oakland-based local activist Huey P. Newton sent an armed convoy of Black Panthers to the state capitol building in Sacramento to protest an impending gun ban in person. The demonstration triggered bursts of panic and near hysteria that simultaneously burnished the young organization's celebrity as it also jeopardized its already slim chances of longevity. The Sacramento protest poised the Black Panthers on a high wire between daring improvisation and reckless bravado, mixing brooding threats of violence with the exhilarating spectacle of street-corner toughs turned political revolutionaries.

In July, Newton issued an executive order in the pages of the mimeographed *Black Panther* newspaper to draft Carmichael into the group. Newton's mandate conferred the rank of field marshal on Carmichael, with a public commission to "establish revolutionary law, order and justice" over the United States to the Continental Divide.[139] It was an unlikely reward, conferred in absentia (Carmichael was out of the country at the time of Newton's executive mandate), for Carmichael's ongoing activism in Lowndes County, Alabama, whose Panther symbol had been eagerly snapped up by scores of militants, thereby forming its most enduring beachhead in Oakland, California.

There was a whiff of desperation to Newton's order. Carmichael scarcely needed to lend his name to a group of revolutionaries who could easily be mistaken for misguided, if colorful, black gangsters. An August 1967 *New York Times* exposé resuscitated the waning buzz of the group's Sacramento adventure by publishing "The Call of the Black Panthers," written by *Ramparts'* assistant managing editor Sol Stern. The story was accompanied by a soon-to-be iconic photo of Huey P. Newton. With an open-collared white dress shirt underneath a black leather jacket, a pensive Newton sat in a flared chair holding a rifle in one hand and a spear in another, surrounded by African shields carefully strewn on the floor. The image evoked poetic juxtapositions between the past and present, the modern and the ancient. It suggested forward-thinking black revolutionaries armed with a potent knowledge of history and politics. However, the Black Panthers would not be treated as such.

For Stern, the Panthers' limited impact on the Bay Area's civil rights scene made them less of a political phenomenon than a sociological one.[140] Against the backdrop of civil disorder in urban cities nationwide, the Panthers—with their melodramatic statements, bombastic posture, and dead serious swagger—demanded attention. The profile suggested that the Panthers were not a cause of urban unrest but merely one of its most potent symptoms. Stern's profile contained all of the ingredients designed to turn the group into a household name. The article lingered over Newton's good looks and smoldering intensity, showcased cofounder Bobby Seale's common touch with ordinary people, and documented the Oakland police department's visceral hatred for the Panthers. It quoted one anonymous officer's wish that both groups engage in "an old-fashioned shootout." With characteristic brio, the Panthers inflated their membership numbers, spoke of mounting a global revolution against American imperialism, and convened sparsely attended rallies where their rage against the police drew more interest from curiosity seekers than new recruits.[141]

While the Panthers searched for regional fame, Carmichael toured the world, burnishing his own international reputation and following in the footsteps of Malcolm X. Hailed as an international ambassador by revolutionaries in Cuba, Algeria, and Vietnam, his trip placed Black Power at the center of global narratives of race, war, and democracy. Critics fumed that he recycled the same anti-American speech into "a first class, round the world airline ticket," while supporters hailed Carmichael as an international emissary whose political platform spanned nothing less than the entire world.[142]

Carmichael arrived in London on July 15 as FBI field offices buzzed with rumors that his actual destination was Moscow.[143] His tour coincided with furious FBI investigations attempting to link him to the Communist Party as well as domestic urban unrest in Newark and Detroit that, Black Power activists argued, offered a mere prelude to a more violent revolution to come. London would be the first stop on Carmichael's five-month international tour.

There, Carmichael impressed intellectuals and activists alike at the 1967 "Dialectics of Liberation" conference. This event featured well-known radical intellectuals such as Herbert Marcuse and Angela Davis, a recent Brandeis University graduate and perhaps Marcuse's most precocious student, who found Carmichael to be erudite and insightful. British newspapers described him as a "phenomenon" whose "slogan is Black Power" and whose skin color constituted "his country."[144] In working-class neighborhoods of Brixton, Hackney, and Notting Hill, he recounted how an early infatuation with Western civilization (in Trinidad and the Bronx) curdled from newfound knowledge of the black world's potential and the white world's historic transgressions. Calling Malcolm X his "patron saint," Carmichael defined America's urban riots as "rebellions" and predicted that domestic violence was inevitable in a nation born in bloodshed.[145]

Detroit burned just as Carmichael arrived in Santiago, Cuba, on July 25.[146] Civil unrest in Detroit, like most urban riots of the era, was sparked by an explosion of tense police-community relations. A police raid of an after-hours spot, or "blind pig," sparked a citywide insurrection as fed-up neighborhood residents spontaneously attacked a police car. Escalating violence turned west-side tenements and private homes into bonfires. Woodward Avenue, one of the city's main streets, burned throughout the night and twenty square city blocks burned along the Grand River. Detroit's riot outpaced Newark's similar conflagration just two weeks before in both scale and destructive grandeur.[147] "It was as if," wrote reporter Louis Lomax, "God himself was on the side of the organized revolutionaries."[148] In the *Omaha World Herald*, Lomax penned a highly speculative account that traced the riot's origins to a group of organized Black Power militants, at least one of whom had been on the scene in Newark. His chronicle characterized looters, police officers, and bystanders all as pawns in a political experiment orchestrated by urban revolutionaries.[149] If Lomax's story exaggerated Black Power's ability to organize urban insurrection, it also accurately reflected the mood of politicians, law enforcement, and a large segment of Americans who correlated riots with radicals. Meanwhile, Carmichael's arrival in Cuba suggested that black radicals might form powerful alliances with guerilla movements surging across Latin America.

The foreign press found Carmichael to be a charming personality. Cuba's *El Mundo* and *Granma*, Paris's *Le Monde*, and the Algerian Press Service carried reports of Carmichael's statements, as did newspapers in Rome, Poland, Yugoslavia, Hanoi, and Dakar, Senegal. In interviews and press conferences, he proved himself to be an affable raconteur—quick-witted, spontaneous, and articulate. In a sports shirt and dark sunglasses, Carmichael matched wits with Latin American and European journalists, who by all accounts found him irresistible. In fact, *Le Monde*'s special correspondent described him as possessing the bearing of "an athlete at rest," and Vienna's *Arbeiter-Zeitung* characterized him as the "strangest Latin American" at the Cuban conference.[150] In truth, Carmichael's speeches and interviews in Cuba gave pause to all sides of the Cold War. This included the Chinese, who sanguinely quoted his words of praise for Mao without reporting a word about the conference; the Soviet Union, who were upset over OLAS's rejection of Moscow's line of "peaceful co-existence" with imperialism; and European leftists who were uncomfortable with his talk of revolutionary violence.[151]

In Santiago, Carmichael sat down in a place of honor as Castro, in a speech that lasted two hours and twenty minutes, singled him out as the leader of black Americans fighting for freedom. But perhaps the most significant aspect of Castro's annual keynote anniversary speech concerned his pointed references to racial conflict in the United States. Castro began his "relatively brief" address by describing Carmichael as "one of the most prestigious leaders for civil rights in the U.S." [152]

Domestic concerns dominated the bulk of Castro's speech, but themes of racial violence in America surfaced in his conclusion. "The U.S. colored population, victim of discrimination and exploitation," said Castro, "is rising up more and more with astonishing valor and heroism to demand its rights and resist force with force." With one final "heartfelt embrace for the representatives" of black Americans, Castro completed his speech. If his words buoyed Carmichael's spirits, they also gave American officials further pause. Secret State Department files noted that Castro's closing statement accorded "Carmichael the ultimate honor of listing this slogan before his closing salutation to the Vietnamese people."[153]

The next day, on the floor of Congress, at least four members of the House of Representatives publicly declared Carmichael a traitor.[154] Newspaper banners turned provocative snippets from Carmichael's interview with *Prensa Latina* into headlines that promoted unrestrained panic. "Carmichael Sees Long, Hot Summer" and "Black Power Leader Vows 'Fight to Death'" conveyed fevered alarm about the state of race relations in America while it also turned Carmichael into a grotesque specter of anti-American sentiment.[155] Cuba's *Radio Havana* tied Carmichael's political growth to his first encounter with the revolution via Fidel Castro's historic Harlem visit in 1960. Fidel's visit highlighted the manner in which black Americans and Cubans fashioned enduring bonds through a joint struggle against a common enemy. "This event," recalled Carmichael, marked "a moment" in American history that blacks would never forget.[156]

Rowland Evans and Robert Novak, influential Washington-based political reporters whose column made for required reading inside the Beltway, alleged that SNCC represented nothing less than "Fidel Castro's arm in the United States."[157] Breathless FBI reports seemed to confirm such suspicion, with confidential bureau informants suggesting that Carmichael planned to use insurrection techniques learned in Cuba after returning to the States.[158] In fact, Carmichael's visit to Cuba produced no such tangible conspiracies. Although the trip did mark his first opportunity to meet with Third World revolutionaries, his actual goals were more modest and successful. What Cuba offered—and what Carmichael warmly accepted—included provisional networks of communication with Latin American revolutionaries, the reflected glory of Castro's international stature, the chance to personally witness the inner workings of a recently installed revolutionary government, and travel assistance to other parts of the Third World.

From July to December, Carmichael's search for an international model for political revolution suitable for black Americans would take him from Cuba to Vietnam and beyond. With the State Department in hot pursuit, he lunched with Ho Chi Minh in Vietnam, met with guerrilla leaders in Algiers, and arrived in Conakry, Guinea, in time to meet three of Africa's most respected figures: Sekou Toure, Kwame Nkrumah, and Amilcar Cabral.[159] SNCC's new chairman, Hubert "Rap" Brown, temporarily filled the void left in Carmichael's absence. Brown's penchant for verbal bombast turned him into a made-for-television black militant as well as a favorite target of authorities. However, his notoriety paralleled SNCC's decreased effectiveness at the local level. Plagued by staff defections, ideological disputes, and a lack of resources, Brown's tenure as SNCC chairman from 1967 to 1968 would mark the organization's last year of national influence.

By 1967, Algeria had become shorthand for a kind of revolutionary vision that mixed the horrors of guerilla warfare with a kind of left-wing romanticism. Radical intellectuals trumpeted Frantz Fanon's support for the FLN, and Carmichael's presence in Algiers unfolded as a sort of *cinema verite*. They hailed him as a black American revolutionary who had waged nonviolent war in the Deep South now traveling all the way to Africa to be tutored by guerillas who had managed to liberate and rule a nation.

Mustapha Bouarfa, head of the Algerian delegation to the Organization of Latin American Solidarity Conference, arranged Carmichael's September visit under the auspices of the National Liberation Front (FLN). FLN officials carefully orchestrated Carmichael's visit, providing access to virtually all government offices and generous press coverage.[160] For ten days, Carmichael toured agricultural and industrial fields, met with high-ranking Algerian officials, and starred in the role of Black Power revolutionary in a country that prided itself as a citadel of anticolonial struggle. At the Algiers airport, Carmichael described the country as his "homeland" and "one of the most revolutionary countries in Africa."

Carmichael's first weekend in Algeria would prove momentous. Algerians, like much of their country, still bore the scars of a long and bloody independence struggle. A Saturday visit with Ahmed Ghozali, head of the government-owned energy company Sonotrach, led Carmichael to remark that the nationalization of American oil interests represented a unique kind of welcome gift. That same day he met with the Syrian ambassador at the Algerian International Trade Fair, attended a lunch hosted by North Vietnamese ambassador Nguyen Van Phat, and explored the Kasbah, which included a tour of the homemade bomb- and grenade-making factories used during the war of independence. The next day Carmichael traveled to Oran, where he addressed a conference of Algerian government representatives.[161]

In a three-page interview published in the official FLN publication, *Revolution Africaine*, Carmichael again cited urban guerilla warfare as the key to a domestic revolution in America. The FLN's high-profile support for Carmichael sparked rumors among FBI informants that he was negotiating to set up SNCC offices in Algeria financed by the government.[162]

At conferences in Algiers and Oran, Carmichael described Black Power as part of a worldwide struggle against imperialism. He also expressed support for Arabs regarding conflicts raging in the Middle East.[163] Through gestures such as these, Carmichael's rhetoric seemed to reflect the energy of his audience, and Algeria proved a particularly well-suited match.

State Department officials chronicled Carmichael's exploits with reports that expressed rage, hostility, and awe. Damage control remained paramount for officials trying to protect and burnish America's image in countries already skeptical of the promise of democracy. American embassy officials in Algiers summed up Carmichael's presence with a resigned admission of the trip's consequences: "It would be extremely difficult to measure how much harm he generated for the United States; it is abundantly clear that he did no good."[164]

From there, Carmichael landed in Conakry, Guinea, on Tuesday evening, September 26, aboard an Aeroflot from Algeria. He arrived as an honored guest of the Eighth Congress of the Democratic Party of Guinea, although he did not address the Congress. Throughout this visit, Miriam Makeba, a South African singer as internationally recognized for her voice as her beauty, became Carmichael's constant companion. He participated in a round of grenade and rifle practice with African women who comprised the Fifth Battalion of Guinea's local militia. After years of nonviolence and shedding only his own blood in search of higher democratic values in the United States, Carmichael now upheld revolutionary violence as the cure to a planet ensnared in suffering. "The correct road is the one you have chosen under the leadership of Sekou Toure," he told members of the local militia, "taking up arms and being ready to kill the enemy who has killed so many patriots throughout the world, such as Lumumba and Malcolm X."

Carmichael's meetings in Conakry would prove especially fruitful. In correspondence from Guinea, he admonished SNCC workers to resist the temptation of petty squabbles and infighting. "Our people are dying in the streets of Detroit, Vietnam, Congo . . . and all over," he wrote, thereby casting the Third World in racial solidarity with black freedom struggles. "I hope my trip and future trips make things HOTTER for you all," Carmichael insisted, since this would separate serious revolutionaries from pretenders. "I wish most of you would wake up and catch up with your people. They are ahead of you."[165]

Guinea's president Ahmed Sekou Toure presided over a one-party state that advocated a form of African socialism that retained indigenous cultural flourishes appealing to black nationalists. An outspoken and charismatic proponent of pan-Africanism, Toure impressed Carmichael as a steadfast and unpretentious leader. The two developed a close rapport.[166] Guinea was also the residence of deposed Ghanaian leader Kwame Nkrumah. Ousted in a coup the previous year, Nkrumah was a living legend among pan-Africanists, a status he retained in spite of his recent political misfortunes. Conakry's coastal surroundings, low-rise buildings, and arid climate dotted with mango trees and coconut palms reminded Carmichael of his native Port of Spain. Even more, Nkrumah's scenic coastal villa contrasted with the grim reality of political exile. The *Osagyefo* (or redeemer of his native land) and Carmichael took an instant liking to each other. In wide-ranging, candid conversations, Nkrumah recounted his efforts to secure Ghana's independence while Carmichael came away with renewed pan-Africanist impulses. Even as he prepared for the next stop on his global tour, Carmichael made plans to return to Africa.

If Carmichael's tour through Africa struck outsiders as revolutionary in its militancy, his radical statements about Vietnam sounded alarm bells back in the States. In Norway, he addressed a capacity crowd of over 1,000 at the Oslo Student Union where he spoke in measured tones about the Vietnam War. His detailed foreign policy criticisms, which called for Norway to withdraw from NATO, impressed participants and journalists. Five days later, he then appeared before university students in Sweden and capped off his Scandinavian tour with an evening talk at a large concert hall in downtown Stockholm.[167] On Wednesday, December 6, he spoke at an antiwar rally in Paris. Then, at a press conference there he reiterated his support for North Vietnam in caustic tones. "If Ho Chi Minh cannot sleep," Carmichael explained at one point, "Lyndon Johnson shall not sleep." Black Americans and the Vietnamese people, though separated by 10,000 miles, shared a common enemy. Excerpts of Carmichael's comments in Paris made the CBS evening news's Thursday telecast, as correspondent Harry Reasoner summed up the Black Power leader's speeches as "a violently anti-American" jeremiad "to audiences from Havana to Hanoi."[168]

On Monday, December 11, at around 3:30 p.m., Carmichael arrived in New York from Paris. A U.S. marshal representing New York's Eastern District immediately confiscated his passport as over one hundred supporters greeted him.[169] Three days later, Carmichael flew to Washington to attend a meeting at Howard University. A two-minute standing ovation greeted Carmichael as he entered Crampton Hall, where Ron Karenga delivered the evening's keynote speech. Following a brief meeting with Karenga, Carmichael autographed copies of his recently released book, *Black Power: The Politics of Liberation in America*, coauthored with political scientist Charles Hamilton.[170]

Five days before Christmas, Undersecretary of State Nicholas Katzenbach delivered a confidential memo to Lyndon Johnson regarding plans to prosecute Carmichael. "You asked that I examine possible avenues for the criminal prosecution of Stokely Carmichael," began Katzenbach. His sharp legal mind and keen sense of history uncovered a statute dating back to 1799, the Logan Act. This act made it a crime to consort with foreign officials for the purpose of "defeating the measures of the United States." It was under this statute that they hoped Carmichael might be prosecuted. Carmichael's actions in Havana and Hanoi made him ripe for criminal prosecution on these grounds. However, public relations and legal obstacles abounded because the Logan Act remained a "dead letter" that had never been a basis of prosecution for the past 168 years. As such, they ran the risk that the Supreme Court might reverse such a conviction because "hundreds of American citizens probably violate the broad language of the Logan Act every year" and were not prosecuted. Charges of sedition and passport violation were moot for the reason that Carmichael's passport bore "no visas or entry stamps" from the countries he visited, and a trial would turn him into an even bigger celebrity. "After reviewing the grounds of criminal action from the points of view of law and domestic and foreign relations," Katzenbach recommended against prosecution.[171] The U.S. government would have to find other avenues to stymie Carmichael.

The year 1968 found Stokely Carmichael at the height of his public notoriety. However, it would also mark his last year of full-time residence in the United States. Nevertheless, before leaving the country, Carmichael would play a pivotal role in helping to organize the Black Panthers. Although his public utterances increasingly contemplated the meaning and utility of revolutionary violence, he would abandon America as a partial result of witnessing too much bloodshed. Further, his presence in Washington, D.C., that year placed him at the center of the growing controversy surrounding Martin Luther King Jr.'s Poor People's campaign. King had announced the previous summer in his third book, *Where Do We Go From Here: Chaos or Community?*, that massive civil disobedience would have to be the crux of a national movement for social and economic justice.

King's new tactics gave supporters and opponents alike great cause for concern. His full plans to organize a massive tent city at the nation's capital struck Black Power militants as foolish, Washington politicians as quixotic, and local authorities as trouble. Journalists alternately described the campaign as a reckless stunt as well as a last-ditch effort that anticipated the demise of nonviolence as a force for social change.[172]

However, King's determination to organize a mass protest in the nation's capital did renew the combative yet friendly relationship with Carmichael that had been forged in the tumult of 1966's Meredith March. Twice during the first week of February, Carmichael and King met to hash over disputes, discuss areas of mutual agreement, and massage political differences. During a closed meeting of two hundred activists at Washington's Church of the Redeemer, King disclosed more detailed plans of the Southern Christian Leadership Conference's upcoming Poor People's Campaign. For his part, Carmichael expressed support for the campaign's goals while also maintaining SNCC's organizational autonomy. Press reports glossed over the complexity behind these negotiations in favor of characterizing the meeting as part of King's effort to neutralize violent threats posed by Black Power militants.[173] Behind the scenes, however, Carmichael assured King that SNCC's intentions were positive. "Stokely, you don't need to tell me that," replied King. "I know you." Privately, King expressed reservations, confiding to advisor Stanley Levison that, although Carmichael was now "sweet as pie," he tried to "pull a power play on us in Washington" in an attempt to gain leverage over the planned Poor People's March.[174]

Two days after meeting with King, Carmichael unveiled a more sensitive side to his customarily confrontational personality at a conference of Methodist ministers in Cincinnati, Ohio. An astonished group of 250 clergymen listened to a Bible-quoting Carmichael who held up Jesus's dual commitment to saving souls and ending poverty as the contemporary challenge facing the clergy. Quoting the book of Acts, he urged the ministers to "turn the world upside down" in pursuit of social justice. He then deployed snippets of Jeremiah to relay the message that social upheavals to root out injustice proved consistent with tenets of the Christian faith. Reverend James Lawson, chair of the National Conference of Negro Methodists, informed skeptical reporters that "Stokely has the basic compassion called for in the Christian faith," thereby supporting Carmichael's presence as presenting a message that black Methodists needed to hear.[175] Carmichael's ability to speak in the language and rhythm of the clergy dated back to his days as an organizer in the delta. The black church stood at the center of the summer project in 1964 and efforts to organize Lowndes County the following year. During mass meetings in churches, Carmichael could be seen singing freedom songs and, when called upon, would lead groups in prayer. Although he remained critical of SCLC's political strategies, he nonetheless maintained a respect and admiration for King that would endure. Although we will never know what kind of political alliances King and Carmichael may have forged, over time their personal friendship withstood the stresses of Black Power controversy and the Poor People's campaign.

Since returning from his international tour, Carmichael had attempted to return to local organizing in Washington, D.C. However, efforts to forge a Black United Front with the city's leaders stalled, and activists inside of SNCC's Washington Field Office grew resentful over Carmichael's star power. His growing alliance with the Black Panthers proved more promising, and two public speeches in California in February on behalf of the "Free Huey Movement" left no doubt that he remained the biggest speaking draw among black militants in the nation. Furthermore, Carmichael's private life also attracted intense public scrutiny after his engagement to South African singer Miriam Makeba. Almost ten years older than him, Makeba was an international star whose close professional contacts included entertainer Harry Belafonte. Critics charged Carmichael with entering into a marriage of convenience, and thus ignoring the couple's genuine affection toward each other in favor of stories that chronicled Makeba's declining concert schedule due to their impending marriage.[176]

Then, on Thursday, April 4, Martin Luther King Jr. was shot by sniper fire while standing on the balcony of his room at the Lorraine Hotel in Memphis, Tennessee. King's Thursday-afternoon assassination came in the midst of his efforts to aid the city's striking sanitation workers. The night before, in his last public speech, King had delivered a tremendous address during a standing-room-only mass meeting, where he seemed to prophesy his impending death. Against a backdrop of tornado warnings in the region, King laid out a summary of his political accomplishments and the finer points of Memphis's local struggle, certain only that more work remained to be done. "We've got some difficult days ahead," he correctly predicted.[177]

Carmichael heard the news of King's death in SNCC's Washington office. As news of King's death spread, Carmichael, along with staff workers Cleve Sellers and Lester McKinnie, led a group of angry protesters down Washington's U Street corridor of drugstores, supermarkets, and theaters, asking store owners to close. Walter Fauntroy, one of King's advisors, practically dragged Carmichael by the arms, pleading with him to stay calm. Small, attentive crowds gathered around transistor radios that were sifting information from disjointed news stories, recounting the details of King's death. As passersby shattered the windows of the Republic Theater, an unusually diplomatic Carmichael screamed, "This is not the way!" backed by a chorus of SNCC workers repeatedly chanting, "Take it easy, Brothers!" Unable to control the crowd, they eventually retreated a few blocks away, back to Carmichael's apartment. SNCC activists passed the night sharing bittersweet memories, with Carmichael leading tearful reminisces of his friendship with King.[178]

On September 5, 1968, Carmichael and Miriam Makeba flew to Dakar, Senegal, from New York City. Over the next several weeks, they made preparations to relocate to Africa. They also traveled to Conakry, Guinea, where Carmichael met with Kwame Nkrumah for the second time in a year. In conversations with Nkrumah, Carmichael presented the Black Panthers as a group of revolutionaries committed to the deposed leader's triumphant return to Ghana. With the entitlement of a former ruler, Nkrumah preached patience, reminding Carmichael that "without a base we can do nothing."[179]

Three days after Carmichael arrived in Africa, Huey P. Newton was convicted in Oakland, California, of manslaughter. Both Newton's conviction and Richard Nixon's narrow presidential election two months later accelerated Carmichael's plans to seek a new political headquarters. His marriage to Miriam Makeba and hopes for the future collided with concerns for his own safety. Privately, he feared becoming the victim of a political assassination. There were good reasons to be afraid. FBI surveillance of Carmichael had reached comic proportions. After an agent's inquiry into his travel itinerary resulted in a bomb scare following a miscommunication with a TWA flight clerk, Carmichael laughed off the incident, unfurling a huge poster of Che Guevara as he traded barbs with reporters. Nevertheless, the harassment exacted a toll.[180]

That December, Carmichael made plans to move to Guinea for good.[181] Before leaving, he made a series of controversial appearances at Southern colleges where he openly discussed revolutionary violence. At North Carolina

A & T, Carmichael's address, "A New World to Build," announced that the period of "entertainment" had passed in order to introduce concrete strategies in service of a political revolution. Black people, he declared, suffered through both racial segregation and psychological colonization, which was also discussed in Frantz Fanon's *The Wretched of the Earth*. Fanon's analysis of colonialism's damaging effect on the black psyche had an American equivalent in an unspoken compulsion for white standards of beauty. W. E. B. Du Bois's notion of seeing the world through a veil—the possession of a double consciousness that gifted blacks with prophetic powers as it likewise burdened them with internal conflicts—formed the basis of Carmichael's discussion of black self-determination. Pathological behavior in the form of drugs, gangs, and criminal activity were the most visible manifestation of black self-loathing. Denial of African identity and all traces to a continent considered uncivilized left black Americans a people without a history who were ashamed of their own culture. There was difference between Negroes and blacks, Carmichael argued. He reasoned that the former clung to the antebellum era's notion of the good slave, while the latter recognized contemporary symbols of bondage and set out to transform the society that produced slavery. Nevertheless, he maintained that "every Negro was a potential black man," ready to be patiently converted toward an "undying love" for the community rather than privately ridiculed or publicly attacked.[182] With this enunciation of his mature political views, Carmichael departed the United States for good.

In 1969, a reporter for London's *Sunday Times* found Carmichael in Africa and in a playful mood, lounging with his wife, Miriam, and her fifteen-month-old grandson. He was an elder statesman at age twenty-eight. Over dinner, Carmichael candidly discussed his recent split from the Panthers, the decision to relocate to Guinea, and his ongoing search for new political strategies.

If the Panthers represented a political dead end, Carmichael remained unsure of the proper vehicle for the political revolution he still hoped to lead. "I do not know how to begin to cope with the problems" in the United States, he admitted, "so for me to stay there and to pretend that I do is for me to deceive myself and my people." On a hotel balcony in Algiers, he wistfully contrasted his friendship with the late Martin Luther King Jr. with his newfound enmity with exiled Black Panther Eldridge Cleaver. Cleaver's open admiration for Carmichael in early 1967, which had resulted in a flattering essay in *Ramparts*, turned sour after Carmichael resigned from the Panthers.

Political disagreements over strategy and tactics had turned personal, and Cleaver targeted Carmichael in a highly publicized open letter that variously accused his onetime hero of being antiwhite, a government spy, and a fool.[183] For Cleaver, enmity was the flip side of admiration. Over time, Cleaver came to believe that Carmichael occupied a position of national influence that ill-suited him. Possessed of enormous self-regard, Cleaver came to see Carmichael as more of a competitor than a friend. In the aftermath of these charges, ad hominem attacks against Carmichael in the pages of *The Black Panther* newspaper became common. Asked if they could remain friends despite political differences, Carmichael answered, "With Eldridge maybe not." In this, he correctly anticipated no end to a torrent of criticism emanating from the Panthers. As the conversation shifted to talk of the future, Carmichael then extolled Nkrumah as Africa's true leader, a statesman bold enough to encourage pan-Africanism in a continent that had been divided by ethnic and regional differences. The romantic side of Carmichael made it all sound so exciting that the reporter briefly joined the euphoria before stepping back and diplomatically noting that most African leaders did not share Carmichael's enthusiasm for Nkrumah's leadership.[184]

By August 1969, both Carmichael and Cleaver claimed Africa as a political base for far-reaching revolution. From Algeria (soon to be officially recognized by the government as the Black Panther Party's International Section), Cleaver plotted political insurrection in the United States by remote control. He also welcomed a fashionably eclectic band of exiles from the States that included black militants, hijackers, and other colorful and questionable characters.

From the Congo Republic, on the other hand, Carmichael announced his intention to return Nkrumah to Ghana. "Dr. Nkrumah," he informed reporters in Brazzavile, "was the first man to realize the urgency of forming an organization of African unity." The declaration followed an earlier appearance on British television in which Carmichael sketched the international makeup of political struggle and vowed to use Africa as a base for a worldwide revolution.

If Carmichael's activities in Africa made him an icon in world affairs, they simultaneously distanced him from the immediacy of domestic Black Power struggles. But in October 1969, he made a comeback of sorts. He did this by giving an interview to the black press and allowing Ethel Minor, a former SNCC news staff director and close advisor, to report in *Muhammad Speaks* on his international travails.[185]

By 1981, Carmichael changed his name. To honor his mentors Kwame Nkrumah (who died in 1972) and Sekou Toure, he became Kwame Ture. Soon after, he divorced Miriam Makeba and married Marliatou Barre, a doctor, and had a son the next year, whom he named Boabacar "Bocar" Biro.[186] Specks of gray marked the now forty-year-old Ture's hair. He also now sported a more notable accent, which was a combination of francophone West Africa, Trinidad, and the Deep South. Ture snatched moments of domestic tranquility in between frequent tours around the world in order to raise money and political consciousness. Despite modest success recruiting new members into the All African People Revolutionary Party, Ture's dreams of mobilizing a political revolution through pan-Africanism receded against a backdrop of a conservative resurgence in the United States and abroad.

A diagnosis of advanced prostate cancer in 1996 would, in Ture's recollection, "bring out the best" in former colleagues and friends who raised funds for medical treatment in the States and abroad. Old friends chipped away at the mask of political certainty in interviews, conversations, and fetes so as to reclaim fleeting intimacies that were now buried by Ture's obsession to single-handedly ignite a political revolution. Charlie Cobb, a former SNCC worker and onetime confidant, encountered glimpses of "the old loose Stokely" who was full of energy and eager to laugh. More often than not, however, Ture remained inside a cocoon of political certainty, filled with catchy phrases (he routinely answered his phone with "ready for the revolution") and a coterie of loyal admirers.[187]

If Ture created and lived in a political reality of his own making, it was a world that grew larger as his illness progressed. Treatment took him to New York hospitals, Cuban clinics, and a holistic healing center in Honduras. Further travels, for sentimental reasons, found him back in Guinea and then on to Ghana, Egypt, and South Africa. There were other trips as well. Perhaps the most notable of his travels was Ture's return home. On June 12, 1996, he made his first public appearance (he had returned clandestinely before this) in Trinidad in three decades. Dressed in an aqua green robe, he spoke to two hundred students at the National Heritage Library, imploring them to use books as a gateway toward the creation of a more just society.[188]

The race to tie up loose political ends included efforts to complete a long-overdue autobiography that, with the assistance of former SNCC worker Mike Thelwell, would be published five years after his death. Old friends and ex-colleagues from SNCC and the Black Panthers called to inquire about Ture's health. The Nation of Islam provided financial assistance for medical treatment and an ad hoc committee of family and advisors provided treatment options in the United States.

Like his friend Martin Luther King Jr., Ture had ignored opportunities to build financial independence. Annual speaking tours provided subsistence, but his health crisis left him economically bereft and totally dependent on the goodwill of the black community that he affectionately referred to as "my people." Jesse Jackson stopped by Ture's bedside, and Louis Farrakhan kept in regular contact from Chicago. A visit from former Black Panther Communications Secretary Kathleen Cleaver and her two children was followed, coincidentally, by a phone call from Eldridge Cleaver, who was living his final lonely year in California.

Between 1996 and 1998, Ture spent more time in America than he had over the previous two decades. His illness reunited veterans of the civil rights and Black Power movements in organized tributes to the man whose activism indelibly shaped both eras. On Friday, July 5, 1998, Ture departed, for the last time, New York City on route to Guinea. Emaciated and weighing less than one hundred pounds, Ture died in Guinea, on the west coast of Africa, where he called home.

If Martin Luther King Jr. is rightfully considered the avatar of the civil rights movement's heroic period, then Kwame Ture represents, after Malcolm X, the embodiment of the Black Power era. Uncovering the ways in which Ture's legacy ultimately transformed American democracy revises our understanding of the course of postwar American history. Ture, perhaps better than any single postwar historical figure, provides a singular bridge that helps to better illuminate and understand the era's regional differences and racial scandals, gender controversies and class struggles, multiracial makeup and challenge to white privilege. He also helped us see the way in which ordinary people and powerbrokers (sometimes in unison and sometimes at cross purposes) remade America and much of the rest of the world.[189]

Through civil rights activism among poor sharecroppers in the Mississippi Delta and rural woods of Alabama, Kwame Ture sought to extend America's democratic traditions to black citizens who toiled in anonymity. Democratic breakthroughs collided with heartbreaking failures that assaulted Ture's youthful sense of idealism. These turned him toward a pursuit of power that mixed hope and anger, rage and optimism in a quest for a new America and, over time, a new world. Near the end of his life, American democracy's glaring contradictions seemed to pale in comparison to the crisis of African nation-states that unfolded in the post-Black Power era. But for Ture, opportunities remained hidden beneath each setback and, even at its worst, Africa held untold potential. Although such patience struck some as naive, Ture remained confident that his political path had helped shape a better world. Up until his final breath, he believed in—indeed remained ready for—revolution.

Ture's activism and influence spanned from Harlem to the Mississippi Delta, out west to California's Bay Area, and then on to the wider worlds of Europe, Africa, Latin America, and the Caribbean. Most often, however, Ture's presence (except for the obligatory recounting of the Meredith March) is either ignored or demonized in the increasingly vast literature on the civil rights movement. The young Stokely Carmichael's pivotal role in challenging, scandalizing, and transforming American democratic traditions is, inevitably, lost. In fact, Ture's own reticence to acknowledge the depth and complexity of his political journey (even in his own autobiography) at times contributed to the lack of serious scholarly interrogation of his extraordinary life. But there were other reasons as well. Most notably, Ture's unapologetic commitment to a style of black radicalism made him seem out of touch with the political austerity that followed the heady years of the 1960s.

It is now over four decades since the twenty-five-year-old Stokely Carmichael unleashed words sharp enough to cut through the thick humidity of a Mississippi evening. If we can begin to understand the political experiences that led to this momentous declaration—as well as the events that followed—we can also truly begin to comprehend not only the civil rights and Black Power era, but also the larger postwar freedom struggles that inspired and shaped these movements.

4

"A PLACE WHERE ALL THINGS ARE POSSIBLE"

Barack Obama and Dreams of Democracy

Barack Obama's unexpected and meteoric ascent to become the nation's first black president reflects the complex evolution of black politics since the civil rights and Black Power era. Born in 1961, the same year Freedom Riders faced prison to desegregate interstate travel across the nation, Obama nevertheless stands aloof to the culture wars. Whether they are based in racial, gender, or ethnic politics, these struggles remain a cornerstone of the legacy of the 1960s. "I think America is still caught in a little bit of a time warp," Obama confessed in the summer of 2007, going on to state that, "the narrative of black politics is still shaped by the '60s and black power."[1] For Obama, Black Power represents a kind of racial anachronism incapable of confronting the complex and messy realities of America's multicultural present.

Obama's understanding of the Black Power Movement shares in a common public misconception about the nature of its aims and the breadth of its achievements. Black Power activists fought for bread-and-butter issues that impacted the everyday lives of all Americans. These problems included good public schools, decent housing, health care, and robust employment. Although activists looked for racially specific solutions to problems that were rooted in slavery, a variety of multiethnic and racial groups saw in the movement a broad template for social and political justice goals. In this sense, contemporary discussion of multiculturalism and diversity is rooted in the radically democratic ethos of the Black Power era. Ironically, the key to achieving the broad, racially transcendent impact that his soaring rhetoric often reaches for may lie in lessons taught by a Black Power Movement whose legacy Obama is unlikely to ever publicly claim.

While Obama never embraced the legacy of the 1960s, he did acknowledge its crucial role in shaping contemporary American politics. "Despite a forty-year remove, the tumult of the sixties and the subsequent backlash continues to drive our political discourse," he wrote, two years before winning the presidency.[2] Although Obama's personal biography remains deeply rooted in the political legacy of the 1960s, he insisted that the lessons drawn from the era encompassed far more than pitched battles over racial, political, and social equality. Instead he argued that Americans held common dreams that required shared commitment and sacrifice. In Obama's conception of America, issues such as Affirmative Action, gay marriage, and school prayer inspire needless rancor. Indeed, for him they ultimately may require less attention than more universal themes such as health care, job creation, and a clean environment.

But despite Obama's best efforts to move beyond "the psychodrama of the Baby Boom generation,"[3] the social and political upheavals of the 1960s provide the historic context for understanding his 2008 election as the nation's first African American president—forty years after 1968, remembered as one of the most violent years in postwar history. Perhaps the thorniest part of this legacy continues to be Black Power.

Black Power-era radicalism loomed over 1968. That year was marred by the untimely assassinations of Martin Luther King Jr. and Robert F. Kennedy in the spring, followed by the election of Richard Nixon as president in the fall. Urban rebellions—what the media and law enforcement officials referred to as riots—gripped dozens of cities that year, in what was the sixth straight summer of civil disorders. Radicalized college and high school students staged raucous antiwar demonstrations, walkouts, and campus takeovers that sent shockwaves through much of the nation.

Black radicals stood at the center of these upheavals. More specifically, advocates of Black Power would scandalize and, ultimately, transform American democratic institutions through gritty and often provocative street demonstrations, campus takeovers, and community organizing tactics that challenged mainstream black leaders as much as government officials. Over four decades have passed since King was cut down by an assassin's bullet on Thursday, April 4, 1968, in Memphis, Tennessee. It's worth remembering how King's latterday push for economic justice, critique against the Vietnam War, and efforts to rouse the nation's poor stood, in part, as a response to criticism from black militants. During the same decade that thrust King in the spotlight, black radicals, led by Malcolm X, confronted democracy's sharp edges of poverty, police brutality, crumbling schools, unemployment, and an emerging urban crisis. They did so through militant protests in places such as Harlem, Detroit, and Los Angeles. Although they were critical of the civil rights movement's focus on desegregating public accommodations and what many considered an overreliance on voting rights as a racial panacea, many of these Northern activists drew inspiration from these struggles and participated in both movements simultaneously. Malcolm X and early Black Power radicals drew strength and power from the international arena, paying particularly close attention to the 1955 Bandung Conference in Indonesia, Ghanaian independence in 1957, and 1959's Cuban Revolution. When Fidel Castro toured Harlem in 1960, the first leader he met with was Malcolm X. In February of 1961, the movement that would be dubbed Black Power several years later made its national debut. They came on the national scene through an organized UN demonstration in protest of the assassination of Patrice Lumumba, the prime minister of the Republic of the Congo.

In 1966, Stokely Carmichael, a young civil rights organizer who had done impressive work in some of the most dangerous parts of the South, gave name to a preexisting movement by calling for "Black Power" in the heat of the Mississippi Delta. Black Power would fire up black radicals, but it quickly came under fire—then and now—for advocating what critics argued was a racially separatist philosophy that promoted antiwhite sentiment, violence, and misogyny.

Although certain Black Power activists were guilty as charged, the major strains of the movement represented a far more nuanced and radical critique of American society. Black Power activists harbored a deep cynicism about America's ability and willingness to extend full citizenship to African Americans. They openly questioned the power, resiliency, and depth of American democracy. Indeed, Carmichael's radical pursuit of political, economic, and cultural power came only after suffering years of physical abuse at the hands of ordinary white citizens while trying to promote voting rights among sharecroppers.

The year of 1968 was also when the Black Panthers came into their own as perhaps the most enduring symbol of 1960s radicalism. Contemporary mythology surrounding the Panthers focuses on the group's bravado, flashy clothes, guns, fiery polemics, and open advocacy of armed confrontation against the government. Brandishing shotguns and sporting bandoliers, they exuded a kind of reckless nonchalance that made them dangerously romantic heroes of what many considered to be a new revolutionary age. However, what is often forgotten is the fact that cofounders Huey P. Newton and Bobby Seale were college students and fledgling community organizers who cared deeply about the survival of the black community. Just as community organizing in the South inspired interracial teams of young people to start voter registration drives during the early 1960s, inner-city youth in cities such as Oakland applied the same lessons to their own local concerns. Along these lines, the Black Panthers launched a host of "survival programs" during their relatively brief (1966–1982) existence that focused on bread-and-butter issues, including health care, housing, food, clothes, and the treatment of prisoners.

But the Panthers represent only the most spectacular manifestation of the Black Power era's call for radical democracy. The momentum of the movement took a variety of other forms, and its sheer breadth remains impressive. Black college and high school students from New York City to Greensboro, North Carolina, then out west to the Bay Area cities of San Francisco and Oakland successfully transformed university curricula and founded Black Studies programs and departments around the nation. Trade unionists in Detroit and other cities attempted to organize workers caucuses in order to challenge the entrenched racism of white-controlled labor unions. Cultural workers helped to redefine black identity through a Black Arts Movement that, through poetry, theater, dance, music, and style, reimagined America's cultural and political contours. Black feminists challenged both the movement's and the nation's sexism, and through this, they argued for a more inclusive vision of Black Power that promoted a human rights agenda. Prisoners from Attica to San Quentin agitated for better living conditions, programs, and fair treatment before the criminal justice system. Welfare mothers from New York City to Las Vegas dreamed of a guaranteed income and lectured Dr. King on the intricacies of public policy. Finally, hundreds of thousands of ordinary local people backed a new generation of black politicians and successfully elected them as mayors of a range of urban cities in the 1960s and 1970s: Cleveland, Ohio; Gary, Indiana; Newark, New Jersey; Atlanta, Georgia; Detroit, Michigan; and Philadelphia, Pennsylvania.

Barack Obama is a direct beneficiary of this rich legacy. Far from being a relic of the 1960s, Black Power's legacy resonated in Harold Washington's historic 1983 mayoral victory in Chicago and Jesse Jackson's robust 1984 presidential campaign. At times the media's refusal to acknowledge Black

Power's contemporary significance blunted this legacy. But something else happened to black politics in the post-Black Power era: The activists and politicians whose careers and strategies were forged during the Black Power era almost didn't accept Obama as their candidate.

The conventional path to prominence in the post-Black Power era, between 1975 and 1995, is best exemplified by Jesse Jackson's own meteoric rise from insurgent outsider to the most recognizable black powerbroker within Democratic Party circles. Jackson's route in turn followed a trajectory taken by venerable activists such as Andrew Young, John Lewis, and other civil rights veterans. These political activists came to define King's increasingly radical dream as accommodation with powerful white interests. This aging civil rights vanguard, with the complicated exception of Jesse Jackson Sr., proved cool to Obama's candidacy. Instead, they opted for a temporary refuge in the familiar figure and patronage of Hillary and Bill Clinton. Jackson's rise in American politics merged civil rights-era racial symbolism with power politics. In effect, Jackson served as perhaps the most influential powerbroker linking white politicians to the black community. Obama, in contrast, broke this mould of leverage politics by disagreeing with its premise. Obama's campaign implicitly supplanted the need for the kind of racial conduit that Jackson historically offered white politicians.

At the start of the 2008 campaign, Obama appeared to be more the leader of a symbolic movement than a bona fide presidential candidate. Victory in the Iowa caucuses, however, swiftly catapulted Obama into the position of front-runner. Alarmed by their newfound second-place status, the Clinton campaign responded with a series of racially tinged attacks via various proxies. These assaults brought up Obama's substance abuse as a teenager, characterized his antiwar record as a "fairy-tale," and indirectly impugned Dr. King's legacy by asserting that it took Lyndon Johnson to actually pass civil rights legislation.

The charges briefly shifted the Democratic primary contest from one of substantive political issues to a crass debate over which representative of two historically oppressed groups (blacks or women) most deserved the nomination. Feminist icon Gloria Steinem's *New York Times* op-ed piece, published in the aftermath of Hillary Clinton's Iowa loss, set the tone for this narrative. In it, she argued that black men had received the right to vote fifty years before white women. This argument conveniently ignores the fact that most black men could not actually exercise that right until 1965 because of racial apartheid in the South.

As attacks on Obama mounted, the black community rallied with the latent sense of racial solidarity that is always simmering beneath the surface. In the South Carolina primary in late January, Obama came perilously close to being characterized as the *black* candidate. This was the very moniker his entire campaign had previously avoided. By promoting a robust version of the American Dream—albeit in Technicolor—Obama's campaign sought to avoid the perception of being regarded as a boutique label in contrast to the Clinton brand name. Out of necessity, he sought to gloss over the political legacy he was actually inheriting.

Obama's complicated—indeed at times tortured—relationship with America's sordid racial history is at the core of his best-selling memoir, *Dreams From My Father*. Subtitled "A Story of Race and Inheritance" and originally published to modest sales in 1995, the memoir wrestles with the legacy of the civil rights and Black Power eras in shaping Obama's racial identity and subsequent political destiny. But Obama's very existence attests to the possibilities of postwar American democracy, in which an expansive liberal state teemed with new, unprecedented opportunities for good jobs, higher education, and affordable homes. Yet the New Deal and its aftermath remained a largely two-tiered affair. In this, one level of services and hopes and dreams for whites and another, more tenuous, halting, and largely inferior one for blacks.[4]

Obama's white mother, Stanley Ann Dunham, came of age in this divided world. She was a budding feminist and independent thinker who found herself transplanted to Hawaii. This was the result of her father's itinerant search for satisfying work that took him from Kansas, Texas, and Seattle before arriving in the nation's newest state. As an undergraduate at the University of Hawaii, Stanley Ann met Barack Obama, Sr., an ambitious Kenyan graduate student who her parents more or less accepted, despite his exotic racial origins.[5] In short order they were married, had a son, and Obama's father moved to Cambridge, Massachusetts, to attend Harvard on a scholarship, destined to remain a spectral figure in his son's life.

Like an increasing number of black men of his generation, Obama would be raised by his mother and extended family. Hawaii proved tolerant enough in its own multicultural background to accept the brown boy—with his white mother and doting Midwestern grandparents. If Obama's grandmother—Madelyn Lee Payne Dunham, affectionately known as "toot"—housed unspoken prejudices against black men, his grandfather, Stanley A. Dunham, had a natural affinity toward underdogs that made him receptive to his daughter's daring personal choices.[6]

A product of an improbable and ultimately short-lived union during the last half of the civil rights movement's heroic era (1960–1965), Obama spent much of his early years wrestling with questions of race, identity, and power.[7] Transplanted to Indonesia after his mother's second marriage, young Barry noticed race's uncanny grip on society. He remembers a magazine story about blacks who experienced botched chemical peels in ill-fated efforts to lighten their skin, and he became aware of the paucity of brown faces on the American-imported television shows that he watched as a boy. All this paralleled Ann Dunham's efforts to convince Barry that "[t]o be black was to be the beneficiary of a great inheritance, a special destiny, glorious burdens that only we were strong enough to bear."[8]

Obama confronted much of these burdens in an adolescence that brought him back to Hawaii to attend an exclusive private school. His entry had been greased by the wheel of nepotism (his grandfather pulled some strings) that he would wryly describe as his "first experience with affirmative action."[9] Raised in an overwhelmingly white environment, Obama embarked on what would be a lifelong search for a positive racial identity. Intermittent bouts of fear, self-loathing, and racial resentment haunted this quest. Regardless, Obama sought to avoid being defined by prevailing racial stereotypes that cast black men as violent, angry, and dangerous.

As he searched for a stable identity, the young Obama found refuge in black history books and particular comfort in *The Autobiography of Malcolm X*. For Obama, Malcolm's "repeated acts of self-creation" inspired a belief that he, too, could transform himself through sheer force of his personality and indefatigable will. Perhaps the most important self-made man of his generation, Malcolm X doggedly pursued political goals that would simultaneously lift himself and the wider black community from degradation and stifling poverty. Obama's admiration of Malcolm rested on the Black Power leader's uncanny ability to reinvent himself at crucial points in his life. However, while admiring Malcolm's political self-determination, Obama also distanced himself from the Nation of Islam's racial orthodoxy just as Malcolm himself did toward the end of his life.[10]

Like most Americans, Obama's interpretation of Malcolm X is constrained by a hidebound national script. In this, the black nationalist is cast as ill-tempered and angry, a prophet of rage whose scare tactics contrasted with Martin Luther King Jr.'s more sober plea for racial equality. In reality, due to his complicated engagement, dialogue, and confrontation with the idea of American democracy, Malcolm remains one of postwar America's most controversial, important, and invigorating figures. Popular memory couches Malcolm as an outsider who only belatedly recognized the universality of the human spirit during his final days. In fact, secular impulses guided Malcolm's political activism for over a decade, leading to tensions that accelerated his departure from the NOI.

However, as much as he remained bound by conventional wisdom, Obama's willingness to engage with Malcolm's legacy is important. Striking biographical and political parallels emerge from the lives of Malcolm X and Barack Obama. Both men were raised by single mothers in unenviable circumstances and would spend most of their young adolescence and early adulthood in search of black male role models. As teenagers, both Malcolm and Obama dabbled in recreational drug use and, like sociologists, both enjoyed reaching out and talking to people who lived on the margins. In Malcolm's case, the big-city underworlds of Boston, Detroit, and New York provided an eye-opening real-world education that would serve him for the rest of his life. Obama's own global travails took him from Hawaii's sunsplashed environment all the way to Indonesia's bracing poverty and, eventually, to the gritty streets of Chicago.

At a certain point, however, the two lives diverge. One of the most defining differences from Barack Obama was Malcolm's incarceration in 1946 at the age of twenty-one. Buoyed by the kind of familial stability that Malcolm would only experience as an adult, Obama achieved the kind of educational opportunities usually reserved for elites. Yet in his memoir, Obama expresses ambivalence about the opportunities his unique background afforded him. Aware that, despite his grandparents' unconditional love, "men who might easily have been my brothers could still inspire their rawest fears."[11] Thus, the pitfalls of black anger remain a recurring theme throughout *Dreams From My Father*. Painfully aware of how race marked the outside world's expectations of him, Obama deployed Du Bois's "double-consciousness" trope in order to navigate Hawaii's largely white world: accommodating and deferential around older whites—especially his grandparents—and resentful and diffident around his small coterie of black peers.

From Hawaii, he found a new community in Pasadena, but one that still offered no easy answers to confounding questions about his racial identity. Enrolled at the prestigious Occidental College in 1979, Obama encountered a generation of black college students who were too young to have participated in civil rights demonstrations and Black Power-era campus protests. Nonetheless, they remained uneasy about their status among the predominantly white and wealthy surroundings. Just a few short years earlier, many of the politically minded students Obama befriended at Occidental would have hidden their racial and class angst behind a full-throated endorsement of nationalism. Now they lurched uneasily for a usable identity in a post-Black Power era. Obama adapted to these new circumstances by tapping into latent black nationalist sensibilities among the most race conscious students. He felt envious of his African American counterparts from Chicago who were in possession of what he considered to be a more racially authentic experience, and he craved a kind of acceptance that his mixed-race heritage seemed to perpetually deny. For Obama, his freshman year at Occidental "seemed like one long lie, my spending all my energy running around in circles, trying to cover my tracks."[12] Obama's college-era identification with black nationalism opened up new a world, one that would serve as an entrée to larger ports of social and political activity.

In the process, he uncovered some enduring truths. Efforts in the United States to end apartheid in South Africa had long roots that could be traced back to the anticolonial heyday of the Great Depression and the Second World War era, through to the civil rights movement's high tide, and then gaining footholds on college campuses during the Black Power epic. Unaware of this longer backstory, Obama recalls his involvement in antiapartheid activism as a youthful lark that, almost by accident, transformed into a rite of passage in which political integrity came at the cost of searing experience. Active in the college's local antiapartheid campaign, Obama gave a brief speech at a rally that left him invigorated and yearning for more opportunities to share his views with larger audiences. But a part of him remained disillusioned by the moment's artifice as well as his own culpability in cultivating the kind of political theater that made one popular on campus but didn't necessarily ignite real social change. Like Malcolm X, Obama was beginning to discover the power of words to shape political stages, but longed to use their force to inspire political transformation.

Malcolm had found his voice in prison, by poring over countless books and becoming well versed in history, politics, and religion. In Elijah Muhammad, Malcolm encountered the father figure and political mentor whom he had spent his whole life searching for. In his autobiography, Malcolm describes Muhammad as the most powerful figure to ever enter his life, a man whom he thought possessed "the power of the sun."[13] Around the time that civil rights leaders took on school desegregation, Malcolm preached the Nation of Islam's gospel of black self-determination and racial and cultural pride on gritty urban street corners in Boston and Philadelphia on his way to establishing a more permanent base in Harlem.

Whereas Malcolm's epiphany came via a dingy jail cell in Massachusetts, Obama's true turning point took place in New York City after transferring to Columbia University in 1981. It was the dawn of the Reagan era, when the city's high-rise glamour could no longer hide deteriorating neighborhoods, escalating crime, and economic misery. In New York, Obama began to appreciate in a very concrete manner the way in which race and class politics impacted the city's civic health. Visits to prestigious museums in Manhattan's midtown neighborhood, walks through Harlem's 125th street corridors, and moments spent attending African street fairs in Brooklyn failed to conceal the city's glaring racial disparities. Indeed, they made them all the more conspicuous. After graduating from Columbia in 1983, Obama moved to Chicago to work as an organizer.

Obama arrived in Chicago at a time of great excitement and promise for the black community. The recent mayoral election of Harold Washington in 1983 had buoyed black activists who were disillusioned by Ronald Reagan's ascent. In fact, Washington's successful campaign would itself soon provide inspiration for Jesse Jackson's 1984 presidential run. In Chicago, Obama came to see that "[c]ommunities had to be created, fought for, tended like gardens."[14] Newsreel images of the civil rights era's high tide rattled in his mind, punctuated by the faces of activists as they sang freedom songs, SNCC workers canvassing in the Mississippi Delta, and brave college students igniting a sit-in movement by simply asking for service at an all-white lunch counter in the Deep South.[15]

But civil rights struggles were more than just a romantic montage of episodic moments where courageous black faces, along with a smattering of white allies, braved mob violence in order to expand American citizenship. Like most Americans, especially those coming of age in the aftermath of the movement's peak, Obama at times conflates popular memory of the era with actual history in his reminiscences of the period. As we have seen, the civil rights movement did not suddenly begin with the *Brown* Supreme Court decision or even the Montgomery Bus Boycott, nor did it end with Lyndon Johnson's signing of the Voting Rights Act in 1965.

Modern civil rights struggles grew out of the ferment of social, political, and cultural activism of the Great Depression and Second World War. African Americans led a national movement for radical democracy that stretched from coast to coast. It featured alliances with labor, civic, religious, and secular groups that demanded the simultaneous defeat of fascism abroad and Jim Crow at home.[16] In an age when American democracy's potential seemed far reaching, liberal civil rights groups such as the NAACP found kinship with radical organizations such as the Council on African Affairs in an effort to promote human rights through the United Nations and a global peace movement.[17]

Black activists, most notably Ella Baker, Paul Robeson, W. E. B. Du Bois, and Asa Philip Randolph, organized movements for radical democracy. These efforts plumbed the depths of local concerns, confronted regional diversity, and culminated in national ambitions that found common cause with international developments. The Cold War, however, transformed American democracy, narrowing paths toward citizenship in favor of a broader national interest to defeat Communism. Thus, the reality of the civil rights era that transfixed Obama's dreams are far more complicated than America's historical memory often allows.

Black Power remains perhaps the most controversial legacy of postwar movements for racial, economic, and social justice. In the popular imagination, Black Power evokes images of angry black militants, armed with shotguns and rifles who stoked racial fears, provoked white racial resentment, and successfully destroyed the civil rights era's dream of interracial reconciliation. From this perspective, Black Power emerged from the cauldron of unspoken black anger and resentment that reached a boiling point in the mid-1960s. This is exactly the kind of rage that the young Obama mostly avoided, being gripped by fears of alienating his family and becoming the grotesque embodiment of prevailing racial stereotypes. But Black Power's roots run deeper than such a portrait suggests. Its modern roots go back to Marcus Garvey's movement for racial pride and intertwine with the civil rights movement's call for equal citizenship.

As conceptualized in *Dreams From My Father*, Black Power remains anachronistic, a relic of a distant, unusable past that's populated with aging black nationalists such as a dashiki-wearing elder from his Hawaii youth.[18] In one telling anecdote, Obama recalls attending a lecture by Black Power advocate Kwame Ture (Stokely Carmichael) at Columbia University in the early 1980s. Tellingly, Obama's sharpest recollection of the speech details Ture's rebuke of a young woman's pragmatic question concerning the difficulties of transforming soaring rhetoric into practical reality. According to Obama, as Ture dismissed the question, "his eyes glowed inward as he spoke, the eyes of a madman or a saint."[19]

The passage reveals Obama's lack of awareness of Ture's foundational role in efforts to transform American democracy during the 1960s, when he was known as Stokely Carmichael. For Obama, Ture cut an anachronistic—if also dashing—historical figure whose rhetoric of pan-African unity against the backdrop of a national conservative political ascendance amplified the irrelevance of the social movements of the 1960s. For Obama, each word Ture spoke served as a eulogy for his brand of moribund politics. "The movement had died years ago," Obama laments, "shattered into a thousand fragments."[20] But the movement did not end. After Ture left America, it passed into the hands of latter-day civil rights and Black Power activists like Amiri Baraka and Jesse Jackson. Black political struggles in the 1970s and 1980s comprised a different—but no less important—chapter to an ongoing struggle for racial justice and economic equality.

I n 1972, three years after Kwame Ture left the United States for Africa, Amiri Baraka (formerly named LeRoi Jones) emerged as America's premier Black Power organizer. Born in Newark, New Jersey, on October 7, 1934, Baraka spent short-lived stints at Howard University and in the air force before becoming one of the most promising literary and artistic voices of his generation. Dubbed by critics as the "King of the Lower East Side," mainstream appreciation for Baraka's fiery poetry and incendiary prose culminated in a 1964 Obie Award for the play *Dutchman* and critical praise for his collection of essays the following year, *Home*.

Baraka's vision was not limited to art, but embraced activism as well. During the summer of 1965, he founded the influential but short-lived Black Arts Repertory Theater and School in Harlem with activists such as Sonia Sanchez and Rolland Snellings. After this, Baraka returned to Newark as a community organizer. For the next several years, he helped spearhead a series of local groups that played a critical role in electing Newark's first black mayor, Kenneth Gibson, in 1970. In the early 1970s, Baraka's vision for Black Power wedded community organizing to electoral politics, a trend within black nationalist and pan-Africanist circles that culminated in the March 10 through 12, 1972, National Black Political Convention in Gary, Indiana.

Black Power politics, as the *Washington Post* editorialized at the time, "came of age" during the three-day convention in Gary, Indiana. The city's first black mayor, Richard Hatcher, ordered that Gary be decorated for the occasion in the black nationalist colors of red, black, and green. In addition to Baraka and Mayor Hatcher, Michigan congressman Charles Diggs—a stalwart supporter of African independence movements—served as an official coconvener. At Gary, a diverse array of Black Power activists, ranging from welfare mothers and trade unionists to Black Panthers, all gathered in the spirit of "unity without uniformity." They sought to construct a pragmatic coalition that included civil rights activists, black business and civic leaders, and elected officials. For Baraka, the convention offered the opportunity to harness Black Power's tremendous energies in a workable vehicle for political empowerment. The convention's expansive program, dubbed the "Gary Agenda," outlined ambitious domestic and foreign policy agendas. More than this, however, the spirit of unity of purpose at Gary made even the loftiest goals seem eminently attainable.

Baraka's pragmatic approach to Black Power activism would, ironically, find a more robust and enduring voice in an unlikely figure—Jesse Jackson. Jackson electrified the convention with a speech inspired by a Baraka poem ("It's Nation Time!") that extolled the virtues of black self-determination. Up until this moment, Jackson, despite his flashy style, hip demeanor, and dazzling oratory, was more easily identified as an ambitious young militant within the Southern civil rights movement. His presence in Gary reflected his personal attempts to straddle civil rights and Black Power modes of activism that dated back to the mid-1960s. Born in Greenville, South Carolina, on October 8, 1941, Jesse Louis Jackson came of age in the segregated South, a child of America's rigid system of Jim Crow racism. A star high school athlete, he participated in civil rights demonstrations as a college student in North Carolina. By his early twenties, he had become one of Chicago's most respected young rights leaders.

During the height of the public transition from civil rights to Black Power, Jackson made a name for himself as a community organizer in Chicago and head of the Southern Christian Leadership Conference's Operation Bread Basket. For the last two years of Martin Luther King Jr.'s life, Jackson became an especially close surrogate. In fact, Jackson was among the handful of advisors with King at the Lorraine Motel on April 4, 1968, the day of his assassination.

After King's death, Jackson struggled to find an organizational vehicle for his brash mixture of hip, street-style vernacular that was wedded to themes of self-help, racial uplift, and community organizing. Ordained as a Baptist minister the same year as King's assassination, Jackson characterized himself as a "country preacher" who was inspired by a call to service that was polished during the civil rights era's heyday. His organization PUSH (People United to Save Humanity) advocated a national civil rights agenda grounded in the gritty realities of 1970s-era black urban America. At Gary,

Jackson stole the show sporting a towering afro and wearing a huge medallion of King's likeness around his neck. "What time is it?" he repeatedly asked the convention. "Nation Time!" they emphatically replied.

Nevertheless, unity at Gary eventually fractured along both ideological and practical fault lines. Community organizers and politicians interpreted politics, social justice, and reform in very different ways. Local organizers stressed issues of accountability, social justice, and public policy that remained focused on the redistribution of American wealth toward the inner city and rural areas dominated by poor blacks. Black politicians countered with a more pragmatic outlook, one that specialized in building and expanding black urban political machines.

By 1974, Baraka had come to take sides with the former perspective. He openly embraced Communism, a stance that led to his removal from the National Black Political Assembly, the ongoing vehicle produced by the convention. In contrast, many black elected leaders who had participated in the conference at Gary—and flirted with the idea of forming an independent black political party—soon found themselves firmly entrenched within Democratic Party machine politics.

Jesse Jackson proved more agile than Baraka at navigating the new political realities that emerged in Gary's aftermath. Between 1972 and 1983, Jackson's national and international profile grew enormously, even though he held no official title and had never run for public office. He emerged as an almost ubiquitous national black leader in the diffuse, post-civil rights landscape. Jackson's rise as an unelected independent activist was all the more remarkable considering the important strides black elected officials were making at the local and national level. For example, by 1983 African Americans had been elected as mayors of big cities such as Atlanta, Los Angeles, and Philadelphia, and the Congressional Black Congress boasted increased membership and influence.

Harold Washington's 1983 election as mayor of Chicago proved a particularly historic triumph. Run by Mayor Richard J. Daley for decades, Chicago was well known for its legendary political corruption and intransigent racism. The idea that Harold Washington, a black progressive with ties to community organizers, could actually emerge as mayor remained impossible to many political observers. His victory depended on an improbable coalition of grassroots activists, community organizers, veteran political operatives, and a historic get-out-the-vote effort that galvanized some of Chicago's poorest residents. Black militants proved to be a key part of Washington's electoral success, which hinged on a citywide effort that registered almost 200,000 new African American voters. His election culminated in what historian Manning Marable characterized as "Black Power in Chicago."[21]

Meanwhile, Jesse Jackson's powerful rhetoric provided something that Harold Washington and other elected officials did not. He found himself in the post-King age of simmering racial grievances, concerted assaults on Affirmative Action, and other race-based public policy, as well as skyrocketing rates of black incarceration, poverty, and community and economic decline. From this, Jackson appropriated the swaggering self-determination of Black Power activists and tied it to soaring, civil rights-era rhetoric that openly challenged powerful and entrenched interests. Long before Obama came onto America's political scene, Jackson openly implored Americans of all colors to "keep hope alive."[22]

Jackson's July 18, 1984, speech to the Democratic Convention in San Francisco was a tremendous milestone. For the first time, a black man who had won presidential primary contests addressed the convention in a major speech. Moreover, it took place two decades after the party had resisted efforts led by the sharecropper Fannie Lou Hamer for integration in Atlantic City. "From Fannie Lou Hamer in Atlantic City in 1964 to the Rainbow Coalition in San Francisco today; from the Atlantic to the Pacific," Jackson proclaimed, "we have experienced pain but progress, as we ended American apartheid laws. We got public accommodations." He extolled the profound social change that had occurred in America since the 1960s, reciting a roll call of martyrs who paid the price with blood. "We secured voting rights. We obtained open housing, as young people got the right to vote. We lost Malcolm, Martin, Medgar, Bobby, John, and Viola. The team that got us here must be expanded, not abandoned."[23]

Jackson's eloquent speech evoked powerful symbols of civil rights memories that remained raw in the national consciousness. He held up 1964's Freedom Summer and the infamous murders of three civil rights workers—James Chaney, Andrew Goodman, and Mickey Schwerner—as the events that helped to catalyze the civil rights movement. Just as the broken bodies of Schwerner, Chaney, and Goodman were "dredged from the depths of a Mississippi river," Jackson's own speech sought to elevate the legacy of past struggles for racial justice on behalf of a new political movement. This is what he called a "Rainbow Coalition," one that drew strength in diversity and redefined America as a multicultural democracy.

Thus, Barack Obama arrived in Chicago during a pivotal moment. In 1984, around the same time as Jackson's momentous speech and when a groundswell of opposition to the Reagan Revolution helped usher in watershed victories for African Americans at the local level, the time was further highlighted by Harold Washington's 1983 mayoral victory and Jackson's historic presidential campaign in 1984.[24] Obama still maintains an open fascination—even admiration—for Reagan's uncanny ability to craft a national vision that called Americans to a higher purpose. This is not to suggest that Obama found Reagan's public policy appealing. In fact, Obama's first trip to the White House occurred in 1984 as part of a delegation from City College's Harlem campus, opposing the Reagan administration's slashing of student aid.[25]

At the time, a large majority of the African American community regarded President Reagan as an enemy to agendas for civil rights and social change. At the national level, Reagan successfully implemented a repudiation of New Deal liberalism through tax cuts, generous defense spending, and soaring political rhetoric. In his speeches, he promoted self-reliance and rugged individualism as the antidote to the crime and urban decay that conservatives blamed on the failed social welfare policies of the 1960s. Locally, Reaganism's debilitating effects on predominantly black and brown communities ushered in record levels of poverty, unemployment, and incarceration as well as stiff political resistance. In this sense, even as a new generation of histories argue that the 1960s contained the seeds of the coming conservative revolution, the 1980s, at least at the local level, witnessed a continuation of the civil rights and Black Power eras.[26] Indeed, the successful political coalition that elected Harold Washington included veterans from the civil rights era and Black Power militants, along with progressives of all colors. Jackson's "Rainbow Coalition" in effect attempted to duplicate at the national level the success of Chicago's local movement.

Jesse Jackson's 1984 presidential campaign helped to galvanize black voters in order to gain leverage for African Americans within the Democratic Party. He provided the broad template for the kind of expansive, multiracial call for a new politics that would characterize Barack Obama's candidacy over two decades later. As civil rights leader and Georgia congressman John Lewis presciently remarked in June 1984, Jackson helped initiate "the climate for some Black man or Black woman to come along and be elected President of this country."[27]

In a period that has been characterized as the "Age of Reagan," Jackson occupied the political stage alongside the "great communicator." Here, he preached his own unique message of hope, unity, and change. Launched on the twentieth anniversary of the March On Washington, Jackson's candidacy speech touted his ability to introduce a new style of politics, based on a hope and an argument that, at its very core, America was fundamentally a multicultural democracy. "Thus, our perspective encompasses and includes more of the American people and their interest than do most other experiences," Jackson proclaimed during his November 3, 1983, announcement speech.[28] Former Black Power-era activists, including the Reverend Benjamin Chavis, found Jackson's speech to be a religious sermon squarely in the tradition of black liberation theology.[29]

Although it has been seen as a belated extension of the civil rights struggles of the 1960s, Jackson's campaign nevertheless contained extensive ties to Black Power-era activism. His supporters included black nationalists such as political advisor and Howard University professor Ronald Walters, who had been instrumental in helping to organize the 1972 Gary Convention.[30] Jackson, although primarily supported by the black community, advocated a broad-based political message that sought to transcend racial and regional differences by appealing to common themes of unemployment, health care, decent wages, and domestic and global peace initiatives. But Jackson's unapologetic criticism of American foreign policy, bold efforts to lay claim to King's mantle of moral leadership, and alliance with controversial black nationalist Louis Farrakhan made establishment Democrats uneasy.[31]

Jackson's hopeful and expansive message, brilliant campaign strategies, and tactical victories in the Democratic Primary process helped to pave the way for Obama. After successfully securing over 3 million primary votes with little funding, Jackson became the most well-known and respected black leader in America—the unofficial "President of Black America." Four years later, he attracted almost 7 million primary votes and won ten primaries. Additionally, and most importantly for Obama, he secured rule changes within the Democratic Party Primary process that included proportional representation.

Retrospectively, journalists, pundits, and commentators came to view the civil rights leader's historic campaigns as a largely symbolic effort. Jackson's run is now thought to have been based more on individual appeal rather than community empowerment. But this analysis remains incomplete. Jackson's "Rainbow Coalition" emerged at a critical moment in American history and helped to decisively change a political playing field slanted against blacks. He came to represent the symbolic leader of a movement for social justice that drew on a broad array of racial and ethnic solidarity movements. However, his reticence to allow the movement to progress under local and autonomous activist leadership ultimately blunted the "Rainbow Coalition's" potential as a force for social change. Yet despite this shortcoming, during the 1980s, forces led by Jackson won a showdown within the Democratic Party that changed critical primary and caucus rules—a change that would lead to Barack Obama's 2008 presidential nomination.

Obama's experience as an organizer during the same period concentrated on one of the mainstays of the modern civil rights movement: churches. Recruited by a white organizer whose credentials stretched back to the 1960s, Obama gingerly stepped into the maelstrom of Chicago politics. There, Black Muslims, Christian preachers, elected officials, and white unemployed trade unionists all jockeyed for an ever-shrinking municipal pie. Obama's most concerted efforts as an organizer centered on providing better services for Altgeld Gardens, a local housing project. After a steep learning curve, he came to appreciate small, incremental signs of progress, such as securing a meeting with a local official or inspiring a decent turnout at community meetings among public housing tenants.[32]

Throughout his time in Chicago, Obama confronted legacies of both traditional civil rights activism and Black Power-styled nationalism. For a biracial black man with an unusual background, the latter presented particularly complex challenges. "Ever since the first time I'd picked up Malcolm X's autobiography," he recalled, "I had tried to untangle the twin strands of black nationalism" by reconciling self-determination and cooperative race relations.[33] "If nationalism could create a strong and effective insularity, deliver on its promise of self-respect," observed Obama, "then the hurt it might cause well-meaning whites, or the inner turmoil it caused people like me, would be of little consequence."[34]

Unfortunately, the local nationalists whom Obama encountered in Chicago seemed unproductively obsessed with racial resentments that prevented them from accomplishing tangible political goals. With the notable exception of Louis Farrakhan's reinvented Nation of Islam, black nationalists in Chicago lacked the necessary robust organizing base. These foundations could make them powerbrokers beyond the occasional photo-op demonstration or street-corner-style picketing that trafficked in 1960s-styled polemics without corresponding community outrage and organization.[35] Obama traced black nationalism's relative political failures in Chicago to its ideological flaws—most notably a narrow interpretation of American history that discounted democracy's redemptive powers in favor of a narrative of racial oppression that remained brutal, static, and unchanging.

However, Obama's own account of Chicago's local black political scene likewise glosses over black nationalism's subtler manifestations. Indeed, Black Power-era appeals for racial solidarity were as instrumental in ushering in a new wave of African American political leadership in the 1970s and 1980s as was the civil rights legislation of the 1960s. Postwar America's racial politics accorded black nationalism a far more expansive political appeal than Obama imagines. In 1967, even Martin Luther King Jr. acknowledged at the Southern Christian Leadership Conference's annual convention the positive aspects of Black Power's call to redefine African American identity. Against the backdrop of posters that declared "Black Is Beautiful" and "It Is So Beautiful to Be Black," King embraced aspects of black nationalism and criticized stereotypes that attached negative connotations to the word *black* while extolling the virtues of the word *white*.[36] Black nationalism infused aspects of early civil rights organizing in the urban North. Thus, early Black Power activists straddled conventional civil rights organizing and more militant displays of racial pride.[37]

The year of 1968 has come to signify the best and worst impulses of the 1960s. It was marked with tragic political assassinations, the rise of the Black Panthers, Vietnam's Tet Offensive, Czechoslovakia's Prague Spring, and massive civil disorders and social unrest that seemed to leave no corner of American society untouched. While 1968 is most often remembered for the murder in Memphis of Martin Luther King Jr. and the June 5 assassination of Bobby Kennedy in California, violence gripped much of the nation that year, including the Democratic National Convention. There, antiwar protesters squared off against Chicago police officers in a spectacle that helped doom the party's efforts in the November presidential election. In a year plagued by violence, both experts and ordinary Americans were alarmed by riots and civil disturbances and demanded that something be done.

Perhaps the single most important step forward that year is one whose significance has faded over time. In the winter of 1968, the U.S. Riot Commission, better known as the "Kerner Commission," published its Report of the National Advisory Commission on Civil Disorders. The bombshell report, totaling over six hundred pages—complete with charts, graphs, and statistical evidence—offered a comprehensive portrait of the roots behind the previous summer's racial disorders. Appointed in the aftermath of massive racial unrest in Newark and Detroit in July 1967, the commission's report included a stark conclusion: "Our nation is moving toward two societies, one black, one white—separate and unequal."[38]

The Kerner Commission's summary report framed America's racial stalemate as a fundamental threat to democracy. America, suggested the report, continued to ignore black anger even as it remained "deeply implicated in the ghetto."[39] White political, social, and economic power, the report concluded, aided and abetted black impoverishment despite the civil rights victories of the 1960s. An exhaustive investigation of two dozen urban riots in twenty-three cities revealed the depth of the black poverty, alienation, and resentment that stemmed from chronic unemployment, poor schools, substandard housing, and hostile police-community relationships. However, media coverage, politicians, and the general public ignored the black ghetto's structural and historic roots in favor of a morality tale that viewed the riots as rampant lawlessness and conspiracy theories, a tale that traced the violence back to Black Power militants.

The report added flesh and substance to the "typical" rioter. It noted that the bands of young black men who engaged in rioting did so for economic and political reasons. "Rather than rejecting the American system, they were anxious to obtain a place in it."[40] To secure the black community's rightful position within American society, the report outlined a case for massive new public policy proposals that rested on history, sociology, and national self-interest. Unemployment bred conditions that turned the already tenuous existence of the black poor into a jumbled nightmare of dangerous instability. A national call for job creation in urban ghettoes was followed by a plan for educational reform, the transitioning of welfare programs from fostering dependency to empowering the poor, and the creation of federally funded public housing for African Americans on a scale unseen since the New Deal.

The Kerner Commission's devastating candor blindsided President Lyndon Johnson. In response, he refused to meet with his self-appointed panel of experts and ignored their plan of action. The report's searing honesty could have ignited a watershed national conversation about race, democracy, and citizenship, but instead it inspired fear. Much more than an artifact of late-1960s America, the Kerner Commission Report remains one of the most ambitious governmental-inspired assessments of race relations ever conceived. If 1968 offers a historic lesson in how tumultuous domestic and international events shaped the way in which Americans examined race, power, citizenship, and democracy, then the 2008 presidential election suggested how far the nation has come.

Over four decades after the Kerner Commission's findings, it is tempting to view racial progress in America through the sole lens of Barack Obama's extraordinary personal and political biography. Media fascination with Obama dates back to his 2004 speech at the Democratic National Convention in Boston. With charisma and self-assurance, in less than twenty minutes Obama announced himself as the spokesman for a new generation of political leaders, being unbound by the ideological wars of the 1960s and committed to a kind of multiracial, multicultural democracy whose roots remained quintessentially American.

Describing America as a "magical place" where his improbable story could flourish, Obama represented a new kind of advocate of American exceptionalism. His personal biography reflected the breadth and depth of a national commitment to racial and ethnic diversity, democratic pluralism, and an increasingly multicultural future. Standing aloof from the partisan divides of recent presidential politics, Obama spoke of a national consensus already in existence yet ignored by pundits. "We worship an awesome God in the Blue States," observed Obama, "and we don't like federal agents poking around our libraries in Red States."[41]

In the aftermath of Obama's convention speech and subsequent election to the U.S. Senate, media coverage almost immediately began to proclaim the relatively young (he was forty-three years old when elected) politician as a possible presidential contender. His political success fueled a literary boom that began with the reissued *Dreams From My Father* in 2004 as well as a subsequent book, *The Audacity of Hope*, that combined memoir with a call for a new post-partisan style of national politics.

For Obama, the two years between officially joining the Senate in January 2005 and announcing his presidential candidacy in Illinois in February 2007, comprised a national audition of sorts. He used that period to test the breadth of the aura of celebrity that attached itself to his persona on that fateful night in Boston. During this time, he convened a series of successful book tours befitting his status as a best-selling author and rising political star; received a series of critically favorable profiles in national magazines, journals, and newspapers; and became a favorite of corporate media icons, most notably Oprah Winfrey. By the end of 2006, the question was not if, but when Obama would announce his candidacy.

Obama made the announcement on a chilly day in February 2007 at the Old Statehouse in Illinois. The predominantly white faces in attendance that day formed a carefully scripted backdrop for the campaign's explicit argument that his candidacy transcended race. He sought to appeal to white Americans by stressing commonalities over difference, unity over division, and the potential for racial rapprochement over racial war. Regardless of his efforts, however, from the beginning, race formed the underlying focus of the intense fascination and eventual scrutiny of Obama's candidacy.

By the spring of 2007, Obama's dense network of fund-raising made it clear he was in the race to stay. From this, media coverage held up his rise as a national presidential contender to America's embrace of "post-racial" politics. In short, his candidacy represented a modern-day culmination of Dr. King's dream of a color-blind society. In a July 2007 cover profile of the Illinois senator, *Newsweek* exhibited Obama as a new type of political leader whose post-partisan rhetoric proved unsettling to both blacks and whites, albeit for different reasons.

But Obama's "post-racial" appeal only went so far. African American leaders connected to the civil rights movement remained cool to Obama's campaign, and many openly supported his chief rival, New York senator Hillary Clinton, for president. Noted black public intellectual Cornel West chastised Obama at the 2007 State of the Black Union, questioning his political courage and warning him not to take the black vote for granted.[42] Sensing an opportunity, Senator Obama reached out to West, convinced him of his political sincerity, and recruited him as a supporter and unpaid campaign advisor. Despite this convert, however, the majority of black elected officials in the Democratic Party enthusiastically supported Hillary Clinton's candidacy based on their own extensive ties to the Clinton administration of the 1990s and skepticism that America was ready to elect a black president. Despite impressive fund-raising and dazzling exposure in the print and news media, through the summer of 2007 Obama remained a national question mark, with polls showing that even minorities were more inclined to support the better-known Clinton.[43]

Obama's efforts to recruit major civil rights leaders ran into difficulties. These stemmed in part from generational tensions between black leaders who came of age during the 1960s and the subsequent Ivy-League-educated, post-Black Power generation. For political leaders like Jesse Jackson, John L. Lewis, and Andrew Young, America remains far from the "magical place" Obama described in his 2004 convention speech. A two-time presidential candidate himself, Jackson watched Obama's ascendance with a mixture of pride—in having partially blazed the trail—and resentment of the way the media praised Obama's candidacy at his own expense.

Whispers about the black community's muted support for Obama's candidacy grew into open questions about whether the young senator's exotic racial background disqualified him from the black race.[44] Such questions plumbed the depths of America's tragic racial past. Obama's biracial background had, for most of his short political career, been a boon that broadened his appeal to a wider array of constituencies. Now, however, certain critics questioned whether a black man raised by a white mother and grandparents in Hawaii and Indonesia truly understood the African American experience. Education at three of America's best schools—Occidental College, Columbia, and Harvard—further distanced him from the real-world experiences of most blacks. Writer Debra Dickerson dismissed Obama as racially suspect, claiming that his father's Kenyan heritage meant that "he had no part" in America's legacy of racial slavery and lacked a truly comprehensive understanding of the African American experience.[45] Journalist Ta-Nehisi Coates countered, suggesting that the refusal to embrace Obama's candidacy revealed the sophistication of black voters more concerned with issues than race and that his marriage to a black woman, membership in a black church, and work as a community organizer on Chicago's South Side made him a quintessential, if subtle, race man.[46]

Obama's upset win in the January 4, 2008, Iowa caucus turned him from a media phenomenon into the front-runner for the Democratic Party's presidential nomination.[47] This victory produced a national sense of *racial vertigo* that Americans are still dealing with today, one that journalists, scholars, and pundits have yet to fully comprehend.

Racial vertigo feeds off of, while upending, what anthropologist John L. Jackson Jr. has memorably characterized as "racial paranoia." According to Jackson, racial paranoia represents the complex web of hunches, assumptions, and gut-instincts based on race that play out in everyday life. In African Americans, racial paranoia infuses conspiracy theories that imagine New Orleans levees being purposely obliterated by government agencies while whites remain fearful that Affirmative Action-like mechanisms ensure an unequal playing field that perpetually advantages blacks. Tellingly, racial paranoia's main feature is a fundamental distrust of the motives, actions, and integrity of groups based on race.[48]Racial vertigo, then, cuts through this default mode of racial behavior by drastically altering expected or historic racial patterns.

Obama's primary win produced racial vertigo on all sides of America's color line. In his typically understated declaration, he struck a studied pose of humility after the victory. "What I was so pleased with was not just that we won, or the raw numbers," claimed Obama, "but what it showed about the country."[49] Black cynicism regarding the possibility of an African American president faded overnight as whites began to relinquish deep-seated fears that equated a minority commander in chief with a coming onslaught of racial supremacy. The racial subtext to a black candidate winning in an overwhelmingly white state such as Iowa could be seen in the jarring portraits of a beaming Barack and Michelle Obama resplendent among a sea of white faces. Black voters who had once been suspicious of Obama immediately decided to take a second look. Further, the racial loyalty the Clintons took for granted (and that Toni Morrison's notion of Bill Clinton as America's first black president had turned into legend) became an open question.

Over the course of the first half of 2008, Barack Obama became a universal symbol of America's racial progress. He demonstrated the ability to inspire millions of new voters and small donors to participate in a campaign that promoted social change and democratic values above partisan bickering *and* a racially specific totem who encapsulated the hopes and deferred dreams of generations of African Americans. In one fell swoop, Obama appeared on the verge of becoming both the first black president and the unofficial racial leader of black America. For different reasons, such a prospect unnerved and upset Hillary Clinton's white supporters and a generation of civil rights leaders.

Bill Clinton's ease around African Americans, willingness to appoint them to a string of midlevel cabinet positions, and friendship during his impeachment hearings made him a perennial favorite in the black community. Yet despite this goodwill, there were also preexisting tensions in Clinton's relationship with blacks, including his well-publicized denunciation of rapper-activist Sista Souljah during a 1992 appearance at Jesse Jackson's Rainbow Coalition. Castigating the rap artist's caustic remarks in the aftermath of the L.A. riots, Clinton laid down a racial gauntlet, letting whites know that he would not pander to the politics of black rage, no matter the cost. During the same election season, then governor Clinton broke from his campaign schedule to preside over the execution of black inmate Ricky Ray Rector, in a photo-op that instantly burnished his law-and-order credentials while it simultaneously turned him into the reverse Michael Dukakis, the liberal Massachusetts governor who had seen his own presidential ambitions dashed four years earlier on the twin shoals of Willie Horton and his opposition to the death penalty.

If Bill Clinton's racial politics were characterized by bold flourishes designed to bolster his appeal among white working-class "Reagan" Democrats, Hillary Clinton, for the most part, allowed surrogates to broach this volatile subject. Clinton's most powerful—and unpredictable—asset turned out to be her husband. The tremendous political chemistry Bill Clinton forged with the African American community during his eight-year tenure in the White House partially explained Hillary's high approval ratings among black Democrats through much of 2007. But Iowa permanently altered the political calculus shaping the Democratic primaries.

In the aftermath of Hillary Clinton's comeback victory in New Hampshire, South Carolina became a key testing ground of her appeal in the black community. Obama's subsequent decisive victory in the state roiled the Clinton campaign. Bill Clinton ignited a furor in the black community with his dismissive comment that "Jesse Jackson won South Carolina in '84 and '88." This led many to accuse the former president of injecting race into the increasingly bitter primary fight.

The former president's off-the-cuff remark about Obama kindled black support for the junior senator's campaign while also putting Clinton's on the defensive. While three other Clinton surrogates—including two African Americans: corporate leader Bob Johnson, New York congressman Charlie Rangle, and former vice presidential nominee Geraldine Ferraro—would unleash racially tinged tirades against Obama throughout the primaries, it was Clinton's own attacks that resonated the deepest among African Americans. In short order, Obama went from answering questions about his racial authenticity to being perceived as *too* black. Until the last desperate days of her presidential campaign, Clinton managed to stay above the fray of racial politics, a dignified position that came to an unceremonious end when she announced in an interview in May that "hard working whites" were rallying around her candidacy.[50]

Clinton's candor exposed an ugly truth that became more apparent the further the primary season progressed. White working-class voters in Rust Belt states, such as Ohio and Pennsylvania, and Southern states, such as Kentucky and West Virginia, favored Hillary over Obama. Her public skepticism over whether Obama could successfully attract white working-class voters echoed media pundits who alternately fawned over the Illinois senator's historic presidential campaign and fretted over American race relations. But by June 3, Obama had achieved the improbable by successfully securing enough delegates to be the presumptive Democratic Party nominee. For his supporters, the historic nature of this victory was marred by Senator Clinton's pointed refusal to concede, which was then followed by public hints that she hoped Obama would offer her the vice presidential nomination.

In the course of his sixteen-month presidential campaign, Obama went from answering questions about his blackness to becoming the most resoundingly beloved and admired figure in African American public life since Martin Luther King Jr. Ironically, his newfound status propelled him into the role of a young peer of veteran civil rights leaders.

Even an Obama supporter such as Jesse Jackson contained enough anger and resentment toward the candidate to disparage the Illinois senator. In an off-the-cuff conversation that was accidentally recorded, Jackson's comments came in response to Obama's widely publicized speech at a black church where he criticized the lack of fathers in black households and challenged black men to be responsible parents. Jackson stated that Obama was "talking down to black folks" and that he wanted to "cut his nuts out."[51] The fact that Jackson spent much of his career sounding the same themes of personal responsibility made his comments against Obama seem particularly petty.[52] Notwithstanding personal feelings of jealousy and envy that may have animated the elder civil rights leader's comments toward Obama (for which he later publicly apologized), Jackson's anger at the first black presidential major-party nominee in American history reveals deep generational and ideological fissures within the African American community.

Part of this resentment stemmed from the sheer audaciousness of Obama's presidential run. Most seasoned African American political leaders, such as Georgia congressman and civil rights veteran John Lewis and former UN ambassador, Atlanta mayor, and King aide Andrew Young, backed Clinton's candidacy. They viewed the young senator as hopelessly overmatched in a contest that pitted a brash, largely unknown black junior senator against the juggernaut of an impending Clinton dynasty in waiting. Even second-generation black political leaders, those who, like Obama, were too young to participate in civil rights struggles such as Philadelphia mayor Michael Nutter and New York congressman Gregory Meeks, had supported Clinton. Black politicians who were willing to support Obama ranged from liberals such as Illinois congressman Jesse Jackson Jr. to Newark's pragmatic centrist mayor, Cory Booker. These younger black leaders lacked strong patronage ties to Bill Clinton's White House and felt confident enough in post-1960s American race relations to believe that a black man could successfully run for president.

As Obama's victory went from long shot to increasingly likely, some black politicians switched sides. After John Lewis's home state of Georgia handed

Obama a decisive primary win, the representative announced that he would vote as a super-delegate for Obama. Furthermore, in the aftermath of his father's harsh words against Obama, Jesse Jackson Jr. publicly lambasted the civil rights leader and called for him to follow Obama's lead in always choosing his words wisely rather than lashing out in rhetorical flourishes—even in private.

The core of the Jackson-Obama contretemps stemmed from Jackson's belief that Obama was too willing to denounce perceived black pathology— the staggering proliferation of poor, single black households—for political gain while failing to address the larger structural roots of the fractured black family. Obama could score cheap political points with white voters pleased by his insistence on personal responsibility at the expense of fighting for the massive Kerner Commission-inspired social programs that had fallen out of favor in America with the demise of the Great Society.

Jackson Sr., however, did nevertheless support Obama's candidacy earlier than most civil rights leaders. But he also perceived Obama's failure to understand the fundamental legacy of the civil rights movement—social action in service of promoting personal and collective responsibility—as the candidate's greatest weakness. In *Dreams From My Father*, Obama implicitly counters such criticism by outlining in great detail the painful impact that his own fractured family had on him. From this reading, Obama's speeches on the black family and personal responsibility are based on his own biography in a way that transcends naked political impulses.

If Jesse Jackson still retained the unofficial status of the "President of Black America," which had been won over the course of presidential campaigns in 1984 and 1988 and high-profile assaults on institutional racism, Barack Obama's emergence rendered the position altogether obsolete. In effect, Obama, by virtue of winning a major party's presidential nomination, became the de facto leader of black America.

The very notion of a "President of Black America" by now seems anachronistic. It evokes images of old-fashioned corrupt machine politics in black, complete with old-time ward heelers and smoke-filled rooms. In truth, the existence of such a position dates back to at least the antebellum era, when Frederick Douglass represented the quintessential black powerbroker—a position made more remarkable by the fact that he was born a slave. Then, in the early twentieth century, Booker T. Washington and W. E. B. Du Bois competed for this position as the more intellectual Du Bois was out-financed by the elegant and pragmatic "Wizard of Tuskegee." After Washington's death, the Jamaican-born Marcus Garvey assumed this mantle (to the chagrin of Du Bois). By the Second World War, a coterie of influential blacks, from Paul Robeson to Ralph Bunche, vied for this position. During the civil rights movement's high tide, Martin Luther King Jr. occupied this position regardless that Malcolm X made successful inroads in Northern black communities. In the aftermath of King's 1968 assassination, younger leaders, such as Stokely Carmichael, Eldridge Cleaver, and Angela Davis, seemed poised to take over this role. But it would be Jesse Jackson, the self-described "country preacher" and King confidante, who would successfully assume it for practically a two-and-a-half-decade tenure beginning in 1984.

Jackson was not actually the first post-civil rights-era black candidate to run for president. That honor belonged to Brooklyn congresswoman Shirley Chisholm, whose 1972 presidential campaign received the support of the Black Panther Party and a smattering of white feminists. But two factors set Jackson's 1984 campaign apart: its timing and its relative success. Against the backdrop of President Ronald Reagan's successful repudiation of New Deal liberalism, Jackson advocated a return to the bread-and-butter advocacy that had buoyed Americans from the Great Depression through the civil rights era. Moreover, his campaign presented an alternate reality that challenged the Reagan-dominated status quo. Jackson's campaign infrastructure further distinguished his candidacy, replete with credentialed advisors, well-written policy papers, and sprawling yet detailed domestic and foreign policy agendas. Running against better-financed candidates such as former vice-president (and eventual nominee) Walter Mondale and Colorado senator Gary Hart, Jackson managed to earn over 3 million votes in Democratic primaries—an astonishing feat for an African American presidential candidate. Four years later, he practically doubled his vote total while winning over ten primary and caucus states and consolidating his status as black America's premier powerbroker with a powerful speech at the 1988 Democratic National Convention.

Jackson's ambitious attempt to forge a "rainbow coalition" that championed the enormous potential of America's multiracial democracy provided a blueprint for the Obama campaign. Obama's personal biography, Ivy-League education, and generational distance from the civil rights era allowed his theme of change to resonate to a broader spectrum of Americans. Moreover, the Illinois senator's oratory—more charismatic street speaker and college professor than Baptist preacher—smoothed out the rougher edges of Jackson's populist rhetoric.

Important differences abound between the two campaigns. Obama's policy proposals fell far short of the kind of sweeping economic investments in jobs and infrastructure that Jackson proposed in the early 1980s. From the beginning, Jackson's primary base remained the African American community despite the campaign's efforts to appeal to disaffected working-class whites and Latinos. In contrast, Obama's primary base until his victory in the Iowa caucuses consisted of white voters who ranged from upscale professionals to college students.

Obama's surprise victory in the Democratic Party presidential primary has obscured much of this complex history. Mainstream media pundits dismissed Jackson as an angry old black man, upset over his own past political failures and unwilling to gracefully allow a new generation of leadership to emerge onto the world stage. Such criticism ignored the fact that Jackson, warts and all, is a genuine American hero. He is one of the few contemporary leaders who can claim a distinctive and continuous legacy of social justice activism that stretches back to the 1960s.

However, Jackson's off-the-record assertion during the campaign that Obama was "talking down to black people" did reflect the unease of progressive and radical black intellectuals and activists. According to these critics, Obama's election, however historic, does not equal racial equality. For them, any attempts to define it as such seeks to purchase racial rapprochement on the cheap through the monumental symbolism attached to Obama's success.

Just as it has inflected our perceptions of Jesse Jackson's legacy, Obama's meteoric rise has had an impact on black political leadership in all walks of life. For all intents and purposes, Obama's presidency occupies two distinct and historically antagonistic roles: a commander in chief and black America's de facto political leader. Obama became a sort of racial godfather in those predominantly black local congressional districts where African American incumbents who supported Hillary Clinton faced tough reelection campaigns. Obama's support could now virtually guarantee a victory, just as his aloofness would produce great difficulties. Even as his national candidacy inspired premature rhetoric about a post-racial America, his support at the grassroots level has been marked by a fierce sense of racial loyalty. This conflict between the local and national approach would bubble to the surface in the controversy over his relationship with Jeremiah Wright.

Overwhelming African American popular support has served to blunt criticism of Obama's inability to directly confront America's ugly racial past—with the exception of what became know as "The Speech" in the spring of 2008. With his presidential hopes on the line when he came under fire for his association with Reverend Jeremiah Wright, Obama delivered a largely self-written and nationally televised address. This speech, for mainstream Americans, plumbed the nation's racial depths in a way not seen since the torrential political storms of the late 1960s.

The address was rooted in Obama's spiritual journey in Chicago during the early 1980s. This is where he encountered Reverend Jeremiah Wright, pastor of Trinity United Church. Part civil rights advocate and part Black Power firebrand, Wright preached sermons based on Black Liberation Theology that applied the social gospel to society's contemporary ills. Its postwar innovators included Detroit reverend and Malcolm X ally Albert Cleage Jr. and the radical theologian James Cone. Black Liberation Theology pointedly challenged traditional biblical interpretations as flawed based on institutional racism and white supremacy.

Personally, Trinity United offered Obama a chance for fellowship with a broad spectrum of the black community while pursuing the kind of spiritual sustenance that books, politics, and organizing could not deliver. In *Dreams From My Father*, Obama described the church as offering an opportunity for personal redemption: "It was a powerful program, this cultural community, one more pliant than simple nationalism, more sustaining than my own brand of organizing."[53] In the context of Chicago's local black political scene, Obama's membership in Trinity afforded him access to upper-middle-class strivers, working-class community activists, and an assortment of well-connected African American professionals. Implicitly, his relationship with Reverend Wright and Trinity helped to cement his standing in the city's black community.

But what played out well locally proved troubling nationally.[54] Although Obama pointedly thanked Wright during his 2004 Senate election victory speech, the reverend was informed at the last minute that he would not provide the invocation to Obama's presidential announcement in 2007. By the winter of 2008, filmed excerpts of Wright's fiery sermons that criticized the United States became an Internet sensation. From this, right-wing pundits and mainstream media outlets demonized Wright as the worst kind of racial arsonist. Obama's twenty-year personal and political relationship with his pastor and mentor, one that had served him so well up until then, had now turned into his biggest political liability.

Obama responded with perhaps the most sophisticated speech about race ever to be delivered (let alone written) by a major-party presidential candidate. The speech, "A More Perfect Union," was delivered in Philadelphia amid carefully constructed stagecraft that included over a half dozen American flags. In it, Obama candidly discussed slavery as the nation's "original sin," one that revealed the gaps between the rhetoric and reality of democracy. He held out the struggles of generations of Americans from the Civil War to the civil rights movement as hopeful signs that the burdens of the past could be eased through a focus on common dreams and shared faith in democracy. He recounted his personal biography, as the son of a Kenyan immigrant and a white mother with Kansas roots, as a story that could only take place in the United States. For the first and last time in the campaign, Obama rigorously addressed national misgivings about his race. He noted that, "[a]t various stages in the campaign, some commentators have deemed me either 'too black' or 'not black enough.'" Obama then admonished Wright for an overly narrow view of America, one that placed white racism above genuine racial breakthroughs, as he also praised Trinity United Church of Christ as a stalwart community institution in Chicago devoted to antipoverty efforts that included supporting those afflicted with HIV/AIDS.

For Obama, Wright represented the inevitable contradictions of identity and citizenship in a nation scarred by racial wounds with which America was still struggling. This was especially true of the black church. "The church contains in full the kindness and cruelty," said Obama, "the fierce intelligence and the shocking ignorance, the struggles and the successes, the love and yes, the bitterness and bias that make up the black experience in America." He argued that he could "no more disown" Reverend Wright "than I can my white grandmother." In so doing, Obama simultaneously professed undying love for the woman who helped raise him while admitting that she "once confessed her fear of black men who passed by her on the street" and who felt comfortable using ethnic and racial stereotypes.

Moving beyond the personal and political, Obama addressed the tortured history contouring American race relations. After briefly noting the impact of antebellum slavery and legalized segregation, Obama sketched a portrait of the postwar period of Jim Crow America where Reverend Wright came of age. According to Obama, despite racial progress made evident by a generation of middle-class blacks, bitterness and anger over decades of denied opportunity haunted the African American experience and lay at the heart of Wright's worldview. If Wright had the privilege of expressing rage from a vantage point of success, many more blacks continued to enact seemingly scripted lives of desperation and despair that were marked by random violence, premature death, poverty, and prison.

Although black anger stemmed from historic discrimination, white Americans housed a unique set of racial resentments that were rooted in the belief that blacks benefited from government largesse and special programs that amounted to reverse discrimination. In Obama's words, "[a]nger over welfare and affirmative action helped forge the Reagan coalition." Combating such fears required moving beyond easy labels and characterizations in order to understand the "legitimate concerns" that fueled white backlash.

Obama concluded his speech by calling for blacks and whites to come together for common purposes—better schools, jobs, and health care—that would benefit all Americans in race-transcending ways. Specifically, he called for blacks to remain vigilant about past and contemporary discrimination while also realizing their fundamental ability to control their own destinies and reject viewing America from the perspective of a victim. For whites, racial harmony required recognizing the impact of historic racism on the development and evolution of the black community as well as racism's uncanny ability to reappear in modern guise.

Appealing to America's hunger for economic prosperity and domestic safety and security, Obama argued that transcending racial divisions strengthened the nation's collective character. In so doing, he provided individuals with the ability to focus on common dreams and shared goals rather than racial divisions. It was a tremendous speech, masterfully delivered in a mournful tone reminiscent of one of Obama's presidential heroes, Abraham Lincoln.

Yet for all of its bracing candor, "A More Perfect Union" failed to delve into America's nightmarish racial past. Obama feared upsetting a predominantly white electorate already skittish about the prospect of an African American candidate. In stark contrast to the Kerner Commission's searing words about institutional racism and white responsibility for the creation and perpetuation of urban ghettos, Obama's speech absolved the nation of collective blame for past generations' sins. His rhetorical sleight of hand effected a King Solomon-like posture that blamed both sides equally for a predicament that blacks have largely had no part in creating. In fact, Obama glossed over perhaps the best example of institutional racism's modern face—Hurricane Katrina.

Nevertheless, Obama's Philadelphia speech elegantly deflected criticism that declared his connection to Wright to be a harbinger of racial extremism by a candidate dedicated to a race-neutral campaign. More importantly, his deft handling of the Reverend Wright controversy ensured him of black electoral loyalty for the foreseeable future. Wright's own saga came to an unfortunate conclusion the next month through a very public (and self-serving) media tour. During this circuit, he pranced and preened before a grinning, largely white press corps in a vain attempt to not only explain his actions but also to seemingly destroy his onetime protégé's chances of winning the election. Since that time, however, Obama has been reluctant to directly address the racial roots behind black America's perpetual economic crisis, one marked by failing schools, poverty, and crumbling inner cities.

Indeed, Obama's "post-racial" campaign pivoted on an embrace of the symbolic power of his historic candidacy while sidestepping America's racial past. Journalists played a pivotal role in this narrative, openly admitting that "[a] black president in a country that fought a civil war over race might even prove cathartic."[55] For whites, Obama's ability to compartmentalize America's past from its present while boldly symbolizing its color-blind future is both refreshing and inspiring.

Reporters enthusiastically documented this phenomenon, marveling over Obama's visceral impact on middle America and noting that while black listeners in Iowa greeted the senator with reserved pride, "[t]he white people, by contrast, are out of control."[56] Blacks observed Obama's national pirouette on racial politics with a mixture of awe and admiration. Despite overwhelming African American support, there remained a vocal minority of progressive and radical activists, pundits, intellectuals, and writers who have pointedly criticized Obama for failing to speak tough racial truths to his white supporters. Why, for instance, does Obama insist on preaching the politics of personal responsibility and the meaning of fatherhood to black churches without corresponding tough-love symposiums to white law enforcement officials whose eagerness to criminalize black defendants has left the criminal justice system bursting at the seams with African American prisoners?[57]

However, this is not the first time that Obama has found himself distanced from the black community. As a young boy in Hawaii, he purposefully recoiled from his only other black classmate, a plump girl named Coretta, out of fear that "direct contact would only remind us more keenly of our isolation."[58] It is this sense of isolation from a larger black world community—despite his searing efforts to forge one through direct pilgrimage, friendships, sports, even marriage—that inspires skepticism among Obama's harshest black critics.

Within the black community, Obama has been the subject of vigorous criticism from a wide range of thinkers and activists. Writer Glen Ford decried Obama's campaign as an empty shell that mesmerized political progressives through its brilliant deployment of stagecraft. For Ford, Obama represented a doomsday scenario for both African Americans and political radicals of all stripes by substituting the appearance of social transformation without the substance.[59] Others questioned whether Obama's campaign presented an extension of Stokely Carmichael's (Kwame Ture) call for Black Power or the cynical realization that the first major-party presidential nominee largely ignored the racial subtext behind his candidacy.[60]

Talk-show host and "State of the Black Union" convener Tavis Smiley was Obama's most visible black critic during the campaign. Smiley publicly criticized Obama for refusing to attend the February 2008 "State of the Black Union" conference in New Orleans. From this, he then pointedly called on the black community to hold the candidate politically accountable based on policy rather than race pride. Obama responded with an open letter that discussed his recent victory in the Louisiana primary, political support for health care issues that are critical to the black community, and offer to send his wife, Michelle Obama, as a surrogate as proof of his strong support for African Americans.[61]

Smiley's comments touched a nerve in the black community and immediately sparked controversy. Black public opinion ran overwhelmingly in favor of Obama, accusing Smiley of being a "playa-hater," or jealous critic who envied the first black man with a shot at the White House. Stunned, Smiley confessed to surprise and anger at the critical denunciation. He lamented that his relatives in Indianapolis had been harassed by angry Obama supporters.[62] By April, Smiley announced that he was leaving his post as a commentator on the popular Tom Joyner radio show, a move that, according to Joyner, stemmed from hurt feelings over the black community's response during the controversy. Although Smiley publicly denied the Obama tiff as the reason for his resignation, the timing of the decision seemed to indicate otherwise.

The Obama-Smiley controversy presents in miniature one of the reasons a small coterie of black progressives feared an Obama presidency. The black community's inability to distinguish thoughtful criticism from vulgar denunciations places Obama above reproach, a position in which no constituency can afford to put a president. Whatever the intent behind Smiley's aggressive criticism of Obama, the resulting controversy revealed the black community's reluctance to allow this symbol of racial progress to be scrutinized too closely. Of course, part of this stems from very real concerns that Obama's race makes him vulnerable to a host of trumped-up and outrageous charges based on rumors about his racial background, religion, patriotism, and association with foreign powers.

Thus, closing racial ranks behind Obama received its initial boost from the Clinton campaign. As black public intellectual and professor Boyce

Watkins astutely observed, "Bill Clinton made Obama into a King" by virtue of his racially tinged comments after the South Carolina primary. However, danger lurks behind such unanimity, as indicated by the reaction to Smiley. Whatever one may think of Smiley, his commitment to the black community is above reproach, having been solidified through decades of public service that includes philanthropy, civic participation, and a media advocacy on behalf of black issues. On this score, accusations of "selling out" and race betrayal hurled at Smiley in various quarters reveal more about the state of black politics than either Obama or Smiley.[63]

In a very real sense, Obama's election has successfully fused powerful aspects of both the civil rights and Black Power movements. Obama himself represents this duality. His speeches, books, and interviews discuss democracy and the potential for civic renewal in the broad, sweeping language preferred by King. However, they also avoid the slain civil rights martyr's stinging post-1965 denunciations against rampant American materialism, racism, and militarism. Similarly, Obama's presidential campaign and confident personal demeanor mimic the swagger and audacity of Black Power-era militants. His long, lanky frame suggests (aesthetically at least) the lean, upright silhouette of both Malcolm X and Stokely Carmichael. But if Malcolm and Stokely projected the avenging anger of black radicals intent on achieving racial equality by any means necessary, Obama speaks in the language of the law professor turned street speaker in order to project an inner calm even when surrounded by tens of thousands of cheering supporters.

In large measure, Obama has enjoyed the benefits of both the civil rights and Black Power movements while maintaining a safe distance from both. His aloofness is not only politically astute, but inherent in his age. At forty-eight, he is too young to have marched in civil rights demonstrations or participated in Black Power-era campus protests. Instead, Barack Obama came of political age in the late 1970s and early 1980s in an arid political desert of social change. Though there were ongoing movements to protect Affirmative Action, end apartheid, and stave back Reagan-era economic cuts, this was a time when the left and the black movement in general reacted to, rather than set, America's social and political agenda.

Obama's community organizing took shape against the backdrop of diminished national expectations. Promoting good schools, jobs, and housing for poor black residents in Chicago seemed far removed from the romantic civil rights era where stark lines could be drawn in the face of Jim Crow and the denial of voting rights. From the perspective of Obama's generation, the civil rights era's basic victories had provoked satisfaction and ambivalence. The beneficiaries of another generation's dreams and aspirations, the post-civil rights generation came to understand racial politics in a way that distinguished them from their forebears. Chicago's ethnic enclaves and rigidly segregated neighborhoods proved to be a perfect classroom for Obama to learn harsh lessons about race and American democracy.

Obama's arrival in Chicago coincided with the high point of local black political power. The election of Harold Washington had proved, once again, that racial progress, despite daunting odds, could be achieved through grass-roots political organizing. Washington's political coalition, notwithstanding its multiracial ambitions, drew its core strength from an invigorated and inspired black community. Yet black political power, regardless of Washington's victory, remained elusive. Chicago's city council stalled needed reforms. City Hall's ability to rapidly and substantively change the misery experienced by blacks proved more limited than at first imagined.

Nationally, Jesse Jackson's presidential campaigns seemed to muster one final advance by the armies of the 1960s who had waged a heroic struggle against more powerful foes. By the late 1980s, however, Harold Washington's death ended the dream of black political power in Chicago just as the defeat of Jackson's second presidential campaign signaled the limits of the ability of civil rights-styled leaders to gain actual political power at the national level.

Meanwhile, the twenty-seven-year-old Obama was still searching for an identity in Chicago. In 1988, he simultaneously traced his ancestral roots even as he worked to master the intricacies of a political system he wished to dominate. The summer before entering Harvard Law, Obama visited Kenya for several weeks. Just as it had been for Malcolm X and Stokely Carmichael, the trip to Africa would prove to be life-altering. Tracing the tangled roots of his father's personal and political odyssey transformed Obama. It cemented his evolution from diffident youth to community activist, civil rights lawyer, and politician. Impressed by his father's towering intellect but determined to practice the personal and professional discipline that had eluded his father, Obama came away from Africa with a better sense of his own identity and a clear sense that he had a larger political destiny to fulfill. But if Malcolm X and Carmichael departed Africa intent on exploring the possibilities of pan-Africanism and racial solidarity, Obama tapped into universal impulses that would lead him to consistently stress human commonalities that transcended borders and boundaries, countries and continents.

At first blush, it may be hard to see how and why civil rights-era leaders—or any other Americans for that matter—could quarrel with such an expansive worldview. Although it is difficult to find fault with the destination that Obama lays out for the national future, critics have pointed out that the road leading toward "one America" requires heavier lifting than his lofty rhetoric suggests. Racial reconciliation without public policy that specifically addresses contemporary discrimination may represent more high-minded rhetoric than the type of transformative change Obama's presidential campaign promised.

In his best-selling second book, *The Audacity of Hope*, Obama spends an entire chapter discussing race. The bulk of this essay probes the roots of black poverty, alternating between addressing structural issues such as unemployment, health care, and schools and cultural issues including teen pregnancy, absentee parents, and unsupervised children. Obama's stress on personal behavior and responsibility echoes the sentiment of a generation of civil rights-era middle-class African Americans. Bill Cosby gave voice to this perspective during a 2004 NAACP speech commemorating the fiftieth anniversary of the *Brown* Supreme Court desegregation decision. In that address, he lashed out at the inner-city black poor for failing to take advantage of the doors of opportunity opened up by civil rights struggles. Cosby's words ignited a firestorm of controversy in the black community. Critics, most notably black public intellectual Michael Eric Dyson, castigated Cosby as an armchair activist, courageous enough to blame the poor while ignoring the larger forces that marginalized African Americans. Supporters such as journalist Juan Williams countered that, far from airing the black community's dirty laundry in front of white folk, Cosby spoke blunt truths that young blacks, especially those enamored with hip-hop culture, chose to ignore at their own peril.[64]

In *The Audacity of Hope*, Obama attempts to confront this discussion holistically. That is to say, rather than treating them as an either-or discussion, he addresses both structural racism and individual responsibility. That he exhibits more passion and eloquence for the latter reflects his status as a black politician and his own optimism in the inexorable march toward racial justice in America despite the nation's tangled and messy racial history.

For Obama, racial progress in America can be measured through his own startling political rise and in the personal stories of redemption and reconciliation shared by colleagues and constituents old enough to remember the dark days of the not-so-recent past.[65] Obama argues, "To think clearly about race requires us to see the world on a split screen," one that observes America as it ought to be along with the nation's more painful contemporary face.[66] Yet, he insists, blacks should not ignore the remarkable economic and political strides they have accomplished in a relatively short amount of time. Obama is especially impressed by record levels of black entrepreneurship, including financial independence that benefited his own Senate campaign, as a mark of progress.

Obama suggests that the key to racial progress lays in universal support for better schools, health care, and education. He claims that economic uplift has allowed Americans to transcend race, even as he admitted that, in Chicago's case, black migrants entered a segregated world filled with dead-end jobs, dilapidated housing, and inadequate schools. And this indeed is Obama's conundrum when he attempts to have a frank discussion about race.

The reverberations of what Obama rightfully characterizes as the nation's "original sin" of slavery casts an enduring shadow over contemporary America. Perhaps the biggest example is not the psychological scars of racial segregation to which Obama and others often point. Instead, it could be the persistent gap in wealth and ownership. Despite providing the labor that transformed the United States into an industrial power, African Americans were both denied their fair share of the profits and punished for a century after slavery through the denial of basic citizenship rights. Over four decades after the passage of the Voting Rights Act, African American wealth and political and economic influence is miniscule in comparison to the group's population, contributions to American society, and length of duration in the country. Such hard truths are difficult to discuss under the best of circumstances. In large measure, *The Audacity of Hope* evades confronting hard racial truth in favor of embracing race-transcendent themes of national unity.

In certain instances, Obama paints an overly optimistic picture of race relations and social progress in order to give whites an inordinate measure of credit. At one point, he discusses how "white guilt has largely exhausted itself"[67] in contemporary America. This presumes that such a thing as white guilt actually exists. Obama describes a civil rights movement fought by equal numbers of blacks and whites, regardless that such a portrait contradicts the historical record. Most white Americans stood on the sidelines during the civil rights era. Black progress was earned at great personal cost by poor and unlettered African Americans at the grassroots level and with black women providing much-needed and too often overlooked leadership and organizational prowess.

The very programs that Obama supports rarely provide legitimate and unbiased relief for poor blacks. If history is our judge, too often the very universal programs Obama endorses as keys to uplifting poor blacks have contained ongoing inherent biases that continue to prevent African Americans from receiving their full benefits. The New Deal's alphabet soup of programs and GI benefits were so unequally distributed that scholar Ira Katznelson has referred to the postwar era as a period "When Affirmative Action Was White."[68]

This is not to suggest that Obama ignores racism's structural face. Instead, he discusses public policy initiatives, from the Clinton administration's Earned Income Tax Credit to more unspecified but presumably far-reaching legislation. These acts hold the potential to confront the deep-seated poverty exposed by the ravages of Hurricane Katrina. Obama is simply guilty of trying to have it both ways: He offers kind words about Katrina victims and acknowledges the dangers of wasteful federal spending without taking the kind of firm political stance that would alienate large swaths of the electorate. For instance, in *The Audacity of Hope* he praises welfare reform while acknowledging the legislation's devastating impact on the working poor. He empathizes with employers unwilling to hire ex-felons yet singles out an African American businessman who made it his life's work to provide former inmates with precious job opportunities.

When Obama does take a stand, he displays a lack of awareness of history that is at times stunning. He has defended Daniel Patrick Moynihan's infamous 1965 report on the black family from accusations of racism, ignoring the fact that the report proved to be both racist and sexist.[69] It contributed to the still-widespread assumption that black poverty resulted from a breakdown of family structure rather than racial discrimination in America's social and political institutions. Civil rights activists blasted the report as a diversion while white liberals and certain black nationalists embraced much of its aspects, albeit for different reasons. Liberals admired the idea that government did not have the solution to this latest crisis plaguing African Americans while nationalists conceded the lack of patriarchy in their community as one of its most glaring weaknesses. Moynihan's thesis of black matriarchs undercutting the role of black men successfully demonized black women's struggles to maintain healthy familial bonds and shifted discussion of the future of American race relations from social policy to behavioral pathology.[70] Obama's embrace of black poverty as something that is both structural and deeply rooted in personal behavior helped him present an image of political centrism to the wider American public. At his most enigmatic, Obama came across as a political changeling whose views reflected the beliefs of whatever particular audience he was addressing at any given moment. His most inspiring moments recalled the extraordinary dignity of political struggles for a more expansive vision of American democracy rooted in the social movements of the civil rights era. But it is also important to keep in mind that the media, as much a part of the narrative of the 2008 election as they were narrators, obscured and at times amplified Obama's contradictory persona and message.

Media coverage of Obama's ascendancy has indulged in a kind of racial schizophrenia. On the one hand lauding the fact that a black man has accomplished so much, on the other hand critics and commentators downplay race as the definitive factor in his political success.[71] To a certain extent, this tendency is reflected in the overwhelming emphasis on Obama's individual achievement.

If racial progress is measured by the success of specific individuals, a black president represents a watershed achievement: the breaking of a racial glass ceiling once thought to be impenetrable. Historically, African American civil rights activists have measured racial progress by group rather than individual success stories, even as they celebrated every hard-won "racial first" achieved. From this perspective, Obama's political ascent proves to be more ambiguous. This is because it comes against the backdrop of deteriorating economic conditions for African Americans that include skyrocketing incarceration, unemployment, and disease.

Obama's pointed refusal to propose far-reaching and expensive solutions to intractable, systemic issues in *The Audacity of Hope* in part made him a hero to mainstream news magazines. *Time* magazine's October 2006 cover story, "Why Barack Obama Could Be The Next President," represented the unofficial announcement of his candidacy and excerpted portions of his second book.

In many ways, Obama's candidacy represented an idiosyncratic synthesis of civil rights and Black Power ideologies. While the former is readily apparent in Obama's soaring appeals to racial inclusion, citizenship, and democracy, the latter may seem, at first blush, a bit of a stretch. Black Power militancy is most popularly associated with the fiery rhetoric of Malcolm X, Stokely Carmichael, and Huey P. Newton; the swaggering machismo of the Black Panthers; the poetry of Sonia Sanchez; and the iconic imagery of Angela Davis's afro and Tommy Smith's and John Carlos's black-gloved salute at the 1968 Mexico City Olympics. But the movement had a more buttoned-down side as well. Although Barack Obama is hardly the kind of black politician who would garner the approval of 1960s-era militants, his candidacy represents a strand of Black Power too often ignored.

Black politicians, business leaders, and corporate aspirants defined Black Power as a quest for economic and political power rather than a Third World revolution. Obama's willingness to seek the nation's highest office after barely two years on the national political scene embodies the boldness and politics of self-determination that were a hallmark of Black Power-era politics, much in the same way that Obama's much-publicized former church, Trinity United, and pastor, Jeremiah Wright, also did.

Trinity United Church, whose motto declared it "unapologetically black and Christian," was guided by a pastor firmly entrenched in Black Liberation Theology, which itself was rooted in the 1960s-era Black Power Movement. Wright's sermons reflected a belief in the transformative power of social, political, economic, and spiritual self-determination in combating worldly ills such as poverty, racism, crime, and hunger. A Trinity member for two decades, Obama undoubtedly listened to (and he publicly admitted as much in his Philadelphia race speech) sermons by Wright that criticized American racism, foreign policy agenda, and domestic ignorance of long-suffering black communities in urban centers such as Chicago.

Much has been made of Wright's sermons and their impact on Obama. Critics who chided Obama's membership in Trinity cited his willingness to listen to Wright's anti-American sermons as proof that the young senator was a chameleon capable of appealing to all while remaining beholden to none. In actuality, the most telling aspect of his membership in Trinity and his twenty-year relationship with Reverend Wright is Obama's ability to personally express faith and optimism in the American Dream while also attending a church whose leader openly questioned the nation's capacity for inclusion and its willingness to extend full citizenship to African Americans. In many instances, Wright's fiery sermons and ability to speak truth to power offered Obama a window into the black community's unvarnished sentiments about American society. Obama experienced the pain and anguish, hopes and dreams, and the ambivalence and alienation of the African American community in Chicago by sitting in the pews of Trinity United Church. If this fellowship helped to buoy his status as a rising local politician in Chicago, it later threatened his presidential hopes by hinting that the very candidate who promised a full break from America's racial past harbored his own deeply entrenched biases.

The public reaction to Wright's sermons illustrated contemporary America's shocking lack of racial maturity. Critics conflated Wright's unabashed criticism of American foreign policy as a lack of patriotism. They replayed severe snippets of particularly hard-hitting sound bites in an endless loop that was inappropriately characterized as "hate-speech." Over the next year, as the media and politicians went back to business as usual, any hope that Obama's race speech would spark a national conversation about race relations receded as the issue was then only addressed as a consequence of crisis or in the context of spectacle—or both.

Over the past four decades, America's discourse about race has developed unevenly. This ranged from the jarringly candid policy prescriptions of the Kerner Commission to rancorous debates over bussing and Affirmative Action, to the intermittent eruptions generated by post-Black Power riots in Miami and Los Angeles as well as the more high-minded debates surrounding proposals for a King holiday and a host of civil rights memorials and remembrances. Racially charged criminal cases, demonstrations, and even natural disasters have, like car accidents, momentarily riveted the nation's attention, but failed to prick its conscience.

The 2008 presidential election sparked, for perhaps the first time since 1968's Kerner Commission, a sustained national discussion about race. Obama's two books remain perennial best sellers and his race speech jump-started dialogues about the issue and democracy that have been reminiscent of the 1960s. However, Obama's campaign and early presidency minimized race because of the all-too-real and tragic belief that a frank discussion of difference threatened his universal appeal. Nevertheless, his status as icon has still sparked renewed interest in addressing contemporary American race relations.

The Wright episode exposed deep fissures in American race relations, the kind that politicians no longer make any pretense of addressing. One of the most important and perhaps least enduring legacies of the 1960s and early 1970s is the manner in which social movements forced the nation to publicly—if fitfully—wrestle with institutional racism. Civil rights leaders and Black Power militants both contributed to this robust national dialogue. Martin Luther King Jr. displayed a particular genius for addressing racial inequality in starkly moral terms, comparing black America's racial struggles to the ancient toils of Old Testament prophets who rescued entire nations from bondage. Malcolm X issued searing indictments against American racism, exposed democracy as hypocritical, and exhorted African Americans to cultivate racial pride and self-determination as shields against Jim Crow, antiblack violence, and poverty. By the late 1960s, the nation's racial dialogue then took on a new sense of urgency as Black Power militants expressed the depth and breadth of black rage, anger, and disillusionment with unexpected power and poignancy. Leaving behind the measured tones he perfected in his

1963 March On Washington address, King turned into one of the nation's sharpest critics, speaking out against the Vietnam War and sympathizing with the anger—if not tactics—of Black Power militants. Interest in race then turned into a publishing and media boom, with countless books, memoirs, and autobiographies directly addressing the nation's racial crisis, and no less than the *New York Times* providing space for black radicals in their editorial opinion pages.[72]

The conservative counterrevolution, manifestly visible during the 1980s, spurred a shift in this conversation. Over the past quarter century, a conversation that once centered on the potential for restorative public policy measures to address racial inequality changed quite dramatically. Racial discourses now centered on white resentment over perceived black special treatment. Conservative think tanks produced impressive policy papers and books that, paradoxically, extolled King's dream of a color-blind society while repudiating Affirmative Action as reverse racism.[73] Thus, it comes as no surprise that Obama's somber address on race relations discussed both black anger over racial discrimination and white resentment at perceived special treatment. African American grievances over America's shameful history of slavery, lynching, and Jim Crow no longer occupy the moral high ground in the media, among politicians, or the general public.

Barack Obama's significance as a symbol of America's racial progress and reconciliation is belied by hard facts. America remains more segregated than ever, with dreams of integrated public schools receding with each passing year. African American treatment before the criminal justice system remains a national scandal, and the face of HIV/AIDS has become increasingly black. African American wealth lags behind whites and, despite Obama's election, black representation at the highest levels of the nation's corporate and political industries remains inadequate.[74]

Yet regardless of the litany of social and economic indicators pointing to racism's stubborn intractability, the pat narrative of Obama's ascendance threatens to substitute one man's remarkable journey for an entire group's continuing travails. From this perspective, Obama stands in for African Americans—past and present. His enormous achievements represent the possibility for national redemption on issues of race and inequality. This prospect of a racial *tabula rasa*, however, comes at a heavy cost.

In a controversial *New York Times Magazine* cover story, writer Matt Bai raised the provocative question of whether an Obama presidency would mean the end of black politics.[75] Bai focused on the perceived generational divide between black elected officials who came of age in the civil rights era and post-Black Power politicians embodied by Obama. The new black politics, suggested younger leaders, was post-racial to the extent that its politicians, such as Newark mayor Cory Booker, Massachusetts governor Deval Patrick, and Philadelphia mayor Michael Nutter, eschewed explicitly racial appeals for votes in favor of a more universal approach. While "Old Guard" leaders such as Congressmen John Lewis and Jim Clyburn had agonized over whether to support Obama, younger black politicians dispassionately chose to support him—or not—based more on pragmatism than racial loyalty. Off the record, black leaders (presumably from the civil rights generation) confessed that an Obama presidency "might actually leave black Americans less well represented in Washington." This would be the ironic result of the nation's first black president bending over backwards in order to not play favorites.[76]

The notion that the first African American president would lead to the death of black politics mistakes individual achievement for collective empowerment. This analysis discounts the way in which history is made through a collective process full of fits and starts, and it is always incomplete even at moments of great transformation.[77]

Obama's meteoric rise in American politics mesmerized a wide variety of liberals. The majority of these supporters felt uneasy about Affirmative Action even as they reveled in the historic nature of the 2008 Democratic primaries. Obama's tepid support for Affirmative Action fuels dreams that as president he might end racial preferences backed by the kind of political cover no white president could ever possess. But black politics have always transcended individual leaders. Conventional narratives of black history, like most of American history, remain anchored in stories of heroic men and select women, such as Harriet Tubman and Sojourner Truth, who helped lead movements for social justice. This top-down vision of postwar African American history credits Martin Luther King Jr. with virtually single-handedly ending segregation. It marks his death as creating a void that has remained unfulfilled until recently. Obama's ascent as the most popular black leader since King renews this narrative of "great black leaders," but with a twenty-first-century twist.

As a symbol of America's multicultural future, Obama is both a black leader and a post-racial icon, both the ultimate insider and racial outlier. This unique position allows him, in his own words, to "serve as a blank screen on which people of vastly different political stripes project their own views."[78] Historically, the black community has been led not by any single individual leader, but by ordinary sharecroppers, teachers, workers, preachers, and community organizers, all of whom demanded equal citizenship, good schools, decent jobs, and affordable housing.

Most contemporary discussions of Black Power fixate on the politics of racial identity at the expense of chronicling the movement's ambitious and at times ruthless pursuit of power in all facets of American life. Although Obama has been lauded as an extension of the civil rights era's quest for integration into the mainstream of American life, his efforts at political self-determination borrowed from Black Power proponents' audacious pursuit of power. They are, however, stripped of Black Power's calls for racial solidarity. Between 1991, when he graduated from Harvard Law School and returned to live in Chicago full-time, and 2004, when he was elected to the U.S. Senate, Obama plotted an ambitious course that culminated in his ascent to the highest echelons of political power. Over a thirteen-year span, he led voter registration drives, practiced civil rights law, served in the state senate, and lost a bitterly contested congressional election to ex-Black Panther Bobby Rush. Along the way, he also learned hard lessons about politics, navigated Chicago's long-simmering intraracial tensions, and crafted a staggeringly diverse interracial coalition of influential friends and supporters who cultivated his political career even during times of crisis.[79]

Barack Obama, therefore, does not signal the death of black politics so much as the evolving character of race and American democracy. Yet the debate itself provides an important point of departure when reflecting on Obama's tenuous relationship with a style of black politics that predominated in the 1960s and 1970s and still exists today.

Obama confronted the kind of politics many hope his election ends in person during an August 1, 2008, rally in St. Petersburg, Florida. During his speech, about a dozen protesters from a local Black Power group stood up in an organized disruption, holding a large sign that read "What About the Black Community Obama?" During the question-and-answer session, they asked him pointed questions about his reticence to specifically advocate on behalf of issues related to the black community, including police-related shootings, Hurricane Katrina, and more. Visibly caught off guard, Obama responded by reiterating his civil rights record as a legislator and lawyer.[80]

The widely reported incident was replayed on cable news for days. His antagonists, members of St. Petersburg's local Uhuru Movement, parlayed their widely publicized demonstration into a series of meetings, conventions, and demonstrations. These criticized Obama as a modern-day "House Negro" who was enthralled by "white power" and unmoved by the depths of poverty, racism, and misery that is experienced by poor blacks. Media fascination with the incident centered on the stark visual and temperamental contrasts between the casually dressed and mostly youthful militants and Obama's button-downed confidence.

In fact, Obama's hecklers represent the legacy of one strain of Black Power-era militancy. Rooted in the pan-Africanism of Malcolm X and Kwame Ture, a small but robust segment of black activism continues to organize around Black Power-era principles of radical self-determination, political empowerment, and anti-imperialism.[81] For such activists, Obama's rise signals a repudiation of their long struggle for racial justice rather than its ultimate affirmation. At first blush, this complaint may seem like the empty ravings of political activists caught in a time warp: dashiki- and medallion-clad urban warriors who, in the face of genuine racial breakthroughs, conjure up past racial ghosts so that they can continue to ply their trade. Their criticisms, however, are more widespread than many Obama supporters realize.

Black radicals believe that Obama will do little to alter the structural forces plaguing the black community. His unwillingness to candidly address the gritty issues facing inner-city America, denounce contemporary white racism and police brutality, and offer a plan to empower African Americans is clear enough proof of his uneasiness around such subjects. During the campaign, some went as far as to argue that, by lulling black activists to sleep while the first black president safely ignores the political interests of the black community in order to further his personal political ambitions, his election would do more harm than good. Black activists have a legitimate point here, though they miss the broader picture regarding the watershed significance of Obama's election. The sheer power of Obama's daily public image as the first black American president shields him from major criticism in a black community aware of the magnitude of what they perceive as a collective achievement.

Indeed, judging by his published books, speeches, and interviews, a case can be made that Obama's campaign and early presidency remains broadly tailored to pleasing the majority of white American voters. But there is something peculiarly narrow about racial interpretations designed to not offend whites rather than being concerned with both universal justice and the historical grievances of blacks. As a result, Obama's presidency presents the black community with very real challenges, ones that, his critics correctly point out, necessitates more vigilance—not less. But Obama's critics may overstate aspects of their case, especially his connections to Black Power.

Black Power was never a monolithic movement. If Stokely Carmichael and Malcolm X represented one strain, then black elected officials, from Richard Hatcher to Harold Washington, represented another. Within the movement itself, revolutionaries and political pragmatists existed alongside one another. Over time, black politicians did distance themselves from grassroots activists who were too idealistic to understand the rough-and-tumble world of machine politics. In response, community organizers denounced electoral politics, largely abandoning the electoral arena in favor of community-building and consciousness-raising. The impact of this fractured relationship can be witnessed in inner cities across America. It is especially poignant in the fact that Obama's election helped to reestablish these frayed ties by inspiring community organizers to participate, many for the first time, in presidential politics.

This leads to perhaps the most important question related to Obama's election: Was there, in fact, an Obama movement? The answer, based on the millions of small online donations, new registered voters, and first-time political participants at the grassroots level, must be a resounding yes.

Contemporary Black Power activists have every right to criticize Obama and openly question his commitment to racial justice and civil rights. Yet at the same time they must also concede that Obama's campaign unleashed the kind of political energy within and beyond the African American community not witnessed since the late 1960s and early 1970s—the high tide of the Black Power, women's, and antiwar movements.

If Obama's overwhelming support in the black community exposed mainstream black politics as vulnerable, it has also revealed much of what considers itself to be radical and progressive as virtually bankrupt. This is not to deny the existence of tens of thousands of local, community-level organizations, as well as hundreds of thousands of activists performing heroic work in churches, athletic centers, libraries, and street corners across the country. The success of the October 16, 1995, Million Man March and the subsequent follow-up demonstrations attest to the viability of modern-day, Black Power-era mobilizing principles. Likewise, the more recent coordinated efforts to assist victims of Hurricane Katrina and the Jena 6 illustrate the legacy of radical movements for social justice. However, the lack of an organization, power base, or clearinghouse for black radicals to effectively challenge Obama has been stark. That there is a lack of centralized strategy should come as no surprise, since Obama managed to snub Tavis Smiley—whose corporate connections and financial base far exceed that of black radicals—and come out of the ensuing controversy more popular than ever. In fact, the black leader powerful enough to negotiate with Obama proved to be another post-racial icon—no less than Oprah Winfrey herself.

Lacking the media, financial, and institutional resources to effectively criticize Obama, black radicals have taken to the Internet and YouTube postings to voice dissatisfaction. However, much of this sound and fury has been overwhelmed by the unremitting pro-Obama coverage found in the black media. During the 2008 presidential election, black radio, television, and media outlets enthusiastically promoted Obama's candidacy and raised voter awareness through popular talk shows that reached millions of African Americans.[82] His inspirational message of hope, optimism, and democratic renewal enthralled multitudes of both black and white voters on a scale unprecedented in American history. His radical critics, however, point out the *realpolitik* behind much of this message and the gap between America's promise and reality. Indeed, Obama's preference for spending much more time extolling national triumphs over tragedies dovetails with the spirit of American exceptionalism that animates postwar America. Regardless, his critics have been unable to effectively develop an alternate reality that can be embraced by black Americans or build institutions strong enough to challenge the Obama movement's growing hegemony in black politics.

Barack Obama's election represents, in contrasting and converging instances, a validation of the legacy of both the civil rights and Black Power movements. Obama's call for multiracial democracy free of America's tortured history of racial bias and discrimination echoes the civil rights movement's enduring belief in the capacity for national change. Civil rights leaders appealed to universal impulses in service of racially specific goals that included promoting equal opportunity in housing, employment, the criminal justice system, corporate America, as well as social, cultural, religious, and economic institutions. At times, he emphasized the universal at the expense of the specific, a situation that led civil rights leaders to question his commitment to black issues and journalists to wonder whether his ascent signals the demise of black politics in America.[83] Both of these assumptions miss a larger point about Obama's election and its relationship to historic civil rights struggles. A forgotten but all-too-important aspect of the civil rights movement is the fact that it was, at its core, a movement for radical democracy.

More than any single group in American history, blacks have promoted a deep, broad, and expansive vision of democracy. On this score, black-led social movements during the postwar era fundamentally transformed American democracy through nonviolent civil disobedience, mass demonstrations, and sit-ins. Struggles for racial justice interacted with, and gave inspiration to, trade-unionism, feminism, and a "rainbow radicalism"[84] that drew multicultural ethnic groups into coalitions with black activists, all of whom pursued a more humane society.

Too often, we forget African American involvement in these movements to transform democracy. Struggles for racial justice cannot be separated from antiwar movements, the push for workers' rights, and women's equality. Antiracist civil rights struggles formed beachheads in virtually every major American city during the civil rights era. They did so in ways that reverberated at the local, regional, national, and international levels. In this sense, civil rights represents not simply a struggle for black equality, but also for a deeper and more meaningful definition of democracy, one that continues to animate contemporary struggles for social, political, and economic justice.

Obama's symbolism, then, amounts to far more than just being the historic milestone of America's first black president. His rise speaks to the very possibilities of American democracy. Postwar America featured radical movements for social justice that included a wide array of black activists and white allies, all of whom envisioned an America free of institutional racism and a beacon for oppressed people all over the world.[85] For a time, this vision seemed possible—even probable. Buoyed by the New Deal and war-time antifascism, the rhetoric of American democracy became capacious enough to embrace controversial figures such as Paul Robeson and W. E. B. Du Bois as patriots. But the Cold War swiftly sapped the strength of this burgeoning movement. Both Martin Luther King Jr. and Malcolm X entered the political arena a decade later in the mid-1950s in a nation that was already vastly changed.

King and Malcolm contended with the new realities of activism in Cold War America with contrasting strategies that were, in different ways, both right and wrong. King responded by focusing on the moral, spiritual, and psychological dimensions of racial oppression, while Malcolm offered a stinging indictment of American democracy as nothing more than rhetorical hypocrisy. King's initial approach for the first ten years of his public life pragmatically adapted to the status quo even as Malcolm's envelope-pushing polemics gave the more reasonable preacher vital room to operate.

Neither King nor Malcolm were infallible. Both men committed grave political errors that, too late, they attempted to correct. In Malcolm's case, this centered on his static view of American society. In spite of the litany of crimes committed against black America, African Americans had fought for—and produced—meaningful change that made the nation more racially progressive. During the last year of his life, Malcolm seemed more in tune to these transformations and exhibited a willingness to form coalitions with groups he once admonished. On the other hand, King's belief in American democracy's ability to transform itself on behalf of African Americans proved a bit too optimistic. One biographer has suggested that in the aftermath of the 1965 Voting Rights Act, King turned into a "pillar of fire," castigating the Vietnam War, repudiating American imperialism and military violence, and organizing a massive Poor People's March On Washington.

After King's 1968 assassination, both civil rights and Black Power activists focused on power politics through the election of black politicians, the creation of black businesses, as well as the entrée into corporate America, the federal government, and higher education through Affirmative Action programs. Civil rights struggles, then, animate the soaringly optimistic rhetoric of Obama's candidacy and its hopeful belief in America's capacity for social and political transformation. His efforts to become America's first black president extended the by now virtually lost politics of integration into the twenty-first century even as Black Power's call for political self-determination and willingness to take risks on long odds infused Obama's campaign as well.

On Tuesday, November 4, 2008, at 11:00 p.m. eastern standard time, Barack Obama was elected the first black president of the United States. Long lines at polling booths around the nation hinted at the levels of excitement and enthusiasm sparked by his candidacy. Many voters waited several hours at polling places in order to cast a vote in an election universally regarded as historic.

His unprecedented victory over Republican candidate John McCain featured a comfortable electoral college victory buoyed by the largest popular vote (over 68 million votes) in American history. Obama's resounding national victory, including 43 percent of white voters, refuted gnawing skepticism regarding the nation's willingness to elect a black president.

The opening line of President-elect Obama's victory speech in Chicago's Grant Park addressed the lingering doubts, both domestically and abroad, that had attended his candidacy from the beginning. "If there is anyone out there who still doubts that America is a place where all things are possible; who still wonders if the dream of our founders is alive in our time; who still questions the power of our democracy, tonight is your answer."[86] As Obama spoke these words, Jesse Jackson stood in Grant Park openly weeping at a sight that seemed unimaginable two generations earlier.

Obama's unprecedented victory sparked waves of spontaneous celebrations nationwide. Record crowds gathered in parks, on street corners, at college campuses, and for private parties to celebrate the election. New York's Times Square, Harlem 125th Street corridor, and Washington, D.C.'s famed U Street strip featured throngs of multihued revelers. International sentiment echoed America's domestic euphoria, with celebrations stretching from Europe to Africa, and the Middle East out to Asia and far corners of the globe.

Major media outlets characterized Obama's election as a national breakthrough in race relations. "RACIAL BARRIER FALLS IN DECISIVE VICTORY" reported the *New York Times* in a headline that succinctly summed up much of the 2008 campaign's underlying subtext. His election, the *Times* proclaimed, "amounted to a national catharsis" in a time of war and looming economic crisis that doubled as a sweeping repudiation of America's sordid legacy of racism. Baby Boomers who came of age during the civil rights era shed bittersweet tears and struggled to reconcile the roiling days of the 1960s with the election of a black president. African Americans danced in the streets of Harlem, wept tears of unabashed joy, and extolled pride in citizenship and democracy that would have seemed unimaginable before this election.[87] "Obamaism," according to one postelection analysis, was "a kind of religion" steeped "in a deep faith in rationality" that unleashed a new kind of political idealism, inspiring citizens of a twenty-first-century multicultural America to believe in the impossible.[88]

Major media outlets joined in the celebration. *Newsweek* dubbed the coming era "The Age of Obama." It portrayed the president-elect as a once-in-a-generation leader whose successful election had pivoted on an unpredicted historical wave fueled by hope instead of fear and animated by inspiration rather than rage.[89] *Time*, in a commemorative issue that featured a suitably iconic portrait of the president-elect, hailed Obama's election as a sign that King's dream "is being fulfilled sooner than anyone imagined."[90] *Ebony* magazine named Obama its first-ever "Person of the Year," hailing him to be a bold oracle of change poised to transform the entire world.[91] Luci Baines Johnson, LBJ's youngest daughter, recounted how her father's signing of voting rights legislation paved the way for an Obama presidency.[92]

Obama's public image, formidable since his 2004 Democratic National Convention speech in Boston, reached astounding new levels after his victory. Print, radio, television, and Internet coverage of his victory inspired a historic media frenzy that extended to the tabloid press, Internet marketers, and even infomercials hawking commemorative items featuring the president-elect.

The most iconic president-elect since George Washington, Obama's victory increased newspaper sales. This led many to reprint special commemorative election issues and forced conservative outlets such as the *New York Post* to display more balanced reporting about the event than its readers had come to expect.

Obama's election symbolically passed the torch of American democracy to a new generation even as it evoked past historical triumphs and tragedies. Comparisons between King and Obama, however, while understandable, proved to be inaccurate. This is because the "young preacher from Georgia," as Obama often describes him (to the chagrin of progressives who would prefer King's name to be more forcefully invoked), led a movement for social justice and aspired to no elected office in his lifetime. King's moral stature as a political leader rested in large part on his intuitive ability to transcend political parties and interest group ideology for larger themes that encompassed civil and human rights. On the other hand, Obama's disciplined pursuit of the nation's highest political office steered clear of King's call for world peace, redistributive justice, and the end of global poverty.

Icons at relatively young ages (King by the time he was in his late twenties and Obama by the time he was in his early forties), both men did share a resounding faith in the transformative capacities of ordinary people and American democracy. In contrast, whereas King's pointed critiques of American racism, militarism, and capitalism questioned notions of American exceptionalism, Obama has embraced this idea along with its pitfalls of national strength and moral certitude.

Obama's debt to the civil rights era remains immense. A former community organizer in Chicago's Altgeld Housing project in the 1980s, Obama has written passionately about his experiences helping poor African Americans feel a sense of political empowerment amid the bleak physical and political landscape of the Reagan Revolution. For Obama, the work of a community organizer "held out an offer of collective redemption."[93]

This symbolic offer was solidified during Obama's final campaign rally. On November 3, 2008—election eve—Barack Obama confronted the legacy of America's antebellum past. That evening he held his last campaign rally in Manassas, Virginia, the site of the Civil War's first major battle. It was the kind of symbolic gesture that the historian in Obama relished throughout the campaign. He was fully aware that the image of a man on the cusp of becoming America's first black president visiting Dixie's citadel signaled a new chapter in the nation's history. Over 100,000 people came to listen to Obama that evening in what was the largest gathering of its kind in American history. As he strode onto the stage at 10:30 p.m., Obama must have sensed that Virginia was poised to buck forty years of tradition and vote for a Democratic candidate—a feat not accomplished since 1964.[94] In Manassas, Obama's thoughts surely must have conjured up images of the distance America had traveled from Lincoln's age to his own.

The idea of redeeming America's promise through his very biography successfully catapulted Obama to the White House. His success illustrates the major strides that African Americans have made since the civil rights era, just as it also showcases the narrow parameters of this progress. In the popular imagination, the civil rights movement petered out as a result of urban riots, Black Power's separatist politics, and a white backlash. In truth, the civil rights era's decline paralleled the movement's search for redistributive justice. By the late 1960s and early 1970s, the era of major rights legislation gave way to bruising neighborhood, state, and national struggles over employment, housing, schools, social services, and political and economic power. King's efforts to redeem America's soul came with a staggering cost attached, one that the majority of white citizens, politicians, and powerbrokers found too steep to bear. During his last three years, King's national political stature waned, his once cordial relationship with Lyndon Johnson turned fractious, and his outspoken denunciation of the Vietnam War led former liberal allies to denounce him as something of a kook.[95]

For this reason, much of his 2008 presidential campaign projected Obama's candidacy as a chance for national redemption. If King's penchant for discussing hard truths alienated powerful allies and turned off once stalwart constituencies, Obama's deft ability to highlight themes of national unity successfully deflected long-standing racial and economic divisions. His election unleashed waves of latent patriotism both domestically and around the world. The ideal of America remains a powerful force for social justice and an important source of inspiration for those in search of hope, dignity, and second chances.

That a nation founded in racial slavery, nurtured on Jim Crow, and steeped in the color-line could elect a black president speaks to American democracy's capacity for reform, innovation, and evolution. Nevertheless, the nation's racial trajectory has been far from linear. In the aftermath of Reconstruction, a whole generation of African Americans—including the first class of elected officials in the late nineteenth century—were shut out of the political process, economically coerced into sharecropping and menial labor, and denied basic civil, legal, and human rights.[96] In a very real sense, then, the postwar era of civil rights and Black Power offered the nation a Second Reconstruction. It was an opportunity to fulfill democracy's broken promises. Indeed, the most potent (and perhaps least-quoted aspect) of King's celebrated "I Have a Dream" March On Washington Speech evoked the notion of reparations due to blacks for centuries of racial oppression. On August 28, 1963, at the Lincoln Memorial, King spoke of a "promissory note" that linked the descendants of slaves to the Founding Fathers. Despite the nation's deep economic and spiritual reserves, African Americans had been given a "bad check," one stamped "insufficient funds." "But we refuse," noted King, "to believe that the bank of justice is bankrupt," and instead African Americans appeared before the nation in impressive numbers in an effort to make good on American democracy's promise.[97]

As a presidential candidate, Obama largely avoided the charged topic of American race relations. But his very biography inevitably made race a core part of each debate, campaign speech, and interview of both the Democratic primary contests and the general election. Journalists, pundits, intellectuals, and ordinary citizens countered Obama's reticence with a full-throated—if not always fully informed—conversation about race. This dialogue ranged from pride in a history-making candidate to astonishment that a black man could be president to annoyance that race was being singled out as a potential reason behind the candidate's success or failure. For some, Obama represented a post-racial America, wherein King's dream of a color-blind democracy found its expression, fittingly, in the son of a Kenyan immigrant from Africa and a white woman with roots in Kansas. Others blanched at such romantic descriptions, noting that Obama's unthreatening appearance, placid demeanor, and even temperament soothed white voters who were still uncomfortable with the prospect of voting for a black man.[98]

Obama's election-night victory speech offers an alternative answer. His words evoked a vision of a multicultural America where millions of Americans who had never participated in the political process braved long lines to cast their vote, large swaths of young people chose hope over cynicism, and the chance at fostering racial reconciliation triumphed over those who stoked division and fear. America's ultimate strength, noted Obama, stemmed from "the enduring power of our ideals: democracy, liberty, opportunity, and unyielding hope." By way of example, he recounted the story of Ann Nixon Cooper, a 106-year-old black woman born a generation after slavery in an era ruled by Jim Crow who lived to cast a vote for a black president via a touchscreen ballot.[99]

In many ways, Obama's election as America's first black president represents the culmination of centuries-long struggles for freedom and democracy. Its immediate roots can be traced back to the civil rights era's heroic period, where courageous young blacks and smaller numbers of white allies shook the nation's conscience to its core by demanding racial equality, economic opportunity, and human dignity. Martin Luther King Jr. continues to loom large over this era, seen as a modern-day prophet who powerfully extolled the dynamic convergence between the nation's political and moral imperatives. But it was the less glamorous figures who made King's dream possible.

Thousands of students, from elementary schools to colleges and universities, embarked on a political crusade in the early 1960s that fundamentally changed American democracy. The sit-in movement ignited the direct-action phase of the efforts and inspired a dormant Congress of Racial Equality to renew its Freedom Rides. It also pushed the thirty-one-year-old King into a more boldly confrontational posture. Southern black sharecroppers risked their lives and property in search of citizenship that reporters too often boiled down to the vote. This pursuit, however, encompassed not only the ability to cast a ballot, but also to succeed in accordance with the vastness of one's imagination. Obama himself acknowledged the debt owed to these activists in his choice to become a community organizer. Just as SNCC activists argued that citizenship required service, Obama conjured a definition of organizing that was expansive enough to pull the disparate threads of his background into a coherent identity. "In the sit-ins, the marches, the jailhouse songs, I saw the African-American community becoming more than just the place where you'd been born or the house where you'd been raised," he writes. Work as a community organizer required "shared sacrifice" and a belief that "the larger American community, black, white, and brown" could remake itself. "It was," Obama recalls, "a promise of redemption."[100]

The Black Power Movement paralleled and intersected with the epic struggles for civil rights that Obama holds as sacred. Beyond human dignity and the right to vote, black militants sought political power by any means necessary. Malcolm X's impassioned speeches constituted verbal declarations of war that openly questioned American democracy's jagged edges of racism, segregation, poverty, police brutality, and repression. In addition, Northern civil rights struggles were often no less contentious than the South's more well-chronicled battles.[101] Stokely Carmichael's well-publicized call for Black Power continues to be misunderstood. A tireless civil rights organizer who worked in some of the South's most dangerous areas, Carmichael extolled

Black Power as the political self-determination required to secure black citizenship and promote genuine democracy.

Barack Obama himself has admitted that he possesses "a curious relationship to the sixties."[102] Part of this stems from the fact that, having been born in Hawaii in 1961—the summer of the bloody Freedom Rides—and having spent several years of his childhood in Indonesia, he came of political age at a remove from the raucous cultural and political struggles that defined the era. Lacking an experiential connection to the period, Obama's understanding of this time comes largely through reading and the anecdotal stories told by his mother and maternal grandparents. His sympathetic consideration of the civil rights era evokes a heartfelt—if at times uncomplicated and romantic—portrait of the difficulties experienced by swashbuckling civil rights workers in the South. Similarly, Obama offers a respectful, albeit two-dimensional, critique of black nationalism as too didactic to encompass America's unruly racial makeup.

Despite his debt to historic traditions of black activism, Barack Obama's election rested on a ruthless pursuit of the type of power that both civil rights and Black Power activists were once convinced black people might never wield. Stunning transformations in America's racial, social, cultural, and political landscape paved the way for an Obama presidency. African American elected officials, corporate leaders, entrepreneurs, athletes, hip-hop, and other symbols of black popular culture undoubtedly also shaped the racial landscape that helped elect Obama. Perhaps the most important phenomenon in making an Obama presidency possible is the growth of African American Studies. A product of militant Black Power-era protests and building on the towering legacy of activist-intellectuals such as W. E. B. Du Bois and Ida B. Wells, the evolution of Black Studies since the 1960s has touched virtually every aspect of American society. Beyond ivory and ebony towers of elite universities, the rigorous study, debate, and critical analysis of the roles of blacks in American history has reached a critical apex. This is in addition to the mass dissemination through books, documentaries, the rise of a new generation of black public intellectuals, and the Internet. Obama's historic election helped to usher in a new stage of America's democratic evolution and set the stage for an equally historic presidential inauguration.

American democracy's very aesthetics were fundamentally transformed on January 20, 2009. Over 2 million people from a wide range of diverse backgrounds, ethnicities, generations, and countries trekked to the nation's capitol, braving frigid temperatures in order to witness Barack Obama being sworn in as America's forty-fourth president. A global media event covered in minute detail on television, radio, and the Internet, his inauguration represented the culmination of enduring political struggles for racial and economic justice in American society.

Perhaps the most striking feature of the inauguration proved to be the enormous symbolism of the nation witnessing a black man take the oath of office. Journalists immediately heralded the achievement of "a once-inconceivable journey for the man and his country."[103] Both ordinary Americans along with celebrities and entertainers stood on the National Mall to take in what the *Wall Street Journal* described as a "Glimpse of History."[104] Obama's racial biography in effect presented the nation with a democratic moment once considered unimaginable. From a stage that stood high upon the western face of the Capitol building, Obama's every movement and gesture carried enormous symbolic weight. Juxtaposed against Washington's still predominantly white cast of political powerbrokers and economic and social bureaucrats, Obama's physical presence offered both a refreshingly jarring portrait of change as well as a stark reminder of how rigid and enduring America's racial boundaries remain.

Faced with the pressure of a moment universally regarded as a watershed in American history, Obama delivered an inaugural address whose substance matched the day's symbolism. The most striking aspect of his inauguration address was its sweeping appreciation of the complex nature of American history. Asking Americans "to choose our better history," the speech offered a subtle history lesson that spanned the Revolutionary era to the present. From the coerced labor of Americans who "toiled in sweatshops" to the forced conscription of enslaved Africans who "endured the lash of the whip," Obama acknowledged the nation's complex history where immigrants and slaves, laborers and landowners, rich and poor have sought to remake their world. Rather than papering over divisions of class and caste, race and religion, region and ideology, he squarely confronted them, noting that Americans had "tasted the bitter swill of civil war and segregation, and emerged from that chapter stronger and more united."

Obama's address implicitly rejected Ronald Reagan's notion that a sprawling federal government sapped American ingenuity through high taxes and welfare. "The question we ask today is not whether our government is too big or too small," said Obama, "but whether it works—whether it helps families find jobs at a decent wage, care they can afford, a retirement that is dignified." Amplifying John F. Kennedy's famous 1961 promotion of national service, Obama called for "a new era of responsibility" in which civic matters comprised "duties that we do not grudgingly accept but rather seize gladly" in service to larger democratic aspirations.

Race loomed large over the day's entire proceedings. With typically understated eloquence, Obama explicitly addressed racial themes in three different instances. But even before addressing racial matters, he summarized with poetic power the historical currents that buffeted his own assumption of office. "Yet, every so often the oath is taken amidst gathering clouds and raging storms," he said. "At these moments, America has carried on not simply because of the skill or vision of those in high office, but because We the People have remained faithful to the ideals of our forebears, and true to our founding documents."

Obama first touched on the subject of race by memorializing those Americans who had "endured the lash of the whip," thereby offering up a poignant acknowledgement of the nation's original sin of chattel slavery. The legacy of America's period of antebellum slavery continues to haunt contemporary race relations. The nation's enduring paradox remains the fact that a state founded on cherished ideals of freedom, liberty, and equality distorted and defamed the very heart of its democratic experiment by promoting, sanctioning, and profiting from the forced labor of generations of black women and men in bondage. Yet the sheer symbolism of a man who could have easily been purchased and sold during the antebellum era being sworn in as the nation's commander in chief gives proof to both the grandeur and travails of America's democratic experiment.

The second explicit reference to race came when Obama briefly discussed the Civil War and Jim Crow period of racial segregation as a "dark chapter" in the nation's history that, paradoxically, left the nation more united and strong. His sanguine words about the era of Jim Crow stuck to the conventional script regarding the civil rights era's heroic period. In this popular, widespread, but ultimately naive and historically inaccurate narrative, racial segregation represented a moral and political evil that had been wiped away by the soul power of Martin Luther King Jr. and the canny legislative brilliance of Lyndon Johnson. Without in any way diminishing the towering legal and legislative victories of the era or dismissing the courageous marchers, demonstrators, and ordinary citizens who braved violence, jails, and death for larger democratic ideals, racial segregation persists in twenty-first-century America. That it is characterized by the term *de facto*, which refers to happenstance rather than malicious segregation, makes it perhaps more insidious than Jim Crow's ancient regime.

Obama's last reference to race evoked the personal and political. Near the end of his speech, he spoke of the "meaning of our liberty and our creed," noting that "a man whose father less than sixty years ago might not have been served at a local restaurant can now stand before you to take a most sacred oath."[105] These are some of the most powerful lines of the entire address. On one hand, this allusion to race is in fact the second and most pointed confrontation with the nation's tragic racial past, especially its history of Jim Crow segregation. Obama's candid admission that his dark-skinned African father, Barack Hussein Obama Sr., would have suffered the many indignities of American apartheid reminds us that a president who largely shied away from the nation's racial legacy as a candidate nevertheless understands the unique burdens of his biography.

But the words perhaps obscure as much as they reveal. Indeed, Obama's father may have been denied entrée into a local diner far more recently than sixty years ago. For even several years after the passage of the 1964 Civil Rights Act's ban on discrimination in public accommodations, African Americans were still subject to discrimination, harassment, and violence. The popular idea that discrimination ended magically via a stroke of a presidential pen is one of the many civil rights-era fictions that remains a generational touchstone.

Ultimately, however, Barack Obama's inaugural address represented a historical tour de force wherein the first black president served as the nation's "educator-in-chief." He offered a nuanced, bracing, and sober assessment of the nation's past, one sweeping in scope, generous in praise, yet resolute in its acknowledgement of American democracy's enduring racial wounds. These lesions remain etched in the very fabric of America's social, political, and economic culture and are exemplified in the nation's political economy where race continues to shape hope, opportunity, and life chances.

In a general sense, then, Obama's speech served as a bookend to one of his presidential heroes, Abraham Lincoln, whose two inaugural addresses explicitly, though at times opaquely, addressed first the prospect of civil war and, later, the aftermath of a conflict once thought unimaginable. As a meditation on race and democracy, Lincoln's speeches in 1861 and 1865 reflected the tenor of the times, less altruistic paeans to the equality of all citizens than a pragmatic appeal to political reconciliation. Likewise, themes of race and American democracy contoured Obama's address, but did so in ways that Lincoln would have found impossible to articulate. In Obama's vision, race and democracy are less paradoxical notions forced down the throats of a divided nation than proof that ancient grievances are subject to contemporary solutions and that once irresolvable conflicts can be forcefully mediated.

The prospect of racial progress, reconciliation, and even the end of race altogether hovered over Obama's first one hundred days in the White House. Beyond the racial symbolism of the nation's first black president lay multiple political crises that included wars in Iraq and Afghanistan, a looming financial recession that offered the worst economic conditions since the Great Depression, and myriad global crises that ranged from Middle East conflicts to African genocide. Regardless of these issues, race continued to exert an influence on the Obama administration's first three months of power. Two controversies provide vivid snapshots of a nation coming to grips with the reality of electing its first black president beyond the euphoria of inauguration-day festivities.

On February 18, 2009, a *New York Post* cartoon depicting two police officers shooting a chimpanzee sparked a national controversy over Obama and race. "They'll have to find someone else to write the next stimulus bill," noted one of the cartoon officers.[106] At its most benign, the cartoon editorial satirized the recent passage of President Obama's stimulus bill with reports of a wild chimpanzee from Connecticut who had mauled an innocent victim. Critics charged that the chimp represented a caricature of the president and played upon gnawing anxiety that his enormous personal achievement would ultimately end in violence.

Prominent black political and cultural activists, including Al Sharpton and Spike Lee, called for a boycott of the *New York Post*. Their efforts in turn triggered a partial editorial retraction that apologized to those who were offended by the cartoon, though they steadfastly maintained that "sometimes a cartoon is just a cartoon—even as the opportunists seek to make it something else."[107] Obama stayed above the fray of this racial controversy, content to save another "race speech" in reserve for an actual crisis. Meanwhile, the *Post*'s "apology" evasively drew distinctions between Americans who could be properly offended by the cartoon and racial opportunists.

The controversy over the *New York Post* cartoon highlighted race's shifting battleground in the age of Obama. Hopes that his election would usher in an era of "post-racial" American politics have collided with a national history rife with racial doubts, fears, and paranoia. For African Americans, the implicit equation of the nation's first black president with a chimp evoked painful memories of a not-too-distant past where blacks, regardless of their social standing, were compared to animals. During Reconstruction and continuing into the long period of Jim Crow, blacks were caricaturized as brutes, beasts, and savages who were unworthy of citizenship. Far from being cultural artifacts from a buried racial past, such depictions of black Americans persisted well into the twentieth century, when civil rights activists such as Martin Luther King Jr. were characterized as coons and the NAACP was referred to as "planet of the apes."[108] More than simply painful reminders of the past, these dehumanizing portrayals of blacks remain part of the nation's racial imagination.

The same day that the *New York Post's* alleged depiction of Obama as a chimp appeared, Attorney General Eric Holder delivered a remarkable speech at the Department of Justice in commemoration of Black History Month. America's first African American Attorney General, Holder suggested that "to get to the heart of this country one must examine its racial soul." His speech then attempted to do just that. Despite America's multicultural and multiethnic makeup, its citizens remained "a nation of cowards" on the subject of race, too fearful of the consequences of racial candor. Holder discussed the enormous achievements made by the nation since the 1954 *Brown* Supreme Court decision, but nonetheless admitted that America "has still not come to grips with its racial past," and that this reluctance reflected a historic reluctance in confronting race matters.

Black History Month should be accustomed to igniting a national conversation about race, Holder suggested, especially since racial segregation in private remained part of the very fabric of American life. Through a sweeping examination of the role that slavery, Jim Crow, and civil rights protests played in transforming American democracy, Holder argued that Black History provided a context to reimagine the nation's racial boundaries as it moved toward a more robustly multicultural future. The Attorney General's blunt speech concluded with a roll call of figures—including Malcolm X—whom he recognized as providing the "broad shoulders" on which his own professional success stood.[109]

Holder's candor echoed Obama's widely praised "race speech" of 2008 but proved far more controversial. Progressives praised the Attorney General's remarks as the kind of clarity that was needed in order to push race relations forward. Some even suggested that Holder's more pungent remarks about slavery and racism made his speech more powerful than Obama's.[110] Conservative critics, on the other hand, blasted the address as one-sided, overly provocative, and pessimistic.[111] These critics singled out Holder's description of America as a "nation of cowards" regarding racial questions as particularly offensive.

The furor over the *Post* cartoon and Holder's speech illustrates persistent constraints on the national dialogue around race. If the age of Obama promised to usher in a more nuanced, complex, and sophisticated personal and political discussion about American race relations, the reality has not delivered. Instead, we have witnessed a retreat back to a post-civil rights and Black Power-era racial stalemate. The towering symbolism of Obama's election only temporarily managed to contain the politics of racial animus and scapegoating that have fueled America's electoral arena since its founding.

As president, Obama has proven less immune to racism's more mundane features. This includes a national inability to discuss not only America's past racial tragedies but also the nation's unfolding racial history. Narratives of race in America, as told by political candidates including Obama himself, present a largely triumphant story of redemption that stresses universal themes of citizenship, democracy, and national unity. But Eric Holder's remarkable speech distanced itself from themes of triumphant self-congratulation in favor of confronting racism's contemporary face. That Holder's speech produced mixed results is not surprising considering even President Obama's reluctance to focus on race.

Both controversies that took place within the first month of the Obama administration suggest that the shifting grounds of America's racial politics ushered in by the 2008 presidential election remain stubbornly grounded in a national history steeped in mutual recriminations. They also resist facile predictions that Obama's election signaled the "end of black politics." If anything, Obama's election reflects stark lines of demarcation within the black community. The politics of racial solidarity that helped to propel Obama's almost universal support among black voters likewise obscured generational, class, and ideological tensions within the African American community. Upwardly mobile and Ivy-League educated blacks embraced Obama as a symbol of racial transcendence and color-blind politics that dovetailed with their hard-earned efforts to break glass ceilings in corporate America. Black progressives viewed Obama's candidacy as a major bombardment in an enduring—some would say never-ending—campaign against white supremacy. Still others, perhaps most notably Attorney General Holder, attempt to split the difference, lauding the administration's historic achievement while they simultaneously admonish the nation for refusing to confront its racial past.[112]

Considering his public admiration of Abraham Lincoln, Obama's personal reluctance to discuss issues of race is especially ironic.[113] In the popular imagination Lincoln is hailed as a nineteenth-century prophet of racial reconciliation, the "Great Emancipator" who ended slavery and preserved the union amid civil war and unimaginable years of violence. But Obama's contemporary appreciation of Lincoln remains a simplification inasmuch as it largely fails to deal with the sixteenth president's extraordinarily complicated racial views.

There remains a yawning gap between the "Great Emancipator" and America's actual sixteenth president. Lincoln may best be thought of as a "recovering racist." A product of the nineteenth century, he was complex enough to reject slavery as an institution though he remained skeptical about the idea of black social and political equality and supportive of various colonization schemes to deport slaves to tropical countries beyond American shores. If Lincoln's anti-Negro racial attitudes marked him as very much a man of his age, then the evolution of his thinking about race and social equality (however partial and incremental) made him uniquely suited to serve as president during one of the most crucial turning points in American history.[114] Yet the Lincoln who, in Obama's words, singularly "understood the deliberative functions of our democracy and the limits of such deliberation"[115] required the persuasive intervention and moral courage of a former slave.

Frederick Douglass, on the other hand, offered a critical appreciation of Lincoln. A former slave who rose to international prominence as a dazzling speaker, best-selling author, and abolitionist, Douglass's gift for personal and political reinvention boldly complemented Lincoln's more cautious and pragmatic tendencies. If Douglass "established the tradition of the self-made African American,"[116] then Obama's zesty appreciation for this legacy has animated his entire political career. The most well-known antislavery activist of the antebellum era, "Frederick Douglass loved to expose American lies"[117] in a manner that Obama would find uncomfortable. Indeed, for much of his public career, Douglass remained a harsh critic and an outspoken, although friendly, adversary of Lincoln. For Douglass reminds us that, at times, even Lincoln's eloquent words—most notably his 1861 inaugural address—could obscure cruel intentions. On this score, Lincoln's oft-recited closing paragraph to his first inaugural address—one quoted by Obama on election night—has been posthumously lauded as an enduring example of presidential wisdom and statesmanship. In truth, Lincoln's paean to the "better angels of our nature" hid a sinister truth: that Congress had passed a never-ratified

Thirteenth Amendment guaranteeing slavery in existing states and designed to thwart a civil war.[118]

Contemporary Americans, including President Obama, seem unprepared to embrace Lincoln's legacy in all of its complex contradictions. But here again, Douglass offers a mature historical example and, perhaps, a guidepost for the future. He considered Lincoln more than just a political adversary or a simple icon. He regarded Lincoln as a friend. Despite this, eleven years after Lincoln's death Douglass would confess that blacks were Lincoln's "step-children" who were only begrudgingly considered citizens. However, such criticism did not make Lincoln any less of a majestic figure. In fact, because the sixteenth president did possess the popular racial sentiment toward blacks of the day, perhaps it made him more so for having, temporarily at least, overcome ancient prejudices.[119]

If Abraham Lincoln provides Obama with a vision of presidential temperament, FDR offers a model of public policy and governance. Obama's February 24, 2009, speech to Congress, which served as the incumbent president's de facto State of the Union address, prepared the nation for the boldest governmental public policy agenda since Lyndon Johnson's Great Society and Roosevelt's New Deal. The latter set the modern standard for activist presidents. The broad outline of Obama's message, published on the heels of the recently signed $787 billion "American Recovery and Reinvestment Act," appeared on February 26 in a plan called "A New Era of Responsibility: Renewing America's Promise." The most important aspect of the 134-page document's charts, graphs, and outlines for massive investments in health care, energy, and education consisted of Obama's "presidential message." In it, he characterized the contemporary era as an age "that comes along once in a generation," where Americans chart a new future for national progress. Not since the dawn of New Deal liberalism amid the Great Depression has an American president proposed such a boldly imaginative or far-reaching set of policy initiatives. But whereas FDR struck a decidedly combative tone during his first inauguration address by regaling against "unscrupulous money changers,"[120] Obama's redistributive policy prescriptions came wrapped in a call for national unity. His most closely aligned predecessors came to office at crucial moments in national history, but they remained committed to an ever-expanding vision of democracy's capacity for social transformation. In a sense, the greatest attributes these presidents displayed resided in their deep-seated faith that America's story would continue. As a product of civil rights- and Black Power-era movements for social change, Obama shares this forward-looking thinking as well as an abiding knowledge that history is made not simply by world leaders and presidents, but also by ordinary people.

In his first post-election press conference, Barack Obama self-deprecatingly referred to himself as a mutt. The term reflects a long-standing effort to forge a meaningful synthesis around the disparate parts that contour his personal identity as well as America's. His biography, campaign, and early presidency managed to turn the nation's largely tumultuous racial history into a coherent political narrative that grappled with American democracy's troubling paradoxes and redemptive possibilities.

In a very real sense, the Obama era represents the culmination of America's postwar civil rights movement in which ordinary citizens, sharecroppers, preachers, and young people demonstrated, marched, and, at times, died for the cause of freedom. The civil rights era indelibly shaped Obama. His decision to become a community organizer after college was inspired by the iconic images of the civil rights era's high tide that captured his youthful imagination with images of the faces of activists singing freedom songs, civil rights workers canvassing in the Mississippi Delta, and brave college students igniting a sit-in movement by simply asking for service at an all-white lunch counter in the Deep South. As a Harvard Law student, he carried Taylor Branch's *Parting the Waters*—an award-winning history of the civil rights movement—around with him and referred to it as "my story."[121] In the election's afterglow, where Obama represents, in the words of civil rights activist and Georgia congressman John Lewis, "what comes at the end of that bridge in Selma,"[122] it is easy to forget that the "Moses Generation," including Congressman Lewis, at first stood aloof from his candidacy.[123]

The reluctance of the civil rights generation to fully embrace Obama reflects the complexity of postwar black freedom struggles for racial and economic justice. Obama represented the cutting edge of a new era of "breakthrough politicians."[124] His improbable ascendance to the highest levels of America's political sphere has been interpreted as the very culmination of King's dream of multicultural democracy. Obama's victory triggered intraracial vertigo within the black community, as ancient powerbrokers, senior civil rights veterans, and corporate titans who were connected to the civil rights era struggled to maintain a sense of professional and political balance in the face of a watershed historical moment. With the aid of hindsight, it is easy to dismiss these stragglers as a chorus of tone-deaf critics hopelessly unaware of the historical ground shifting beneath them. But this is only partially true.

Perhaps candidate Obama's most audacious move with respect to his relationship to the history of the black freedom struggle came in March 2007. On the thirty-second anniversary of "Bloody Sunday" in Selma, Alabama, he dubbed himself a part of the "Joshua Generation." This phrase, in light of his subsequent election, took on historic dimensions. While the "Moses Generation" identified the path to the promised land, it would take a "Joshua Generation" to lead African Americans—and the rest of the nation for that matter—to the other side.[125] This was a risky gambit. Identifying himself at the forefront of an effort to complete the civil rights era's quest for racial justice seemed a brazen attempt to cast himself among the iconography of King, Malcolm, Carmichael, and other activists who marched, bled, and died for freedom's cause. On that day, Obama, according to writer David Remnick, "explicitly inserted himself in the time line of American racial politics."[126] As a presidential candidate, he positioned himself as both the contemporary embodiment of civil rights struggles for racial achievement *and* the future torchbearer to subsequent generations.

Obama's respect, admiration, and awe for the civil rights era—like his elevation of Lincoln—attests to the movement's enduring importance. In truth, however, civil rights legacies championed by Obama and embodied by the likes of John Lewis and countless others reveal only one side of a far more complex and at times troubling legacy. This includes a wide range of movements and voices that confronted American mythmaking, challenged the vision of the Founding Fathers, and sought to redefine long-standing democratic institutions. Black Power radicalism, no less than civil rights, provided the context for a transformed political and social landscape that would eventually catapult Obama into the White House.

Perhaps no writer more eloquently chronicled America's racial turmoil during the 1960s than James Baldwin. In his 1963 masterwork, *The Fire Next Time*, Baldwin openly fretted about the longevity of a society racked by racial violence, political terror, and social inequality. "Time catches up with kingdoms and crushes them, gets its teeth into doctrines and rends them," warned Baldwin. "Time reveals the foundations on which any kingdom rests and eats at those foundations, and it destroys doctrines by proving them untrue."[127] Several years later, in the wake of the assassinations of Malcolm X and Martin Luther King Jr. and amid proliferating domestic racial riots, Baldwin's words seemed prophetic. Since King's death, Baldwin confessed, "something has altered in me, something has gone away."[128] Ruminating on the national loss of faith and hope following King's assassination, Baldwin ruefully noted the historical revisions surrounding Malcolm X's memory. Malcolm's friends and enemies, his harshest critics and staunchest allies alike, Baldwin observed, "all claim him now."[129] It seemed the whole era was being recast through a haze of posthumous nostalgia that redefined leaders, events, and the movement's very meaning.

Smoothed of the rough edges Baldwin once found so profoundly gratifying, the civil rights era now neatly conforms to myths of national racial progress. But America's journey from Black Power to Barack Obama defies the unreliable narratives of linear democratic progress that have greeted Obama's extraordinary rise. Instead, the journey reflects the arduous road toward racial justice and reconciliation that was littered with as many false starts and betrayals as it was celebrated with improbable victories and climactic marches. The transition of this era from history to mythology has made the Age of Martin Luther King Jr. sacrosanct for politicians and pundits. At the same time, however, it has rendered its meaning far removed from America's contemporary political and racial reality. Baldwin's prophetic words remind us that the age rightfully remembered for King's towering leadership was also an Age of Malcolm X. "Malcolm," explained Baldwin, "was not a racist, not even when he thought he was."[130]

The civil rights movement's heroic period never followed a simplistic narrative arc that saw good triumph over evil, integration defeat Jim Crow, and national unity overcome ancient and bitter racial and sectional divisions. Instead, it careened and lurched, day by day, toward both remarkable victories and more incremental measures, all the while enduring unexpected setbacks and unanticipated crises. In the popular imagination, Black Power presented the movement with its greatest obstacle toward King's vision of a beloved community. But in truth, the two movements served as improbable collaborators and spirited combatants in a joint effort to fundamentally transform American democracy.

If Barack Obama's election permanently altered the aesthetics of American democracy, then the civil rights and Black Power era provided the historical context for this watershed moment. Perhaps the most eloquent valediction for Obama's victory comes posthumously from Frederick Douglass who, in the thrall of the Emancipation Proclamation's impending announcement, found himself momentarily bereft of words. It was not a day for speeches, Douglass asserted, but rather "[i]t is a day for poetry and song, a new song."[131] Similarly, Obama's election signals a new chapter in America's national political and racial saga.

During an April 6, 2009, address to the Turkish Parliament, President Obama used his first trip to a Muslim nation to meditate on democracy's evolutionary potential with respect to race. Noting that he was president of a nation that recently made it "difficult for a person who looked like me to vote," Obama embraced democracy's constantly evolving nature.[132] At the same time, Obama noted, America, like the Turks in regard to Armenian genocide and the events of 1915, also continued to grapple with the legacies of slavery and Jim Crow.

Obama's discussion of America's history of racial slavery in front of the Turkish Parliament was extraordinary for two reasons. First, it represented his fullest discussion of race and slavery as president. Second, the symbolism of an African American president identifying with a Muslim nation facing unresolved questions of ethnic and religious equality while referencing America's long history of racial divisions was nothing less than historic. In this sense, his racial identity, past experiences living in Indonesia, and candid assessments of America's racial past remind us that the international face of the United States, for the first time in history, is represented in the visage of a black man.[133]

April 29, 2009, represented the one hundredth day of the Obama administration. It also marked the anniversary of a darker chapter in American history. Seventeen years earlier, in the aftermath of a not-guilty verdict of officers accused of beating an unarmed black motorist named Rodney King, Los Angeles exploded in racially fueled civil disorder on a scale unseen since the 1960s. In the spring of 1992, smoldering fires and black plumes of smoke dotted parts of the city's landscape. This formed a portrait of urban decay and racial tensions that echoed the worst aspects of the 1960s. At the time, no one could have imagined that less than two decades later America's first black president would be holding a press conference commemorating his one hundredth day as commander in chief.

A poll taken several days before this press conference revealed something extraordinary: Most Americans found race relations progressing in a positive direction since Obama's election.[134] In this sense, his presidency has unleashed profoundly personal and political emotions in the national body politic. If civil rights marches, urban riots, and black militancy sparked a national dialogue on race during the 1960s that at times threatened to go down the slippery slope of racial hysteria, Obama's election has likewise triggered national contemplation over the very meaning of race and democracy in the twenty-first century. Although the future trajectory and ultimate destination of this sense of racial optimism is unknown, its very existence speaks to the politics of hope and racial reconciliation that Obama's election has unleashed in Americans of all backgrounds.[135]

ACKNOWLEDGMENTS

This book has benefitted from numerous conversations with family, friends, and colleagues over the past several years. Yohuru Williams has been an invaluable critic, friend, and colleague, whose own groundbreaking work has provided great inspiration. Rhonda Y. Williams remains a steadfast friend whose brilliant scholarship sets a high standard for historical integrity and analytical acuity. David Oshinsky's gracious invitation to deliver the Littlefield Lectures at the University of Texas allowed me a wonderful opportunity to visit Austin's thriving intellectual community of scholars and to present some of my work.

Sonia Sanchez, the extraordinary and iconic writer, poet, teacher, mentor, and human rights activist, remains a part of my extended family. Sonia's perseverance and ability to thrive under the most unenviable circumstances continues to inspire me and my work.

Many thanks to Wellington Nyangoni for his support and encouragement and to my former Brandeis University colleagues in Afro-American Studies: Ibrahim Sundiata, Faith Smith, and Mingus Mapps. Thanks as well to all of my colleagues in the history department. Dean Adam Jaffe also provided critical support.

Tufts University has enthusiastically welcomed me into its community. Special thanks to all of my new colleagues in the department of history, especially Howard Malchow and Jeanne Penvenne. Annette Lazzara and Margaret Casey have smoothed my transition immensely. Provost Jamshed Bharucha's commitment to professional excellence and a thriving university culture is inspirational. Dean Bob Sternberg's energy and enthusiasm for learning is infectious.

President Laurence Bacow exemplifies the model of a university leader as an active and engaged citizen, scholar, and administrator. Thanks as well to my research assistants, Ian Greaves and Molly Palmer, for all of their assistance. I am grateful to be part of the Tufts community.

Many thanks to the following colleagues and friends: Robin Kelley, Ben Vinson, Julian Agyman, Hasan Jeffries, Winston Grady-Willis, Lewis R. Gordon and Jane Gordon, Leonard Moore, Ed Linenthal, Ken Kusmer, Bettye Collier-Thomas, V. P. Franklin, Kenneth Kusmer, Robert Schneider, Elwood Watson, George White Jr., Donna Murch, Clarence Lang, Sundiata Cha-Jua, Rod Bush, Jeff Ogbar, Kent Germany, Jeanne Theoharis, Komozi Woodard, Robin D. G. Kelley, Michael Simanga, Jimmy Garrett, Fanon Wilkins, Hasan Jeffries, Scot Brown, Tracey K'Myer, Ernie Allen, John Bracey, Bill Strickland, Abdul Alkalimat, Dwayne Mack, Theresa Caldwell, and Tracy K'Meyer.

Manning Marable has been a generous colleague, collaborator, and friend, whose scholarship continues to provide inspiration. Tom Sugrue's latest book was published just in time, and he has been a good friend and colleague.

Since our first encounter in graduate school in Philadelphia, Juan and Stacey Floyd-Thomas have grown from friends into extended family whose incomparable intellectual energy and enthusiasm continues to sustain me.

As lead scholar for the Smithsonian's two-day Black Power Symposium in March 2009, sponsored by the Museum for African American History and Culture, I had the extraordinary opportunity to present some of the ideas presented in this book in earlier form. Lonnie Bunch, director of the museum, showed tremendous leadership and courage in leading this effort. John W. Franklin, Bettye J. Gardner, Marion Gill, Lopez Matthews, and the entire administration and staff of the Smithsonian proved to be brilliant and stalwart collaborators on this project. Thanks as well to the symposium's distinguished participants: Sonia Sanchez, Amiri and Amina Baraka, Michael Thelwell, Charles Cobb, Courtland Cox, Askia Muhammad Toure, Sylvia Hill, Frank Smith, Gregg Carr, James Turner, Howard Dodson, Rhonda Y. Williams, Lateefah Simon, Farah Jasmine Griffin, Johnetta Cole, Yohuru Williams, Ronald W. Walters, and Donna Brazile.

While I was putting the finishing touches on this book, I had the chance to spend a year at Harvard University's Charles Warren Center, where I worked on a biography of Stokely Carmichael. Evelyn Brooks Higginbotham, one of the Warren Center's coconveners, proved to be the consummate intellectual conductor, shepherding the year with grace and wit. Ken Mack's good humor and intelligence provided the perfect complement for the center's theme of "Race and Law in the Making of the Long Civil Rights Movement." Thanks to all the other fellows, especially Zoe Burkholder, Tom Guglielmo, and Matt Countryman. Thanks as well to the center's great administrative staff: Arthur Patton-Hock and Larissa Kennedy.

John Stauffer provided a model of intellectual acuity and scholarly diligence matched by a generous personality. Vince Brown and Tommie Shelby are examples of unassuming intelligence and the light touch.

My agent, Gloria Loomis, remains not only a brilliant professional ally but a good friend as well.

Lara Heimert's passion for publishing high-quality works of nonfiction made Basic Books a perfect home for this as well as future projects. Lara's critical eye for structure and organization enhanced the final product immeasurably. I am grateful for Brandon Proia's expert assistance with the manuscript in its final stages.

My friends and family contributed to this project through conversations, e-mails, and general support. On this score I owe a debt of gratitude to Darryl Toler, Larry Hughes, Mark Barnes, Sal and Jess Mena, Kerith, Dawn, and Caitlin Joseph, Michael and Natalie Williams, Femi Vaughan, Chris and Ina Pisani, and Catarina da Silva. A special thanks to Astrid for everything.

My mother, Germaine Joseph, remains the most important person in my personal, intellectual, and professional development. This book is dedicated to her.

NOTES

INTRODUCTION

1. Thomas J. Sugrue, *Sweet Land of Liberty: The Forgotten Struggle for Civil Rights in the North* (New York: Random House, 2008).

2. http://www.essence.com/news_entertainment/news/articles/air_force_one_essence _exlcusive/?xid=061709-emailpitch-potusnaacp.

3. http://www,washingtonpost.com/wp-dyn/content/article/2009/07/17/AR200907 1701596_pf.html.

4. *New York Times*, July 17, 2009, p. A14, http://www.washingtonpost.com/wp-dyn/ content/article/2009/07/16/AR2009071601929.html.

5. Adam Serwer, "The President and the NAACP," July 17, 2009, *Tapped: The Group Blog of the American Prospect*, http://www.prospect.org/csnc/blogs/tapped_archive?month =07&year=2009&base_name=the_president_and_the_naacp#comments.

6. Peniel E. Joseph, "Our National Postracial Hangover," *The Chronicle Review*, August 7, 2009, p. B6.

7. Fox News commentator Juan Williams mentioned, http://ta-nehisicoates.theatlantic .com/archives/2009/01/are_you_serious.php.

CHAPTER 1

1. Historian Van Gosse has issued an insightful criticism against narratives of the 1960s that frame the era's heyday as being largely over after King's assassination. Gosse's brilliant panoramic essay argues for the historical presence of a multicultural New Left comprised of a mélange of groups (African Americans, whites, students, environmentalists, feminists, gays and lesbians, peace activists, etc.) missing from the historical narrative of the New Left. Although I agree with Gosse's emphasis on a heterogeneous New Left that did not begin and end with the legendary Students for a Democratic Society, I see the Black Liberation Movement as central to radical

activism in the United States and internationally during much of the postwar era. From this vantage point, civil rights and Black Power are not simply a part of a heterogeneous New Left. Rather, New Left groups pivot around the ebbs and flows of a heterogeneous black movement that stretched from Birmingham, Alabama, to Bandung, Indonesia. See Van Gosse, "A Movement of Movements: The Definition and Periodization of the New Left," in Jean-Christophe Agnew and Roy Rosenzweig, eds., *A Companion to Post-1945 America* (Malden, MA: Blackwell Publishers, 2002), pp. 277–302. See also Peniel E. Joseph, "Black Liberation Without Apology: Rethinking the Black Power Movement," *The Black Scholar* 31, nos. 3–4 (Fall/Winter 2001): 2–17; ed., *The Black Power Movement: Rethinking the Civil Rights-Black Power Era* (New York: Routledge, 2006); and *Waiting Til the Midnight Hour: A Narrative History of Black Power in America* (New York: Owl Books, 2007); and Wesley C. Hogan, *Many Minds, One Heart: SNCC's Dream For a New America* (Chapel Hill: University of North Carolina Press, 2007).

2. James Smethurst, *The Black Arts Movement: Literary Nationalism in the 1960s and 1970s* (Chapel Hill: University of North Carolina Press, 2005); Peniel E. Joseph, *Waiting 'Til the Midnight Hour* and *The Black Power Movement*.

3. For example, see Timothy Tyson, *Radio Free Dixie: Robert F. Williams and the Roots of Black Power* (Chapel Hill: University of North Carolina Press, 1999); Komozi Woodard, *A Nation Within a Nation: Amiri Baraka (Le Roi Jones) & Black Power Politics* (Chapel Hill: University of North Carolina Press, 1999); Yohuru Williams, *Black Politics/White Power: Civil Rights, Black Power, and the Black Panthers in New Haven* (New York: Brandywine Press, 2000); Joseph, "Black Liberation Without Apology"; Barbara Ransby, *Ella Baker and the Black Freedom Movement: A Radical Democratic Vision* (Chapel Hill: University of North Carolina Press, 2003); Lance Hill, *The Deacons for Defense: Armed Resistance and the Civil Rights Movement* (Chapel Hill: University of North Carolina Press, 2004); Scot Brown, *Fighting For Us: Maulana Karenga, the US Organization, and Black Cultural Nationalism* (New York: New York University Press, 2003); Jeffrey O. G. Ogbar, *Black Power: Radical Politics and African American Identity* (Baltimore: Johns Hopkins University Press, 2004); Christopher B. Strain, *Pure Fire: Self-Defense as Activism in the Civil Rights Era* (Athens: University of Georgia Press, 2005); Jeanne F. Theoharis and Komozi Woodard, eds., *Freedom North: Black Freedom Struggles Outside the South, 1940–1980* (New York: Palgrave Macmillan, 2003); and *Groundwork: Local Black Freedom Movements in America* (New York: New York University Press, 2005); and Smethurst, *The Black Arts Movement*.

4. Jacqueline Dowd Hall, "The Long Civil Rights Movement and the Political Uses of the Past," *Journal of American History* 91 (March 2005): 1233–1263; Nikhil Pal Singh, *Black Is a Country: Race and the Unfinished Struggle for Democracy* (Cambridge, MA: Harvard University Press, 2004). I first used the term "Long Black Power Movement" in the introduction to my edited anthology. See "Toward A Historiography of the Black Power Movement" in Joseph, *The Black Power Movement*, 4–6. See also Theoharis and Woodard, *Freedom North and Groundwork*.

5. Theoharis and Woodward, *Freedom North and Groundwork*; Hall, "The Long Civil Rights Movement and the Political Uses of the Past."

6. Joseph, *Waiting 'Til the Midnight Hour*, pp. 1–5; Carol Anderson, *Eyes Off the Prize: The United Nations and the African American Struggle for Human Rights, 1944–1955* (Cambridge: Cambridge University Press, 2003).

7. Ransby, *Ella Baker and the Black Freedom Movement*; Thomas Sugrue, *Sweet Land of Liberty: The Forgotten Struggle for Civil Rights in the North* (New York: Random House, 2008).

8. See Gerald Horne, *Black and Red: W. E. B. Du Bois and the African American Response to the Cold War, 1944–1963* (Albany: State University of New York Press, 1986); *Communist Front? The Civil Rights Congress, 1946–1956* (Rutherford, NJ: Fairleigh Dickinson University Press, 1988); *Black Liberation and Red Scare: Ben Davis and the Communist Party* (Newark: University of Delaware Press, 1994); and *Race Woman: The Lives of Shirley Graham Du Bois* (New York: New York University Press, 2000); Anderson, *Eyes Off the Prize*; Mary L. Dudziak, *Cold War Civil Rights: Race and the Image of American Democracy* (Princeton, NJ: Princeton University Press, 2000); Martha Biondi, *To Stand and Fight: The Struggle For Civil Rights in Postwar New York City* (Cambridge, MA: Harvard University Press, 2003); Azza Layton, *International Politics and Civil Rights Policies in the United States, 1941–1960* (Cambridge: Cambridge University Press, 2000); Bill V. Mullen and James Smethurst, eds., *Left of the Color Line: Race, Radicalism, and Twentieth Century Literature of the United States* (Chapel Hill: University of North Carolina Press, 2003).

9. I have described this new scholarship as "Black Power Studies." See Peniel E. Joseph, "Black Liberation Without Apology: Reconceptualizing the Black Power Movement," and all the essays in special two volume issues of *The Black Scholar* 31, No. 3–4 (Fall/Winter 2001) and 32, No. 1 (Spring 2002). See also Peniel E. Joseph, ed., *The Black Power Movement: Rethinking the Civil Rights and Black Power Eras* (New York: Routledge, 2006).

10. Todd Gitlin, *The Sixties: Years of Hope, Days of Rage* (New York: Bantam Books, 1989); Maurice Isserman and Michael Kazin, *America Divided: The Civil War of the 1960s* (New York: Oxford University Press, 2000); Hugh Pearson, *The Shadow of the Panther: Huey P. Newton and the Price of Black Power in America* (Reading, MA: Addison-Wesley, 1994); Gilbert Jonas, *Freedom's Sword: The NAACP and the Struggle Against Racism in America, 1909–1969* (New York: Routledge, 2005).

11. This perspective is best reflected in Taylor Branch's mesmerizing first two volumes of the movement, *Parting the Waters: America in the King Years, 1954–1963* (New York: Touchstone, 1988) and *Pillar of Fire: America in the King Years, 1963–1965* (New York: Touchstone, 1998); David Garrow's Pulitzer Prize-winning *Bearing the Cross: Martin Luther King, Jr. and the Southern Christian Leadership Conference* (New York: Quill, 1987); and Adam Fairclough's critically acclaimed *To Redeem the Soul of America: The Southern Christian Leadership Conference & Martin Luther King, Jr.* (Athens: University of Georgia Press, 2001).

12. Michael Eric Dyson, *I May Not Get There With You: The True Martin Luther King, Jr.* (New York: Basic Books, 2000); Thomas Jackson, *From Civil Rights to Human Rights: Martin Luther King, Jr. and the Struggle for Economic Justice* (Philadelphia: University of Pennsylvania Press, 2007); and Michael K. Honey, *Going Down Jericho Road* (New York: W. W. Norton & Co., 2007). Also see Garrow, *Bearing the* Cross; and Branch, *Parting the Waters*; *Pillar of Fire*; and *At Canaan's Edge: America in the King Years, 1965–1968* (New York: Simon & Schuster, 2006).

13. Peniel E. Joseph, *Waiting 'Til the Midnight Hour*; and Sugrue, *Sweet Land of Liberty*.

14. Joseph, *Waiting 'Til the Midnight Hour*.

15. *Ibid.*, pp. 18–19.

16. Branch, *Parting the Waters*. Branch's second volume, *Pillar of Fire*, pays considerable attention to Malcolm, but starts only in 1962.

17. Joseph, *Waiting 'Til the Midnight Hour*.

18. Branch, *Parting the Waters*, pp. 810–811.

19. George Breitman, ed., *Malcolm X Speaks* (New York: Pathfinder Press, 1989), p. 16.

20. Malcolm X and Haley, *The Autobiography of Malcolm X*, p. 438.

21. My discussion of Nina Simone is indebted to the brilliant work of historian Ruth Feldstein. See Ruth Feldstein, "'I Don't Trust You Anymore': Nina Simone, Culture, and Black Activism in the 1960s," *The Journal of American History* 91, no. 4 (March 2005), http://www.historycooperative.org/journal/jah/91.4/feldstein.htm (Apr. 6, 2005).

22. Nina Simone with Stephen Cleary, *I Put a Spell On You: The Autobiography of Nina Simone* (New York: Da Capo Press, 2003), p. 95.

23. Joseph, *Waiting 'Til the Midnight Hour*, p. 146.

24. Clayborne Carson, *In Struggle: SNCC and the Black Awakening of the 1960s* (Cambridge, MA: Harvard University Press, 1981); Stokely Carmichael with Ekwueme Michael Thelwell, *Ready For Revolution: The Life and Struggles of Stokely Carmichael* (Kwame Ture) (New York: Scribner, 2003); Joseph, *Waiting 'Til the Midnight Hour*.

25. Federal Bureau of Investigation Kwame Ture (Stokely Carmichael) File. FBIKT 100–446080–298, "Stokely Carmichael," June 7, 1967, pp. 1–6.

CHAPTER 2

1. *Life*, March 20, 1964.

2. Louis Lomax, *When the Word is Given: A Report on Elijah Muhammad, Malcolm X, and the Black Muslim World* (Toronto: Signet Books, 1964), p. 24.

3. Tony Martin, *Race First The Ideological and Organizational Struggles of Marcus Garvey and the Universal Improvement Association* (Dover: First Majority Press, 1986); Ula Taylor, *The Veiled Garvey: The Life and Times of Amy Jacques Garvey* (Chapel Hill: University of North Carolina Press, 2002); Steven Hahn, *A Nation Under Our Feet: Black Political Struggles in the Rural South from Slavery to the Great Migration* (Cambridge, MA: Harvard University Press, 2004); Mary G. Rolinson, *Grassroots Garveyism: The Universal Negro Improvement Association in the Rural South, 1920–1927* (Chapel Hill: University of North Carolina Press, 2007); Bobby Hill, ed., *The Marcus Garvey and Universal Negro Improvement Association Papers* (Berkeley: 1983–2006). See also Jeffrey B. Perry, *Hubert Harrison: The Voice of Harlem Radicalism, 1883–1918* (New York: Columbia University Press, 2009).

4. Malcolm X and Alex Haley, *The Autobiography of Malcolm X* (New York: Ballantine Books, 1998), pp. 1–9.

5. Malcolm X FBI File. Hereafter referred to at FBIMX. FBIMX 100–399321–16, "Minister Malcolm X," May 23, 1955, p. 4.

6. William W. Sales, Jr., *From Civil Rights to Black Liberation: Malcolm X and the Organization of Afro-American Unity* (Boston: South End Press, 1994), p. 33.

7. Feruccio Gambino, "The Transgression of a Laborer: Malcolm X in the Wilderness of America," *Radical History Review* 55 (1993): 20–21.

8. Gambino, *The Transgression of a Laborer*, pp. 7–31.

9. *Saturday Evening Post*, September 12, 1964, in FBIMX 100–399321, page number not recorded.

10. "Malcolm K. Little," April 30, 1954, pp. 5–11 in FBIMX 100–399321–7.

11. FBIMX 100–399321–16, "Malcolm Little," May 23, 1955, p. 15.

12. FBIMX 100–399321–19, "Malcolm Little," April 23, 1957, pp. 1–73.

13. Haley, *The Autobiography of Malcolm X*, pp. 230–289; Peter Goldman, *The Death and Life of Malcolm X* (New York: Harper & Row, 1973), pp. 49–91; Bruce Perry, *Malcolm X* (Barrytown, NY: Station Hill Press, 1992), pp. 160–166, 174–186; Peniel E. Joseph, *Waiting 'Til the Midnight Hour: A Narrative History of Black Power in America* (New York: Owl Books, 2007); Taylor Branch, *Pillar of Fire: America in the King Years, 1963–1965* (New York: Simon and Schuster, 1998), p. 15.

14. FBIMX 100–399321–21, "Malcolm Little," April 30, 1958, p. 24.

15. See Goldman, *The Death and Life of Malcolm X*, pp. 55–65; and Benjamin Karim, *Remembering Malcolm* (New York: Ballantine Books, 1995), pp. 45–46; and *End of World White Supremacy: Four Speeches By Malcolm X* (New York: Arcade Publishing, 1971), pp. 2–6, where he claims that Malcolm conflated Johnson's name. In his autobiography, Malcolm refers to him as "Brother Johnson Hinton." See Malcolm X and Haley, *The Autobiography of Malcolm X*, p. 257; Perry, *Malcolm X*, pp. 164–166, 437; FBIMX 100–399321 (Part 3), "Malcolm Little," April 30, 1958, p. 29.

16. Malcolm X and Haley, *The Autobiography of Malcolm X*, p. 255.

17. FBIMX 100–399321, (Part 3), "Malcolm Little," April 30, 1958, p. 79, quoting Malcolm X from *Pittsburgh Courier*, November 9, 1957; Johnson was awarded $70,000. Perry, *Malcolm X*, p. 166.

18. Malcolm X and Haley, *The Autobiography of Malcolm X*, p. 256.

19. See Timothy B. Tyson, *Radio Free Dixie: Robert F. Williams and the Roots of Black Power* (Chapel Hill: University of North Carolina Press, 1998); Lance Hill, *The Deacons for Defense: Armed Resistance and the Civil Rights Movement* (Chapel Hill: University of North Carolina Press, 2004); Christopher B. Strain, *Pure Fire: Self-Defense as Activism in the Civil Rights Era* (Athens: University of Georgia Press, 2005); Simon Wendt, "The Roots of Black Power?: Armed Resistance and the Radicalization of the Civil Rights Movement," in Peniel E. Joseph, ed., *The Black Power Movement: Rethinking the Civil Rights and Black Power Era* (New York: Routledge, 2006), pp. 145–165.; and Joseph, *Waiting 'Til the Midnight Hour*.

20. Thomas F. Jackson, *From Civil Rights to Human Rights: Martin Luther King, Jr. and the Struggle for Economic Justice* (Philadelphia: University of Pennsylvania Press, 2006); and Michael Honey, *Going Down Jericho Road: The Memphis Strike, Martin Luther King's Last Campaign* (New York: W. W. Norton, 2007).

21. Malcolm X and Haley, *The Autobiography of Malcolm X*, pp. 238–239.

22. Ibid., p. 240.

23. Ibid., p. 241.

24. Goldman, *The Death of Malcolm X*, p. 88.

25. Rebeccah Welch, "Black Art and Activism in Postwar New York, 1950–1965." PhD diss., New York University, 2002, p. 2.; Joseph, *Waiting 'Til the Midnight Hour*, pp. 14–15.

26. Branch, *Parting the Waters: America in the King Years, 1954–1963* (New York: Touchstone Books, 1988), pp. 592–593.

27. Joseph, *Waiting Til the Midnight Hour*, p. 123; Manning Marable, *Living Black History: How Reimagining the African-American Past Can Remake America's Racial Future* (New York: Basic Civitas, 2006), pp. 149–161.

28. *Pittsburgh Courier*, December 22, 1956, p. 6 in FBIMX 100–399321-A.

29. *Pittsburgh Courier*, December 15, 1956, p. 6 in FBIMX 100–399321-A.

30. *Los Angeles Herald-Dispatch*, February 13, 1958 in FBIMX 100–399321-A.

31. Hakim Jamal, *From the Dead Level* (New York: Warner Books, 1973), pp. 188–189.

32. FBIMX 100–399321–21, "Malcolm Little," April 30, 1958, p. 27.

33. Joseph, *Waiting 'Til the Midnight Hour*, pp. 53–63.

34. *Los Angeles Herald-Dispatch*, March 27, 1958, in FBIMX 100–399321-A.

35. *Pittsburgh Courier*, August 2, 1958, p. 14 in FBIMX 100–399321-A.

36. *The Miami Times*, September 27, 1958, p. 11.

37. Invitation to Abyssinian Baptist Church, FBIMX (Part 3), "Malcolm Little," April 30, 1958, pp. 74–75, citing *Los Angeles Herald Dispatch*, August 8, 1957; Karim, *The End of World White Supremacy*, pp. 14–15; Goldman, *The Death and Life of Malcolm X*, p. 68; for competition between Malcolm and Powell see Goldman, op cit., pp. 134–135; Perry, *Malcolm X*, pp. 302–304; and Branch, *Pillar of Fire*, p. 96.

38. *Los Angeles Herald Dispatch*, April 3, 1958, p. 8; April 12, 1958, p. 8; April 17, 1958, in FBIMX 100–399321-A.

39. FBIMX 100–399321 (Part 21) Sub A, *Pittsburgh Courier*, January 25, 1958, and *Los Angeles Herald Dispatch*, February 13, 1958; FBIMX 100–399321 (Part 4) Memo, July 2, 1958.

40. FBIMX 100–39321(Part 4), Malcolm Little, October 17, 1958, pp. 1–4; November 19, 1958, pp. 9–10; Jamal, *From the Dead Level: Malcolm X and Me,* pp. 94–122.

41. Brenda Gayle Plummer, *Rising Wind: Black Americans and U.S. Foreign Affairs, 1935–1960* (Chapel Hill: University of North Carolina Press, 1996); Penny Von Eschen, *Race Against Empire: Black Americans and Anticolonialism, 1937–1957* (Ithaca, NY: Cornell University Press, 1997); and *Satchmo Blows Up the World: Jazz Ambassadors Play the Cold War* (Cambridge, MA: Harvard University Press, 2005); Mary Dudziak, *Cold War Civil Rights: Race and the Image of American Democracy* (Princeton, NJ: Princeton University Press, 2000); Thomas Borstelmann, *The Cold War and the Color Line: American Race Relations in the Global Arena* (Cambridge, MA: Harvard University Press, 2001); James H. Meriwether, *Proudly We Can Be Africans: Black Americans and Africa, 1935–1961* (Chapel Hill: University of North Carolina Press, 2002).

42. Joseph, *Waiting 'Til the Midnight Hour*, pp. 18–19. Ghana's recruitment efforts rescued one exceptionally high-profile leader from political oblivion. W. E. B. Du Bois, two years before his death, expatriated to Ghana to start his proposed *Encyclopedia Africana* at Nkrumah's personal request. The long-delayed project—it had been conceived of as the "Encyclopedia of the Negro"—was planned as a multivolume history that would trace the black presence on several continents and in the Caribbean. Perpetually denied funding for this am-

bitious venture, Du Bois, at ninety-three, became a citizen of Ghana and embarked on his lifelong dream of completing the encyclopedia. See David Levering Lewis, *W. E.B. Du Bois: The Fight for Equality and the American Century, 1919–1963* (New York: Henry Holt, 2000), pp. 389, 442–449.

43. Kevin Gaines, *American Africans in Ghana*.

44. *New York Amsterdam News*, December 28, 1957, pp. 1, 3. See also James H. Meriwether, *Proudly We Can Be Called Africans: Black Americans and Africa, 1935–1961* (Chapel Hill: University of North Carolina Press, 2002).

45. *New York Amsterdam News*, August 2, 1958, p. 1; *Baltimore Washington Afro-American*, August 2, 1958.

46. FBIMX 100–399321 (Part 4), Memo, July 16, 1959, p. 1.

47. FBIMX 100–399321 (Part 4), Memo, July 21, 1959, pp. 1–20.

48. Louis Lomax, *To Kill a Black Man* (Los Angeles: Holloway House, 1968), pp. 65–76.

49. *Pittsburgh Courier*, August 15, 1959, in FBIMX 100–399321-A.

50. Ibid.

51. Ibid.

52. Ibid.

53. Marable, *Living Black History*, p. 153; FBIMX 100–399321 (Part 21), *Pittsburgh Courier*, August 15, 1959.

54. *Muhammad Speaks*, November 22, 1963, p. 12.

55. Tyson, *Radio Free Dixie*, pp. 146–148.

56. Scholar Mary Helen Washington offers a penetrating analysis of black women's political and literary radicalism during the 1950s. See Mary Helen Washington, "Alice Childress, Lorraine Hansberry, and Claudia Jones: Black Women Write the Popular Front," in Bill V. Mullen and James Smethurst, eds., *Left of the Color Line: Race, Radicalism, and Twentieth Century Literature of the United States* (Chapel Hill: University of North Carolina Press, 2003), pp. 183–204; see also Ruth Feldstein, "'I Don't Trust You Anymore': Nina Simone, Culture, and Black Activism in the 1960s," *The Journal of American History* 91, no. 4 (March 2005): 1349–1379; Kevin Gaines, "From Center to Margin: Internationalism and the Origins of Black Feminism," in Russ Castronovo and Dana D. Nelson, eds., *Materializing Democracy: Toward a Revitalized Cultural Politics* (Durham, NC: Duke University Press, 2002), pp. 294–313. Black lesbian feminist Audre Lorde received intellectual mentoring from the Harlem Writers Guild in the early 1950s. See Alexis De Veaux, *Warrior Poet: A Biography of Audre Lorde* (New York: W. W. Norton & Company, 2004), pp. 38–39.

57. Historian Komozi Woodard argues that Paul Robeson's elaboration on W. E. B. Du Bois's notion of black culture inspired future Black Arts and Black Power activists, most notably the young Le Roi Jones. See Komozi Woodard, "Amiri Baraka, the Congress of African People and Black Power Politics: From the 1961 United Nations Protest to the 1972 Gary Convention," in Joseph, The *Black Power Movement*, pp. 55–77.

58. Of course Black Power nationalists were among *A Raisin in the Sun*'s and Hansberry's most vociferous critics. Harold Cruse's dismissive analysis of Hansberry in his 1967 classic, *The Crisis of the Negro Intellectual*, served as a capstone to a discourse imposed by Cold War liberals

who defined the play and Hansberry's politics on their own terms and set the stage for a hopelessly distorted debate. See Ben Keppel, *The Work of Democracy: Ralphe Bunche, Kenneth B. Clark, Lorraine Hansberry, and the Cultural Politics of Race* (Cambridge, MA: Harvard University Press, 1995), pp. 177–214 and 227–229. Over twenty-five years later, former critics—including Amiri Baraka—would issue reevaluations, declaring the play to be on "the cutting edge" of the black movement's "class and ideological struggles." See Robert Nemiroff, "Introduction," to Lorraine Hansberry, *A Raisin in the Sun* (New York: Modern Library Edition, 1995), p. xx.

59. Joseph, *Waiting 'Til the Midnight Hour*, pp. 26–28.

60. Marable, *Living Black History*, p. 153; FBIMX 100–399321 (Part 21), *Pittsburgh Courier*, August 15, 1959.

61. *Muhammad Speaks* also generated significant amounts of income. Members hawked copies on urban street corners in an effort to meet demanding sales quotas. Desperately competitive, bow-tie-wearing Muslim entrepreneurs sank or swam based on the number of papers they sold every week, which they had to pay for in advance in bundles of fifty newspapers. Black Muslims earned or lost income in accordance with the *Messenger*'s frugally tough discipline that denied them credit. High sales figures were rewarded with fleeting fame in the pages of *Muhammad Speaks*, while slackers were verbally chided and at times beaten by Muslim enforcers. For hundreds of thousands of readers unaware of the pressures to meet sales quotas or the punishments doled out to those who didn't, *Muhammad Speaks* offered detailed coverage of the era's unfolding events by employing a skillful group of journalists, including many unaffiliated with the *Nation*. The paper's coverage of Africa was particularly informative, offering insight into revolutionary movements breaking out all over the continent. Perry, *Malcolm X*, pp. 220–221; Branch, *Pillar of Fire*, p. 260; Karim, *Remembering Malcolm*, pp. 153–154. See also Von Eschen, *Race Against Empire*, pp. 173–174 and James Edward Smethurst, *The Black Arts Movement: Literary Nationalism in the 1960s and 1970s* (Chapel Hill: University of North Carolina Press, 2005), pp. 181–183.

62. "Malcolm K. Little," May 17, 1960, pp. 1–58 in FBIMX 100–399321–40 (Part 5).

63. *Los Angeles Herald Dispatch*, January 28, 1960, March 17, 1960, and *Pittsburgh Courier*, March 11, 1961, in FBIMX 100–399321–A.

64. C. Eric Lincoln, *The Black Muslims in America* (Grand Rapids, MI: Eerdman's Press, 1994), p. 65.

65. *New Pittsburgh Courier*, October 29, 1960, p. 2.

66. *New Pittsburgh Courier*, March 11, 1961, p. 9.

67. *New Pittsburgh Courier*, February 4, 1961, p. 10.

68. *Baltimore Evening-Sun*, March 29, 1962.

69. *New York Times*, September 20, 1960, p. 1.

70. Rosemari Mealy, *Fidel and Malcolm X: Memories of a Meeting* (Melbourne: Ocean Press, 1993), p. 42.

71. *New York Amsterdam News*, September 24, 1960, p. 34.

72. FBIMX 100–399321 (Part 6), "Malcolm K. Little," November 17, 1960, p. 20.

73. Van Gosse, *Where the Boys Are: Cuba, Cold War America and the Making of a New Left* (London: Verso, 1993), p. 151.

74. *New York Times*, September 20, 1960, p. 16; September 21, 1960, p. 17.

75. William Worthy, "Writer Sees No Need to Stay Out of Cuba," *The Afro-American*, October 8, 1960, p. 1.

76. Maya Angelou, *The Heart of a Woman* (New York: Bantam Books, 1997), p. 111.

77. *The Baltimore Washington Afro-American*, October 1, 1960, pp. 1, 9; *New York Amsterdam News*, October 1, 1960, p. 35; Worthy, "Writer Sees No Need to Stay Out of Cuba," p. 1.

78. *New Pittsburgh Courier*, October 15, 1960, p. 3.

79. John Henrik Clarke, "The New Afro-American Nationalism," *Freedomways* 1, no. 3 (Fall 1961): 285–295.

80. *New York Amsterdam News* (Brooklyn Edition), August 13, 1960, p. 19; August 27, 1960, p. 19.

81. *New York Amsterdam News*, August 6, 1960, p. 4; September 17, pp. 1, 11; October, 1960, pp. 1, 35; and October 22, 1960, pp. 1, 35.

82. Angelou, *The Heart of a Woman*, pp. 169–180.

83. Plummer, *Rising Wind*, p. 282.

84. Joseph, *Waiting 'Til the Midnight Hour*, p. 42.

85. Ibid., p. 43.

86. Ibid., p. 44.

87. Farah Jasmine Griffin, "'Ironies of the Saint': Malcolm X, Black Women, and the Price of Protection," in Bettye Collier-Thomas and V. P. Franklin, eds., *Sisters in the Struggle: African-American Women in the Civil Rights-Black Power Movement* (New York: New York University Press, 2001), pp. 214–229.

88. *New York Times*, March 2, 1961, pp. 1, 17.

89. Ibid., p. 17.

90. *New Pittsburgh Courier*, Sep. 16, 1961, p. 3, and October 7, 1961, p. 17.

91. *New York Amsterdam News*, April 28, 1962, pp. 1, 3.

92. Joseph, *Waiting 'Til the Midnight Hour*, pp. 63–64; Branch, *Pillar of Fire*.

93. Joseph, *Waiting 'Til the Midnight Hour*, p. 64.

94. *New York Mirror*, June 20, 1962, p. 8 in FBIMX 100–399321-A.

95. Joseph, *Waiting 'Til the Midnight Hour*, pp. 66–67; 1962 proved to be a particularly trying year for the NOI with regards to legal trials. Malcolm testified in November in Buffalo during the trial of NOI members. See *New York Amsterdam News*, November 17, 1962, pp. 1–2.

96. Branch, *Parting the Waters*, pp. 738–745.

97. *Chicago Daily Defender*, February 25, 1963, p. 17; February 19, 1963, p. 2; *Chicago Defender*, February 16, 1963, p.1.

98. *Daily Tar Heel*, p. 1 in FBIMX 100–399321-A.

99. *Buffalo Evening News*, April 25, 1963, in FBIMX 100–399321-A.

100. *Chicago Daily Defender*, June 11, 1963, p. 9.

101. FBIMX 100–399321 (Part 8), Memo, May 13, 1963, pp. 1–2.

102. *New York Herald Tribune*, May 10, 1963, p. 10 in FBIMX 100–399321-A.

103. *The Evening Star*, May 10, 1963, p. c-16 in FBIMX 100–399321-A, and Joseph, *Waiting 'Til the Midnight Hour*, p. 77.

104. FBIMX 100–399321-A, UPI "Black Muslims," May 10, 1963.

105. Lomax, *When the Word is Given*, p. 74.

106. *New York Times*, May 10, 1963, p. 9 in NYFBIMX 105–8999–3623 (Part 50).

107. *New York Times*, May 17, 1963, p. 14 in NYFBIMX 105–8999–3628, and *New York Post*, May 19, 1963, p. 7 (magazine) in NYFBIMX 105–8999–3629; *Chicago Defender*, May 25–31, 1963, p. 17 in NYFBIMX 105–899–3607 (Part 50); Joseph, *Waiting 'Til the Midnight Hour*, p. 77.

108. *Chicago Defender*, May 25, 1963, p. 9. Kennedy noted Malcolm's growing presence on the national scene. In an exchange with reporters about the controversy over the government's awarding of defense contracts to build the new TFX fighter plane, Kennedy remarked that, "We have had an interesting six months . . . with the TFX and now we are going to have his brother Malcolm for the next six." See *Chicago Daily Defender*, June 5, 1963, p. 13.

109. *New York Times*, May 10, 1963, pp. 1, 14.

110. *Chicago Defender*, June 1, 1963, p. 2.

111. *Chicago Defender*, June 1, 1963, p. 8.

112. Ibid.

113. *Muhammad Speaks*, June 7, 1963, pp. 11–12.

114. FBIMX 100–399321 (Part 9), Airtel, May 15, 1963, p. 1; Perry, *Malcolm X*, p. 210.

115. *The Militant*, April 29, 1963, p. 3 in FBIMX 100–399321-A.

116. *Muhammad Speaks*, November 22, 1963, pp. 11–15.

117. *Detroit News*, October 24, 1963, p. 6A in FBIMX 100–399321-A.

118. *New York Times*, February 26, 1963, p. 3; *Muhammad Speaks*, March 18, 1963, pp. 3–4.

119. Branch, *Pillar of Fire*, pp. 16–20.

120. *Muhammad Speaks*, July 19, 1963, p. 21.

121. *New York Herald Tribune*, June 30, 1963, p. 6.

122. *Philadelphia Evening Bulletin*, July 1, 1963, p. 3 in FBIMX 100–399321-A.

123. *Muhammad Speaks*, June 7, 1963, pp. 1, 3.

124. Joseph, *Waiting 'Til the Midnight Hour*, p. 75.

125. UPI, "Negro March," August 13, 1963 in FBI 100–399321-A.

126. Branch, *Parting the Waters*, p. 874.

127. *Chicago Daily Defender*, October 10, 1963, p. A28.

128. *Muhammad Speaks*, October 25, 1963, p. 4 in FBIMX 100–399321-A.

129. *Young Socialist*, December 1963–January 1964, p. 3 in FBIMX 100–399321-A; *Muhammad Speaks*, October 25, 1963, p. 4.

130. *Muhammad Speaks*, November 8, 1963, p. 6.

131. Joseph, *Waiting 'Til the Midnight Hour*, p. 210.

132. Joseph, *Waiting 'Til the Midnight Hour*, pp. 88–92; *Chicago Daily Defender*, Nov. 21, 1963, p. 16.

133. Thomas J. Sugrue, *Sweet Land of Liberty: The Forgotten Struggle for Civil Rights in the North* (New York: Random House, 2008), pp. 400–448.

134. Karim, *The End of White World Supremacy*, pp. 121–148.

135. Ibid., p. 145.

136. Ibid., p. 144.

137. *New York Times*, December 5, 1963, p. 22.

138. *New York Times*, June 25, 1963, p. 13.

139. Joseph, *Waiting 'Til the Midnight Hour*, p. 77; *New York Amsterdam News*, July 5, 1963, in NYFBIMX 105–8999–3660 (Part 50).

140. *New York Times*, March 9, 1964, pp. 1, 42 in FBIMX 100–399321-A.

141. Ibid.

142. *New York Times*, March 5, 1964, p. 39 in NYFBIMX 105–8999–4190.

143. Joseph, *Waiting 'Til the Midnight Hour*, pp. 95–97; Branch, *Pillar of Fire*.

144. *New York Times*, March 9, 1964, pp. 1, 42 in FBIMX 100–399321-A.

145. Ibid.

146. Ibid.

147. *National Guardian*, March 12, 1964, p. 4 in FBIMX 100–399321-A.

148. *New York Times*, March 13, 1964, p. 20 in FBIMX 100–399321-A.

149. *The Militant*, April 1, 1964, in FBIMX 100–399321-A.

150. *Newsweek*, March 23, 1964, p. 32 in NYFBIMX 105–8999–4251.

151. *Progressive Labor*, May 20, 1964, in FBIMX 100–399321-A; Joseph, *Waiting 'Til the Midnight Hour*.

152. *The Militant*, April 1, 1964, in FBIMX 100–399321-A.

153. *New York Herald Tribune*, March 15, 1964, p. 31 in NYFBIMX 105–8999–4172.

154. *New York Journal American*, March 13, 1964, p. 6 in NYFBIMX 105–8999–4233.

155. *New York Times*, March 15, 1964, p. 46 in FBIMX 100–399321-A.

156. *Newsweek*, March 23, 1964, p. 32 in NYFBIMX 105–8999–4251.

157. *Life*, March 20, 1964, p. 40 in NYFBIMX 105–899–4245.

158. Joseph, *Waiting 'Til the Midnight Hour*, p. 99.

159. *Chicago Daily News*, March 21, 1964, p. 1 in FBIMX 100–399321-A.

160. *New York Post*, July 17, 1964, p. 32 in NYFBIMX 105–8999–4742.

161. *New York Courier*, March 21, 1964, p. 1.

162. *New York Herald Tribune*, March 23, 1964, p. 2; and Joseph, *Waiting 'Til the Midnight Hour*, p. 100.

163. *New York Times*, March 22, 1964, p. 17 in FBIMX 100–399321-A.

164. *Chicago Sun-Times*, March 27, 1964, p. 4.

165. Branch, *Pillar of Fire*, pp. 257–258, 269; Joseph, *Waiting 'Til the Midnight Hour*, p. 100.

166. *Newsweek*, March 23, 1964, p. 32.

167. *New York Journal American*, March 23, 1964, p. 3 in NYFBIMX 105–8999–4250; *New York World Telegram and The Sun*, March 23, p. 2 in NYFBIMX 105–8999–4249.

168. *The Evening Star*, March 26, 1964, p. A5 in NYFBIMX 105–8999–4257.

169. *New York Times*, March 27, 1964, p. 10; *Washington Daily News*, March 27, 1964, p. 3 in NYFBIMX 105–899–4256; Branch, *Pillar of Fire*, pp. 267–268; Joseph, *Waiting 'Til the Midnight Hour*, pp. 101–102.

170. *New York Journal American*, March 27, 1964, p. 4 in NYFBIMX 105–8999–4265.

171. Airtel, FBI Director to Chicago SAC, April 10, 1964, pp. 1–3 in NYFBIMX 105–8999–4348.

172. George Breitman, ed., *Malcolm X Speaks* (New York: Pathfinder Press, 1989), p. 50.

173. Ibid., pp. 51–52 and 56–57.

174. *The Militant*, April 23, 1964, in FBIMX 100–399321-A.

175. Joseph, *Waiting 'Til the Midnight Hour*, pp. 102–103.

176. Breitman, *Malcolm X Speaks*, p.26.

177. Ibid., p.31.

178. *New York Amsterdam News*, April 4, 1964, p. 2.

179. *New York Amsterdam News*, March 28, 1964, p. 35 in NYFBIMX 105–8999–4268; Joseph, *Waiting 'Til the Midnight Hour*, pp. 97–102.

180. *New York Times*, May 8, 1964, p. 1.

181. *Washington Post*, May 18, 1964, p. A3 in FBIMX 100–399321-A.

182. *New York Amsterdam News*, May 23, 1964, p. 14 in NYFBIMX 105–8999–4512.

183. *New York Times*, May 19, 1964, p. 28 in NYFBIMX 105–8999–4508; *Philadelphia Independent*, May 16, 1964, p. 12 in NYFBIMX 105–8999–4505; *Chicago Courier*, May 16, 1964, p. 1 in NYFBIMX 105–8999–4504.

184. *Dialogue*, May 1962, p. 14 in NYFBIMX 105–899–1B2(1).

185. UPI, "Malcolm X," May 20, 1964, in FBIMX 100–399321-A.

186. *New York Daily News*, May 22, 1964, p. 10 in NYFBIMX 105–8999–4488.

187. *New York Post*, May 22, 1964, p. 3 in NYFBIMX 105–8999–4491.

188. *New York Amsterdam News*, May 30, 1964, p. 49 in NYFBIMX 105–8999–4523.

189. Ibid.

190. Ibid.

191. *New York Amsterdam News*, May 30, 1964, p. 1 in NYFBIMX 105–8999–4522.

192. *Chicago Sunday Sun-Times*, May 24, 1964, p. 12 in FBIMX 100–399321-A.

193. *Chicago Sunday Tribune*, May 24, 1964, p. 5 in FBIMX 100–399321-A.

194. *New York Times*, May 24, 1964, p. 61 in NYFBIMX 105–8999–4514.

195. Airtel From FBI Director to Chicago SAC, June 19, 1964, pp. 4–5 in NYFBIMX 105–8999–4549.

196. Ibid., p. 9.

197. Ibid., p. 23.

198. Airtel from FBI Director to Chicago SAC, June 19, 1964, pp. 29–30 in NYFBIMX 105–8999–4549.

199. Ibid., p. 31.

200. Malcolm X, "We Are All Blood Brothers," *Liberator* 4, no. 7 (July 1964): 5; Breitman, *Malcolm X Speaks*, p. 62; *New York Amsterdam News*, March 20, 1965, p. 39.

201. *Nigerian Daily Express*, May 11, 1964, p. 6.

202. Malcolm X, "We Are All Blood Brothers," p. 6.

203. *New York Times*, May 13, 1964, p. 17 in NYFBIMX 105–8999–4453.

204. Joseph, *Waiting 'Til the Midnight Hour*, pp. 103–107.

205. *Ghanaian Times*, May 18, 1964.

206. *Ghanaian Times*, May 13, 1964, p. 3.

207. *Ghanaian Times*, May 15, 1964.

208. *Ghanaian Times*, May 16, 1964. p. 5; Joseph, *Waiting 'Til the Midnight Hour*, pp. 105–106; Branch, *Pillar of Fire*, p. 314. For analysis of Malcolm's speech at Legon, see H. M. Basner, "Malcolm X and the Martyrdom of Rev. Clayton Hewett," *Ghanaian Times*, May 18, 1964, and Julian Mayfield, "Basner Misses Malcolm X's Point," *Ghanaian Times*, May 19, 1964, p. 2. See also Kevin K. Gaines, *American Africans in Ghana: Black Expatriates and the Civil Rights Era* (Chapel Hill: University of North Carolina Press, 2006), p. 192.

209. "Malcolm X Visits Accra," Dept. Of State Airgram, May 24, 1964, p. 2 in NYFBIMX 105–8999–5280.

210. "Malcolm X Visits Accra," Dept. Of State Airgram, May 24, 1964, p. 3 in NYFBIMX 105–8999–5280.

211. Malcolm X, "We Are All Blood Brothers," p. 4.

212. Malcolm X and Haley, *The Autobiography of Malcolm X*, pp. 374–393.

213. *The Washington Star*, June 14, 1964, p. A-1 in FBIMX 100–399321-A.

214. Ibid.

215. "Malcolm X. Little," June 16, 1964, pp. 1–3 in FBIMX 100–399321 (Part 11); Branch, *Pillar of Fire*, pp. 345–346.

216. *New York Journal-American*, May 7, 1964, p. 4 in NYFBIMX 105–8999–4533.

217. *New Statesman*, June 12, 1964, p. 902.

218. Sales, *From Civil Rights to Black Liberation*.

219. George Breitman, ed., *By Any Means Necessary: Speeches, Interviews and a Letter by Malcolm X* (New York: Pathfinder Press, 1970), p. 38.

220. Ibid., p. 39.

221. Ibid., p. 40.

222. "Malcolm K. Little," July 10, 1964, pp. 1–2 in FBIMX 100–399321 (Part 12).

223. *New York Post*, July 10, 1964, p. 34 in NYFBIMX 105–8999–4776.

224. *Ebony*, July–August, 1964, p. 39.

225. *Chicago Courier*, July 4, 1964, p. 2 in NYFBIMX 105–8999–4793.

226. Joseph, *Waiting 'Til the Midnight Hour*, pp. 110–112.

227. Breitman, *Malcolm X Speaks*, pp. 72–77.

228. Ibid., pp. 81–82.

229. "Malcolm K. Little," January 20, 1965, p. 142 in FBIMX 100–399321 (Part 14); *New York Times*, August 13, 1964, p. 22 in NYFBIMX 105–8999–4873.

230. "Malcolm K. Little," January 20, 1965, pp. 111–117 in FBIMX 100–399321 (Part 14).

231. "Malcolm K. Little," January 20, 1965, p. 118 in FBIMX 100–399321 (Part 14).

232. *East African Standard*, October 19, 1964, p. 1.

233. *Tanganyika Standard*, October 13, 1964, p. 1.

234. "Malcolm K. Little," January 20, 1965, pp. 110–11 in FBIMX 100–399321 (Part 14).

235. *East African Standard*, October 19, 1964, p. 1.

236. Ibid.

237. "Malcolm K. Little," January 20, 1965, pp. 121–123 in FBIMX 100–399321 (Part 14).

238. Sales, *From Civil Rights to Black Liberation*, p. 129; Fanon Che Wilkin, "The Making of Black Internationalists: SNCC and Africa Before the Launching of Black Power, 1960–1965," *The Journal of African American History* 92, no. 4 (Fall 2007): 483; Joseph, *Waiting Til the Midnight Hour*, p. 113; John Lewis and Michael D'Orso, *Walking with the Wind: A Memoir of the Movement* (New York: Simon and Schuster, 1998), pp. 294–298.

239. *East African Standard*, October 23, 1964, p. 17.

240. *Morning Post* (Nigeria), October 31, 1964, p. 2.

241. *Nigerian Daily Times*, October 30, 1964, p. 4.

242. *Liberian Star*, November 9, 1964, p. 5; *Liberian Age*, November 9, 1964, pp. 1–2.

243. *Liberian State*, November 9, 1964, p. 5.

244. *Daily Times* (Nigeria), November 7, 1964, p. 13, and November 10, 1964, p. 6; *East African Standard*, October 13, 1964, p. 1.

245. *New York Courier*, December 5, 1964, pp. 1, 9 in NYFBIMX 105–8999–5221.

246. *New York Herald Tribune*, December 13, 1964, p. 39 in NYFBIMX 105–8999–5264.

247. *The Militant*, December 21, 1964, pp. 1, 3 in NYFBIMX 105–8999–5296.

248. *New York Times*, December 21, 1964, p. 20.

249. Breitman, *Malcolm X Speaks*, p. 108; *New York Times*, December 21, 1964, p. 20.

250. Joseph, *Waiting 'Til the Midnight Hour*, p. 112; *The Militant*, January 11, 1965, in FBIMX 100–399321-A.

251. *Muhammad Speaks*, December 4, 1964, p. 11 in FBIMX 100–399321-A.

252. *Boston Globe*, January 3, 1965, p. 43 in FBIMX 100–399321-A.

253. *Philadelphia Evening Bulletin*, December 30, 1964. Temple University Urban Archives.

254. *The Militant*, January 11, 1965; in FBIMX 100–399321-A. For Malcolm, showing these films was bittersweet. In September 1959, fresh from his first trip to Africa, he had shown home movies to members of the Nation of Islam's Muslim Mosque #25 in Newark, New Jersey. See "Malcolm K. Little," November 17, 1959, p. 6 in FBIMX 100–399321 (Part 5).

255. Joseph, *Waiting 'Til the Midnight Hour*, p. 114; *Washington Daily News*, February 5, 1965, p. 9 in FBIMX 100–399321-A.

256. Branch, *Pillar of Fire*, pp. 596–597; Joseph, *Waiting 'Til the Midnight Hour*, p. 115.

257. Branch, *Pillar of Fire*, p. 597.

258. *The Nationalist* (Tanzania), March 1, 1965, p.1.

259. *Ghanaian Times*, February 25, 1965, p. 1.

260. *Morning Post* (Nigeria), February 23, 1965, p. 16; February 24, 1965, p. 8; February 26, 1965, p. 3; February 27, p. 16; February 28, 1965, p. 2; *Ghanaian Times*, February 23, 1965, pp. 1, 6; February 24, 1965, pp. 1, 4; *West African Pilot* (Nigeria), February 23, 1965; *East African Standard*, February 23, 1965, pp. 1,4; *Ethiopian Herald*, February 23, 1965, p.1; *The Nationalist* (Tanzania), February 23, 1965, pp. 3–4; *Nigerian Daily Express*, February 23, 1965, pp. 1,3; *Nigerian Daily Times*, February 23, 1965, p. 5; *The Liberian Age*, February 23, 1965, p. 8.

261. *The Standard* (Tanzania), February 23, 1965, p. 1, and *The Nationalist*, February 24, 1965, p. 4.

262. *Ghanaian Times*, February 26, 1965, p. 3; for a sampling of global reaction to Malcolm's death, see *New York Amsterdam News*, March 13, 1965, p. 6.

263. Memorandum from Chicago SAC to FBI Director, "Nation of Islam," June 19, 1964, p. 2 in NYFBIMX 105–8999–4592.

264. Manning Marable, "Rediscovering Malcolm's Life: A Historian's Adventures in Living History," *Souls* 7, no. 1 (2005): 20–35.

CHAPTER 3

1. For a comprehensive examination of the movement, see Peniel E. Joseph, *Waiting 'Til the Midnight Hour: A Narrative History of Black Power in America* (New York: Owl Books, 2007). See also Peniel E. Joseph, ed., *The Black Power Movement: Rethinking the Civil Rights-Black Power Era* (New York: Routledge, 2006); Timothy B. Tyson, *Radio Free Dixie: Robert F. Williams and the Roots of Black Power* (Chapel Hill: University of North Carolina Press, 1999); Charles Jones, ed., *The Black Panther Party [Reconsidered]* (Baltimore: Black Classic Press, 1998); Komozi Woodard, *A Nation Within a Nation: Amiri Baraka (LeRoi Jones) & Black Power Politics* (Chapel Hill: University of North Carolina Press, 1999); Matthew Countryman, *Up South: Civil Rights and Black Power in Philadelphia* (Philadelphia: University of Pennsylvania Press, 2005); William L. Van Deburg, *New Day in Babylon: Black Power and American Culture* (Chicago: University of Chicago Press, 1992); James Edward Smethurst, *The Black Arts Movement: Literary Nationalism in the 1960s and 1970s* (Chapel Hill: University of North Carolina Press, 2005); Curtis J. Austin, *Up Against the Wall: Violence in the Making and Unmaking of the Black Panther Party* (Fayetteville: University of Arkansas Press, 2006); Jama Lazerow and Yohuru Williams, eds., *In Search of the Black Panther Party: New Perspective on a Revolutionary Movement* (Durham, NC: Duke University Press, 2006); Rod Bush, *We Are Not What We Seem: Black Nationalism and Class Struggle in the American Century* (New York: New York University Press, 1999); Manning Marable, *Black American Politics: From the Washington Marches to Jesse Jackson* (London: Verso, 1985); Mike Marqusee, *Redemption Song: Muhammad Ali and the Spirit of the 1960s* (London: Verso, 1999); Nikhil Pal Singh, *Black Is a Country: Race and the Unfinished Struggle for Democracy* (Cambridge, MA: Harvard University Press, 2004); Kathleen Cleaver and George Katsiaficas, eds., *Liberation, Imagination, and the Black Panther Party* (New York: Routledge, 2001); Yohuru Williams, *Black Politics/White Power: Civil Rights, Black Power, and the Black Panthers in New Haven* (New York: Brandywine Press, 2000).

2. I use this term to describe the years between 1954's *Brown* Supreme Court decision and the passage of the 1965 Voting Rights Act. This time frame encapsulates the master narrative of the civil rights movement—from the Montgomery Bus Boycott to Emmet Till's lynching; from the Little Rock crisis to the sit-in movement; James Meredith's efforts to enroll at Ole Miss to the March On Washington and the passage of the 1964 Civil Rights Act. However, it is important to keep in mind that a plethora of new scholarship, including my own work, has illustrated the shortcomings of this periodization (some which is cited in the endnotes of this essay). In a fashion, this period represents America's modern-day Iliad, with Martin Luther King Jr. starring as the tragic hero. The cataclysmic events of this time, with

its marches, demonstrations, political assassinations, and interracial cast of powerbrokers, lends the era a cinematic flavor that has made for powerful narratives (both media driven and scholarly). But in the process, it also ossifies the movement's contemporary legacy, downplays its ideological diversity, ignores its radicalism, and demonizes Black Power as its ruthlessly destructive twin. However, I use the term here purposefully to show how historians can transform its meaning by expansively redefining the era's main actors, organizations, geography, and contemporary legacy. See Joseph, *Waiting 'Til the Midnight Hour* and *The Black Power Movement*.

3. Joseph, *Waiting 'Til the Midnight Hour*, pp. 132–204; Stokely Carmichael with Ekwueme Michael Thelwell, *Ready For Revolution: The Life and Struggles of Stokely Carmichael (Kwame Ture)* (New York: Scribner, 2003).

4. See the special issues I edited on "Black Power Studies" in *The Black Scholar* 31, nos. 3–4 (Fall/Winter 2001) and 32., no. 1 (Spring 2002); Joseph, *Waiting 'Til the Midnight Hour* and *The Black Power Movement*; Carmichael, *Ready For Revolution*.

5. Raymond Arsenault, *Freedom Riders: 1961 and the Struggle for Racial Justice* (New York: Oxford University Press, 2006).

6. Carmichael, *Ready For Revolution*, p. 192.

7. Taylor Branch, *Parting the Waters: America in the King Years, 1954–1963* (New York: Touchstone, 1988), p. 483.

8. Carmichael was initially placed in the Hinds County Jail before being moved to Parchman Penitentiary. Carmichael, *Ready For Revolution*, pp. 198–201, 210–211; Kwame Ture (Stokely Carmichael) FBI File. Hereafter cited as FBIKT 100–446080–1166, "Stokely Carmichael: Correlation Summary," February 29, 1968, p. 2.

9. Carmichael, *Ready For Revolution*, p. 194.

10. Gordon Parks, "Whip of Black Power," *Life*, May 19, 1967, p. 79; Carmichael, *Ready For Revolution*, p. 247; Joseph, *Waiting 'Til the Midnight Hour*, pp. 124–127.

11. Carmichael, *Ready For Revolution*, p. 277.

12. For Carmichael's relationship with local people in the South, see Clayborne Carson, *In Struggle: SNCC and the Black Awakening of the 1960s* (Cambridge, MA: Harvard University Press, 1981); Charles Payne, *I've Got the Light of Freedom: The Organizing Tradition and the Mississippi Freedom Struggle* (Berkeley: University of California Press, 1995), p. 335; Carmichael, *Ready For Revolution*; Taylor Branch, *At Canaan's Edge: America in the King Years, 1965–1968* (New York: Simon & Schuster, 2006); Joseph, *Waiting 'Til the Midnight Hour*. See also Stokely Carmichael and Charles Hamilton, *Black Power* (New York: Random House, 1967) and Stokely Carmichael, *Stokely Speaks* (New York: Random House, 1971).

13. Joseph, *Waiting 'Til the Midnight Hour*, pp. 149–161; Carmichael, *Ready For Revolution*, pp. 520–563.

14. Joseph, *Waiting 'Til the Midnight Hour*, p. 124. For black struggles in Mississippi during the civil rights era, see Carson, *In Struggle*; Payne, *I've Got the Light of Freedom*; John Dittmer, *Local People: The Struggle for Civil Rights in Mississippi* (Urbana: University of Illinois Press, 1995); Chana Kai Lee, *For Freedom's Sake: The Life of Fannie Lou Hamer* (Urbana: University of Illinois Press, 1999); Wesley C. Hogan, *Many Minds, One Heart: SNCC's Dream for a New America* (Chapel Hill: University of North Carolina Press, 2007); Branch,

Parting the Waters, Pillar of Fire: America in the King Years, 1963–1965 (New York: Simon & Schuster, 1998), and *At Canaan's Edge*; Adam Fairclough, *To Redeem the Soul of America: The Southern Christian Leadership Conference and Martin Luther King Jr.* (Athens: University of Georgia Press, 2001); David Garrow, *Bearing the Cross: Martin Luther King Jr. and the Southern Christian Leadership Conference* (New York: Harper Perennial, 1999).

15. Stokely Carmichael to Lorna D. Smith, January 15, 1966, pp. 1–4. Stokely Carmichael Lorna D. Smith Papers, Green Library, Stanford University. Hereafter cited as SCLDS.

16. Stokely Carmichael, "Who Is Qualified?" *The New Republic*, January 8, 1966, p. 22.

17. Joseph, *Waiting 'Til the Midnight Hour*, p. 129.

18. *The Movement*, February 1966, p. 8.

19. Ibid., p. 8.

20. Ibid., p. 8.

21. *The Movement*, March 1966, p. 1.

22. Joseph, *Waiting 'Til the Midnight Hour*, p. 130; Branch, *At Canaan's Edge*, pp. 462–465.

23. Branch, *At Canaan's Edge*, p. 465.

24. *Los Angeles Times*, May 25, 1966, p. 10.

25. *Los Angeles Times*, May 24, 1966, p. 16; Joseph, *Waiting 'Til the Midnight Hour*, p. 131.

26. *The Movement*, June 1966, p. 2.

27. For Wilkins's article on SNCC, see *Los Angeles Times*, June 6, 1966, p. A5. For Carmichael and Wilkins's meeting, see Joseph, *Waiting 'Til the Midnight Hour*, pp. 135–136; Carmichael with Thelwell, *Ready For Revolution*, pp. 494–500.

28. *Los Angeles Times*, June 11, 1966, p. 5.

29. Ibid., p. 5.

30. *Los Angeles Times*, June 12, 1966, p. F1.

31. *Los Angeles Times,*, June 19, 1966, p. J4.

32. *Los Angeles Times*, June 24, 1966, pp. 1, 13.

33. Ibid., p. 13.

34. *Los Angeles Times*, June 27, 1966, p. 6.

35. Ibid., p. 13.

36. Joseph, *Waiting 'Til the Midnight Hour*, pp. 132–147; Carson, *In Struggle*, pp. 209–211.

37. Lerone Bennett, Jr., "Stokely Carmichael: Architect of Black Power," *Ebony*, July 1966, pp. 58–68. SNCC reprint of *Ebony* article, p. 1.

38. Ibid., p. 4.

39. Bernard Weinraub, "The Brilliancy of Black," *Esquire*, January 1967, pp. 130, 132–134.

40. *Los Angeles Times*, June 28, 1966, p. 19, and June 29, 1966, p. 4.

41. Joseph, *Waiting 'Til the Midnight Hour*, pp. 146–147; *Los Angeles Times*, July 3, 1966, pp. B1, 3.

42. *Chicago Tribune*, July 1, 1966, p. 6.

43. *Chicago Tribune*, July 2, 1966, pp. A4 and 8.

44. Joseph, *Waiting 'Til the Midnight Hour*, p. 148.

45. Joseph, *Waiting 'Til the Midnight Hour*, p. 149.

46. "Black Power: The Widening Dialogue," *New South*, Summer 1966, p. 68; *Los Angeles Times*, July 3, 1966, pp. B1, 2.

47. FBIKT 100–446080–3X, "Stokely Carmichael: Racial Matter," July 29, 1966, pp. 1–10; FBIKT 100–446080-NR, "Nation of Islam," August 15, 1966, p. 1.

48. *Chicago Tribune*, July 31, 1966, p. 8.

49. *Los Angeles Times*, August 4, 1966, p. 11.

50. Carson, *In Struggle*, p. 227; Joseph, *Waiting 'Til the Midnight Hour*.

51. *New York Times*, August 5, 1966, p. 10; Joseph, *Waiting 'Til the Midnight Hour*, p. 157; See also *U.S. News and World Report*, August 15, 1966, p. 12, which reprinted excerpts from the *Times* stories as the "Inside Story of 'Black Power' and Stokely Carmichael."

52. *Newsweek*, August 8, 1966, p. 54; *Los Angeles Times*, July 13, 1966, p. A5; *Los Angeles Times*, August 8, 1966, p. A5.

53. *U.S. News and World Report*, August 8, 1966, pp. 40–41. David Susskind accused Carmichael of being a Janus-faced leader trying to sweet-talk him in the studio during a taped interview, a baby-faced demagogue who virtually spoke in tongues. Carmichael reminded Susskind that blacks and whites did indeed see the world from two different points of view, and that his most provocative polemics were viewed in stark contrast depending on the race of the listener. See FBIKT 100–446080–78, "Stokely Carmichael," November 18, 1966, p. 6

54. *Los Angeles Times*, July 3, 1966, p. B2.

55. *Muhammad Speaks*, August 12, 1966, p. 4; August 19, 1966, pp. 3–4; August 26, 1966, p. 13; Joseph, *Waiting 'Til the Midnight Hour*, pp. 154–155. See also FBIKT 100–446080–3X, "Stokely Carmichael: Racial Matter," July 29, 1966, pp. 1–4.

56. Joseph, *Waiting 'Til the Midnight Hour*; *Muhammad Speaks*, August 12, 1966, p.4; *Muhammad Speaks*, August 19, 1966, p. 4; *Los Angeles Herald-Examiner*, August 25, 1966, p. A-10.

57. *The Bay State Banner*, August 27, 1966, p. 1; *Muhammad Speaks*, September 2, 1966, p. 5.

58. FBIKT 100–446080-NR, Airtel, Boston SAC to FBI Director, September 9, 1966, p. 5.

59. FBIKT 100–446080–15, "Stokely Carmichael," September 13, 1966, p. 1; FBIKT 100–446080–10, Memorandum, New York SAC to FBI Director, September 1, 1966, p. 1.

60. Joseph, *Waiting 'Til the Midnight Hour*.

61. FBIKT 100–446080–33m, "Stokely Carmichael," October 6, 1966. Transcript of *Meet the Press*, August 21, 1966, p. 4.

62. Joseph, *Waiting 'Til the Midnight Hour*, pp. 156–157; *Los Angeles Times*, August 22, 1966, pp. 1, 10.

63. FBIKT 100–446080-NR, Memorandum, "Student Nonviolent Coordinating Committee," August 23, 1966, p. 2.

64. FBIKT 100–446080–2X, "Stokely Carmichael," July 13, 1966, pp. 1–9.

65. *Chicago Tribune*, August 23, 1966, p. 16, and *Washington Post*, August 23, 1966, p. A12.

66. Joseph, *Waiting 'Til the Midnight Hour*, p. 155.

67. *Washington Post*, October 29, 1966, p. 3; *Chicago Tribune*, October 28, 1966, pp. 1,8; *Chicago Tribune*, October 29, 1966, pp. 1–2; *Los Angeles Times*, October 28, 1966, p. 31; Joseph, *Waiting 'Til the Midnight Hour*, p. 167.

68. *Los Angeles Times*, October 30, 1966, p. C1; *The Movement*, November 1966, p. 2.

69. Ibid.

70. FBIKT 100–446080–395, "Airtel FBI Director to San Francisco SAC," July 13, 1967, p. 7.

71. *Los Angeles Times*, October 30, 1966, p. C1.

72. *Los Angeles Times*, October 31, 1966, p. 3; Joseph, *Waiting 'Til the Midnight Hour*, p. 168.

73. *Chicago Tribune*, October 31, 1966, p. 14.

74. *Washington Post, Times Herald*, November 1, 1966, p. A2; *Los Angeles Times*, November 1, 1966, p. 22.

75. "Student Nonviolent Coordinating Committee: Stokely Carmichael," November 4, 1966, p. 1. Taylor Branch Collection, UNC-Chapel Hill (LBJ Office Files, Office Files of Mildred Stegall, SNCC-Stokely Carmichael, August-December 1966).

76. *Chicago Tribune*, November 3, 1966, p. A11; *Los Angeles Times*, November 3, 1966, p. B10.

77. *The Movement*, December 1966, p. 8.

78. Stokely Carmichael and Charles Hamilton, *Black Power: The Politics of Liberation in America* (New York: Random House, 1967), p. 115.

79. Ibid.

80. All quotes taken from *The Movement*, December 1966, p. 8.

81. Carmichael and Hamilton, *Black Power*, p. 115.

82. *The Movement*, December 1966, p. 9.

83. *The Movement*, December 1966, p. 8; see also, Branch, *At Canaan's Edge*, p. 548.

84. Carmichael and Hamilton, *Black Power*, p. 98.

85. *The Movement*, December 1966, p. 8.

86. *The Movement*, December 1966, p. 9; Carmichael and Hamilton, *Black Power*, pp. 116–118; Branch, *At Canaan's Edge*, pp. 546–547.

87. FBIKT 100–446080–92, "Stokely Carmichael," November 28, 1966, pp. 1–5.

88. *Los Angeles Times*, November 23, 1966, pp. 3, 18.

89. *Los Angeles Times*, November 24, 1966, pp. 1, 33; November 25, 1966, p. B4; November 26, 1966, pp. 1, 15.

90. *Los Angeles Times*, November 26, 1966, p. 15.

91. Ibid.

92. *The Movement*, December 1966, p. 5.

93. *The Movement*, November 27, 1966; Joseph, *Waiting 'Til the Midnight Hour*, p. 171.

94. *Los Angeles Times*, November 30, 1966, p. 7.

95. FBIKT 100–446080–143, "Stokely Carmichael—Research Satellite Matter," March 15, 1967, p. 15; *Los Angeles Times*, November 30, 1966, p. 7.

96. FBIKT 100–446080–471, Transcript of Stokely Carmichael University of Texas Speech, April 13, 1967, p. 30.

97. *Los Angeles Times*, January 30, 1967, pp. 3, 24.

98. *Los Angeles Times*, February 5, 1967, pp. DB, 14.

99. *The Movement*, February 1967, p. 205. CAKC.

100. *Berkeley Barb*, February 10, 1967, p. 3; Eldridge Cleaver, author, Kathleen Cleaver, ed., *Target Zero: A Life in Writing* (New York: Palgrave MacMillan, 2006).

101. Eldridge Cleaver, "My Father and Stokely Carmichael," *Ramparts* 5, no. 10, April 1967, pp. 10–14.

102. FBIKT 100–446080–141, "Airtel From San Francisco SA to FBI Director," February 28, 1967.

103. FBIKT 100–446080–384, "Stokely Carmichael," July 13, 1967, pp. 1–2.

104. FBIKT 100–446080-no serial, "Stokely Carmichael," February 20, 1967, p. 1.

105. FBIKT 100–446080–131, "Stokely Carmichael; Student Non Violent Coordinating Committee (SNCC)," February 28, 1967, pp. 1–2.

106. FBIKT 100–446080–119, "Stokely Carmichael—Teletype," February 16, 1967, pp. 1–2; FBIKT 100–446080–120, "Stokely Carmichael—Teletype," February 18, 1967, pp. 1–3; FBIKT 100–446080–121, "Stokely Carmichael—Airtel," February 21, 1967, pp. 1–2 and pp. 1–6; *Los Angeles Times*, February 16, p. A8.

107. FBIKT 100–446080-no serial, "Student Non Violent Coordinating Committee: Stokely Carmichael," March 3, 1967, p. 1.

108. FBIKT 100–446080–301, *Montreal Gazette*, February 25, 1967.

109. "Stokely Comes to McGill," *Sanity*, May 11, 1967, p. 2; C. L. R. James, "Black Power: Its Past, Today, and the Way Ahead," pp. 1–3. Speech Delivered by C.L.R. James, August 1967. FBIKT 100–446080-no serial.

110. FBIKT 100–446080-no serial, "Stokely Carmichael," February, 28, 1967, pp. 1–2.

111. FBIKT 100–446080-no serial, "Proposed Demonstration Protesting Police Shooting of George Jennings, Negro Male, 3950 West 16th Street, Chicago, Illinois, February 18, 1967, Racial Matter, Stokely Carmichael: Internal Security," February 27, 1967, p. 1; FBIKT 100–446080–125, "Stokely Carmichael Internal Security—Miscellaneous," March 1, 1967, pp. 1–3.

112. FBIKT 100–446080–380. Memorandum, To FBI Director from Albany SAC, "Stokely Carmichael," July 10, 1967, pp. 1–7.

113. FBIKT 100–446080–135, "Airtel: Stokely Carmichael," March 2, 1967, p. 1.

114. FBIKT 100–446080–127, "Teletype," March 3, 1967.

115. FBIKT 100–446080–128, "Teletype," March 3, 1969; FBIKT 100–446080–123, "Teletype," February 27, 1967; FBIKT 100–446080–127, "Teletype," March 3, 1967; FBIKT 100–446080–129, "Teletype," March 4, 1967; FBIKT 100–446080–132, "Teletype," March 3, 1967.

116. FBIKT 100–446080-no serial, "Stokely Carmichael," March 9, 1967, p. 1; *SNCC Newsletter*, March 15, 1967, p. 1; Parks, "Whip of Black Power," p. 76A; *Baltimore Afro-American*, March 25, 1967, p. 1; *Muhammad Speaks*, April 14, 1967, p. 22; *New York Times*, March 26, 1967, p. 29.

117. FBIKT 100–446080-no serial, "Student Non Violent Coordinating Committee: Stokely Carmichael," March 17, 1967, pp. 1–2.

118. FBIKT 100–446080–139, "Appearance of Stokely Carmichael, Student Non Violent Coordinating Committee at Duke University, Durham, North Carolina, March 17, 1967," March 13, 1967, pp. 1–3.

119. FBIKT 100–446080–143, "Stokely Carmichael—Advocate of 'Black Power': Research-Satellite Matter," March 15, 1967, pp. 1–2; FBIKT 100–446080-no serial, "Stokely Carmichael—Advocate of Black Power," March 23, 1967, p. i.

120. FBIKT 100–446080-no serial, "Stokely Carmichael—Advocate of Black Power," March 23, 1967, p. i.

121. Ibid., p. 7.

122. Ibid., p. 15.

123. Ibid., pp. 1–17.

124. *The Movement*, May 1967, pp. 232, 241; *National Guardian*, April 22, 1967, p. 12; Carson, *In Struggle*.

125. *U.S. News and World Report*, April 24, 1967, p. 10.

126. *New York Times*, April 11, 1967, p. 46; *New York Times*, April 16, 1967; *Philadelphia Evening Bulletin*, May 24, 1967. Stokely Carmichael Clipping File. PEBUA. FBIKT 100–446080-NR, *The New Haven Registry*, April 12, 1967; FBIKT 100–446080–468, "Stokely Carmichael—Sedition," August 8, 1967, pp. 1–16.

127. Branch, *At Canaan's Edge*, p. 593.

128. Ibid., p. 603.

129. King had come out against the war as early as 1965 but was quickly pressured into silence. SNCC subsequently became one of the war's leading critics and, from June 1966 to April 1967, Carmichael emerged as the black freedom struggle's most vocal antiwar critic. See Branch, *At Canaan's Edge*, pp. 254–255, 308–309, 591–597; Joseph, *Waiting 'Til the Midnight Hour*, pp. 179–183.

130. Parks, "Whip of Black Power," p. 78.

131. Ibid.

132. Ibid., pp. 78, 80, 82. See also, Joseph, *Waiting 'Til the Midnight Hour*; "King Near to Stokely?" *Berkeley Barb*, May 19–25, 1967.

133. Parks, "Whip of Black Power," p. 82.

134. Branch, *At Canaan's Edge*, pp. 605–606; FBIKT 100–446080-no serial, "Stokely Carmichael," May 5, 1967, p. 2; FBIKT 100–446080–666, Airtel from Director Hoover to Atlanta SAC, November 17, 1967, which notes that Assistant Attorney General Walter Yeagley requested that agents "obtain the names of these 16 individuals, the city where they refused induction, and what action was instituted against them for their refusal."

135. *Los Angeles Times*, May 2, 1967, p. 9.

136. *Los Angeles Times*, May 6, 1967, p. 4.

137. Ibid.

138. FBIKT 100–446080-NR, "Student Nonviolent Coordinating Committee: Stokely Carmichael," May 17, 1967, p. 2. FBIKT 100–446080–197, "Stokely Carmichael," p. 2. FBIKT 100–446080–230, *Chicago Defender*, May 15, 1967. For Carmichael's plans to resume organizing, see Stokely Carmichael to Lorna D. Smith, February 4, 1967, p. 1. SCLDS.

139. *The Movement*, July 1967. SCLDS.

140. Sol Stern, "The Call Of the Panthers," *New York Times Magazine*, August 6, 1967.

141. Ibid.

142. *Time*, December 15, 1967, p. 28.

143. FBIKT 100–446080-no serial, "Stokely Carmichael," July 13, 1967, pp. 1–2.

144. FBIKT 100–446080-no serial, *The Observer Review*, July 23, 1967.

145. FBIKT 100–446080-no serial, *The Observer Review*, July 23, 1967. As Carmichael toured London and its surrounding areas, local police informants suggested that he planned to return to Brooklyn, New York, on July 19, a prospect that placed the FBI on high alert, especially given outbreaks of violence in nearby Newark. The FBI's London liaison reassured American officials that Carmichael planned to stay in Great Britain for a few more days. FBIKT 100–446080–390, "Cablegram for FBI Director to Legat London," July 18, 1967, pp. 1–2; and FBIKT 100–446080–391, "Airtel from Director Hoover to Knoxville SAC," July 19, 1967.

146. FBIKT 100–446080-no serial, "Cuban Clandestine Operation in the United States," Memorandum, July 26, 1967.

147. Joseph, *Waiting 'Til the Midnight Hour*, p. 186.

148. FBIKT 100–446080–466, *Omaha World Herald*, August 6, 1967.

149. FBIKT 100–446080–466, Louis Lomax, "Detroit Proved a Fertile Field For Riot Seed," *Omaha World Herald*, August 5, 1967, and "Agitators Used Twists of Fate, Human Weakness in Rioting," *Omaha World Herald*, August 6, 1967.

150. FBIKT 100–446080–521, "Reportage and Comment on Stokely Carmichael's Activities and Statements Abroad," pp. 32, 49.

151. Ibid., pp. 24–32.

152. FBIKT 100–446080–410, "Stokely Carmichael," July 28, 1967, p. 1.

153. "July 26, 1967: Castro Adds the US to His Revolutionary List," pp. 1–3. U.S. Dept. of State, File No: POL 23–8; 4/1/67, Box: 2605.

154. FBIKT 100–446080-no serial, Memorandum, July 27, 1967. Record of Congressman Bray, Republican of Indiana; Congressman Clausen, Republican of California; Congressman Pucinski, Democrat of Illinois, and Congressman Blanton, Democrat of Tennessee.

155. FBIKT 100–446080–411, "Carmichael See Long, Hot Summer," July 26, 1967; FBIKT 100–446080–424, "Stokely Says Negroes Plan to Fight to Death," no date; FBIKT 100–446080–425, "Black Power Leader Vows 'Fight To Death,'" *Oregonian*, July 27, 1967.

156. FBIKT 100–446080–448, "Stokely Carmichael," August 4, 1967, pp. 1–2.

157. FBIKT 100–446080–466, "Snick—Castro's Arm in U.S.," *Omaha World Herald*, August 6, 1967.

158. FBIKT 100–446080-not recorded, "Student Non Violent Coordinating Committee," August 4, 1967.

159. Joseph, *Waiting 'Til the Midnight Hour*, pp. 191–193; Carmichael, *Ready For Revolution*, pp. 572–582; Carson, *In Struggle*, p. 273.

160. "Visit of Stokely Carmichael to Algeria," Sep. 21, 1967. CIA-FOIA, Case No. E)-1998–00458; Dept. of State Airgram, October 2, 1967, pp. 1–2. POL 23–8; August 1, 1967, Box 2605.

161. "Stokely Carmichael," September 11, 1967, SD Airgram, RG 59, GRDS, SC, 1/1/67, Box 234.

162. "Stokely Carmichael Interview in Revolution Africaine," September 11, 1967, pp. 1–2, and "Stokely Carmichael in Algeria," September 11, 1967, pp. 1–2. RG59/GRDS, FN: SC, 1/1/67, Box 234.

163. "Stokely Carmichael in Algeria," September 18, 1967, pp. 1–2. RG59/GRDS, FN: Carmichael, Stokely, 1/1/67, Box: 234.

164. Ibid.

165. Correspondence from Stokely Carmichael to SNCC, undated. (Probably Fall 1967). SNCC Papers, Reel 51, frame 14.

166. Carmichael, *Ready For Revolution*, pp. 616–618, 622–632; Joseph, *Waiting 'Til the Midnight Hour*, pp. 195–197; *Carson, In Struggle*, pp. 276–277.

167. State Dept. Telegram, November 28, 1967, p. 1; State Dept. Telegram, November 30, 1967, pp. 1–2; State Dept. Telegram, November 30, 1967, pp. 1–2; State Dept. Telegram, December 5, 1967, pp. 1–2, RG 59/GRDS, FN: Carmichael, Stokely, 1/1/67, Box 234.

168. FBIKT 100–446080–1042, "Stokely Carmichael: Sedition," February 1, 1968, pp. 23–24.

169. Joseph, *Waiting 'Til the Midnight Hour*, p. 204; *New York Times*, December 12, 1967, p. 14; FBIKT 100–446080–744, "Stokely Carmichael," December 12, 1967; FBIKT 100–446080–765, "Stokely Carmichael," December 11, 1967.

170. FBIKT 100–446080–821, "Stokely Carmichael," December 16, 1967, pp. 1–2.

171. "Possible Criminal Prosecution of Stokely Carmichael," December 20, 1967, pp. 1–6. RG 59/State Dept. Records, Carmichael, Stokely, 1/1,67, Box 234.

172. For King and the Poor People's March, see Garrow, *Bearing the Cross*; Fairclough, *To Redeem the Soul of America*; Branch, *At Canaan's Edge*; Michael K. Honey, *Going Down Jericho Road: The Memphis Strike, Martin Luther King's Last Campaign* (New York: W. W. Norton, 2007); and Thomas F. Jackson, *From Civil Rights to Human Rights: Martin Luther King, Jr. and the Struggle for Economic Justice* (Philadelphia: University of Pennsylvania Press, 2007).

173. Carmichael, *Ready For Revolution*, pp. 648–650; FBIKT 100446080, "Stokely Carmichael," pp. 77–78; *Muhammad Speaks*, February 23, 1968, p. 22.

174. FBIKT 100–446080-NR, "Washington Spring Project: Racial Matters," February 9, 1968, pp. 1–3.

175. Carmichael's trip was unexpected and a surprise to even his closest advisors. FBIKT 100–446080–1173, "Stokely Carmichael," February 26, 1968, pp. 1–12.

176. *London Observer*, March 24, 1968. SCLDS; *Baltimore Afro-American*, May 11, 1968, p. 21; *Muhammad Speaks*, May 24, 1968, p. 9; Carmichael with Thelwell, *Ready For Revolution*, pp. 652–656.

177. Branch, *At Canaan's Edge*, pp. 758.

178. Carmichael, *Ready For Revolution*, pp. 656–659.

179. Jules Milne, *Kwame Nkrumah: The Conakry Years: His Life and Letters* (London: Panaf Books, 1990), p. 261.

180. FBIKT 100–446080–1915, *Rocky Mountain News*, August 22, 1968, p. 70; Airtel, Denver SAC to FBI Director, August 22, 1968, pp. 1–3.

181. The State Department had returned his passport months earlier after he agreed to stay out of banned countries so he could honeymoon overseas. See *San Francisco Chronicle*, July 26, 1968, and *Oregonian*, August 7, 1968. SCLDS.

182. For these speaking tours and the controversy they elicited, see *Greensboro Daily Times*, December 10, 1968; *Greensboro Record*, January 1, 1969; *Greensboro Record*, January 3, 1969; *San Jose Mercury*, January 3, 1969. SCLDS. *Baltimore Afro-American*, December 28, 1968.

183. Joseph, *Waiting 'Til the Midnight Hour*, pp. 246–247.

184. *Sunday Times* (London), November 3, 1969, pp. 28–29, 31.

185. Ethel Minor, "Black Activist's Activities in Africa," *Muhammad Speaks*, October 10, 1969, pp. 35, 37–38.

186. Carmichael, *Ready For Revolution*, p. 712.

187. Charlie Cobb, "Revolution: From Stokely Carmichael to Kwame Ture," *The Black Scholar* 27, nos. 3–4 (Fall 1997): 32–38.

188. Carmichael with Thelwell, *Ready For Revolution*, pp. 764–767.

189. The new scholarship on the postwar freedom era is dense. Important works include Robin Kelley, *Race Rebels: Culture, Politics, and the Black Working Class* (New York: The Free Press, 1994); Robert Self, *American Babylon: Race and the Struggle for Postwar Oakland* (Princeton, NJ: Princeton University Press, 2003); Martha Biondi, *To Stand and Fight: The Struggle for Civil Rights in Postwar New York City* (Cambridge, MA: Harvard University Press, 2003); Rhonda Y. Williams, *The Politics of Public Housing: Black Women's Struggle Against Urban Inequality* (New York: Oxford University Press, 2004); Scot Brown, *Fighting For Us: Maulana Karenga, the US Organization, and Black Cultural Nationalism* (New York: New York University Press, 2003); Smethurst, *The Black Arts Movement*; Jeanne Theoharis and Komozi Woodard, eds., *Freedom North: Black Freedom Struggles Outside the South, 1940*–1980 (New York: Palgrave Macmillan, 2003); Sundiata Cha-Jua and Clarence Lang, "Strategies for Black Liberation in the Era of Globalization: Retronouveau Civil Rights, Militant black Conservatism, and Radicalism," *The Black Scholar* 29 (Fall 1999): 25–47; Williams, *Black Politics/White Power*; Jones, *The Black Panther Party [Reconsidered]*; Lazerow and Williams, *In Search of the Black Panther Party*; and Joseph, *Waiting 'Til the Midnight Hour*. Some key works that specifically address the way in which history is written and the need for scholars to expansively rethink master narratives of the postwar era include Peniel E. Joseph, "Black Liberation Without Apology: Rethinking the Black Power Movement," *The Black Scholar*, 31, nos. 3–4 (Fall/Winter 2001): 2–17; and "Preface" and "Introduction: Toward a Historiography of the Black Power Movement," in Joseph, *The Black Power Movement*, pp. xi–xii, 1–25. Payne, *I've Got the Light of Freedom*, pp. 413–441; Jeanne Theoharis, "Black Freedom Studies: Re-imagining and Redefining the Fundamentals," *History Compass* 4 (2006): 1–20; Hogan, *Many Minds, One Heart*, pp. 1–10, 235–244.

CHAPTER 4

1. *Newsweek*, July 16, 2007, pp. 24–25.

2. Barack Obama, *The Audacity of Hope: Thoughts on Reclaiming the American Dream* (New York: Three Rivers Press, 2006), p. 32.

3. Ibid., p. 36

4. Ira Katznelson, *When Affirmative Action Was White: An Untold History of Racial Equality in Twentieth-Century America* (New York: W. W. Norton, 2005).

5. David Mendell, *Obama: From Promise to Power* (New York: Amistad, 2007), pp. 28–31.

6. Barack Obama, *Dreams From My Father: A Story of Race and Inheritance* (New York: Random House, 2004), p. 22.

7. Ibid., pp. 72–91.

8. Ibid., p. 51.

9. Ibid., p. 58.

10. Ibid., p. 86.

11. Ibid., p. 89.

12. Ibid., p. 102.

13. Alex Haley, *The Autobiography of Malcolm X* (New York: Ballantine, 1998), p. 231.

14. Obama, *Dreams From My Father*, p. 134.

15. Ibid., pp. 134–135, 163.

16. Peniel E. Joseph, *Waiting 'Til the Midnight Hour: A Narrative History of Black Power in America* (New York: Owl Books, 2007).

17. Joseph, *Waiting 'Til the Midnight Hour* and Thomas J. Sugrue, *Sweet Land of Liberty: The Forgotten Struggle for Civil Rights in the North* (New York: Random House, 2008).

18. Obama, *Dreams From My Father*, p. 98.

19. Ibid., p. 140.

20. Ibid.

21. Manning Marable, *Black American Politics: From the Washington Marches to Jesse Jackson* (London: Verso, 1985), 191–246.

22. http://www.americanrhetoric.com/speeches/jessejackson1988dnc.htm.

23. http://www.americanrhetoric.com/speeches/jessejackson1984dnc.htm.

24. Harold Washington, "It's Our Turn," in Manning Marable and Leith Mullings, eds., *Let Nobody Turn Us Around: Voices of Resistance, Reform, and Renewal* (Lanham, MD: Rowman & Littlefield, 2003), pp. 535–537.

25. Obama, *The Audacity of Hope*, p. 43.

26. Lisa McGirr, *Suburban Warriors: The Origins of the New American Right* (Princeton, NJ: Princeton University Press, 2001); Matthew Lassiter, *The Silent Majority: Suburban Politics in the Sunbelt South* (Princeton, NJ: Princeton University Press, 2006); Kevin M. Kruse, *White Flight: Atlanta and the Making of Modern Conservatism* (Princeton, NJ: Princeton University Press, 2005); Joseph Crespino, *In Search of Another Country: Mississippi and the Conservative Counterrevolution* (Princeton, NJ: Princeton University Press, 2007).

27. Marable, *Black American Politics*, p. 281.

28. Ibid., p. 247.

29. Ibid., p. 271.

30. Ibid., p. 270.

31. Sean Wilentz, *The Age of Reagan: A History, 1974–1978* (New York: Harper Collins, 2008), pp. 172–173; Marable, *Black American Politics*, pp. 282–292; Lucius J. Barker and

Ronald W. Walters, *Jesse Jackson's 1984 Presidential Campaign: Challenge and Change in American Politics* (Urbana: University of Illinois Press, 1989).

32. Obama, *Dreams From My Father*, pp. 227–248.

33. Ibid., p. 197.

34. Ibid., p. 200.

35. Ibid., pp. 200–204.

36. Joseph, *Waiting 'Til the Midnight Hour*, p. 197.

37. Joseph, *Waiting 'Til the Midnight Hour*; Sugrue, *Sweet Land of Liberty*.

38. *Report of the National Advisory Commission on Civil Disorders* (New York: Bantam Books, 1968), p. 1.

39. Ibid., p. 2.

40. Ibid., p. 7.

41. Larissa MacFarguhar, "The Conciliator," *The New Yorker*, May 7, 2007, p. 55.

42. *Newsweek*, July 16, 2007, pp. 23–24.

43. Ibid., p. 25.

44. Ta-Nehisi Coates, "Is Obama Black Enough?," *Time*, February 1, 2007.

45. Debra Dickerson, "Colorblind," *Salon.com*, January 22, 2007.

46. Coates, "Is Obama Black Enough?"

47. Richard Wolffe, "Inside Obama's Dream Machine," *Newsweek*, January 14, 2008, pp. 30–34.

48. John L. Jackson Jr., *Racial Paranoia: The Unintended Consequences of Political Correctness* (New York: Basic Books, 2008), pp. 1–22.

49. Wolffe, "Inside Obama's Dream Machine," p. 34.

50. http://www.usatoday.com/news/politics/election2008/2008–05–07-clintoninterview _N.htm.

51. http://www.nypost.com/seven/07092008/news/nationalnews/jesse_jackson_sharply _criticizes_obama_119161.htm.

52. http://www.latimes.com/entertainment/news/tv/la-et-jackson11–2008jul11,0,164 7731.story.

53. Obama, *Dreams From My Father*, p. 286.

54. Douglas Waller, "Dreaming About the Senate," *Time*, July 4, 2004, p. 34. See also Amanda Ripley, "Obama's Ascent," *Time*, November 15, 2004, pp. 74, 76, 78, 81.

55. Jonathan Alter, "Is America Ready?," *Newsweek*, December 25, 2006–Jan. 1, 2007, p. 30.

56. Joe Klein, "The Fresh Face," *Time*, October 23, 2006, p. 46.

57. The political Web site BlackAgendaReport.com provided some of the most comprehensive and critical analysis of Obama's candidacy. See for example, Tom Grayman, "I Feel Rev. Jesse Jackson's Pain," July 16, 2008; Kevin Alexander Gray, "Why Does Barack Obama Hate My Family," July 16, 2008; Glen Ford, "Obama's Choice of Biden: The Devil Made Me Do It," August 27, 2008; Paul Street, "The Empire's New Clothes," November 12, 2008.

58. Obama, *Dreams From My Father*, p. 61.

59. Glen Ford, "Progressives For Obama Fool Themselves," *BlackAgendaReport.com*, July 30–August 5, 2008.

60. Charles J. Evans, "Where Black Power Meets Progressive Politics," *The Black Commentator*, July 3, 2008, www.blackcommentator.com.

61. Boyce Watkins, "Tavis Smiley vs. Barack Obama," February 17, 2008, http://blog.boycewatkins.com/2008/02/dr-boyce-video-tavis-smiley-vs-barack.html. Mary Mitchell, "Sen. Barack Obama's letter to Tavis Smiley," *Chicago Sun-Times*, February 14, 2008.

62. Darryl Fears, "Black Commenter, Criticizing Obama, Causes Firestorm," Washingtonpost.com, February 16, 2008.

63. See for example, Tavis Smiley, ed., *The Covenant With Black America* (Chicago: Third World Press, 2006).

64. See Michael Eric Dyson, *Is Bill Cosby Right?: Or Has the Black Middle Class Lost Its Mind* (New York: Basic Books, 2005) and Juan Williams, *ENOUGH: The Phony Leaders, Dead-End Movements, and Culture of Failure That Are Undermining Black America—and What We Can Do About It* (New York: Crown Books, 2006).

65. Obama, *The Audacity of Hope*, pp. 234–240.

66. Ibid., p. 233.

67. Ibid., p. 247.

68. Katznelson, *When Affirmative Action Was White*.

69. Obama, *The Audacity of Hope*, pp. 249–254.

70. Paula Giddings, *When and Where I Enter: The Impact of Black Women on Race and Sex in America* (New York: Bantam Books, 1984).

71. Perry Bacon Jr., "The Exquisite Dilemma of Being Obama," *Time*, February 20, 2006, pp. 24–28.

72. Stephen Steinberg, *Turning Back: The Liberal Retreat from Racial Justice in American Thought and Policy* (Boston: Beacon Press, 1995); William L. Van Deburg, *New Day in Babylon: Black Power and American Culture, 1965–1975* (Chicago: University of Chicago Press, 1992); Jane Rhodes, *Framing the Panthers: The Spectacular Rise of a Black Power Icon* (New York: The New Press, 2007).

73. Steinberg, *Turning Back*; Jacqueline Dowd Hall, "The Long Civil Rights Movement and the Political Uses of the Past," *Journal of American History* 91 (March 2005): 1233–1263.

74. Douglass S. Massey and Nancy Denton, *American Apartheid: Segregation and the Making of the Underclass* (Cambridge, MA: Harvard University Press, 1998); Michael B. Katz, ed., *The Underclass Debate: Views From History* (Princeton, NJ: Princeton University Press, 1993); Thomas M. Shapiro, *The Hidden Cost of Being African American: How Wealth Perpetuates Inequality* (New York: Oxford University Press, 2005).

75. Matt Bai, "Post-Race," *New York Times Magazine*, August 10, 2008, pp. 34–41, 50, 54–55.

76. Ibid., p. 55.

77. Gwen Ifill, *The Breakthrough: Politics and Race in the Age of Obama* (New York: Doubleday, 2009), p. 16.

78. Obama, *Audacity of Hope*, p. 11.

79. Mendell, *Obama*, pp. 93–246; Ryan Lizza, "Making It: How Chicago Shaped Obama," *The New Yorker*, July 21, 2008, pp. 49–65.

80. http://uhurunews.com/.

81. St. Petersburg activist Omali Yeshitela (formerly Joe Waller) is an exemplar on this score. A former SNCC activist, Kwame Ture ally, and founder of the *Burning Spear* newspapers, Yeshitela is the founder of the African People's Socialist Party. See http://omaliyeshitela.org/.

82. *New York Times*, July 27, 2008, p. 1.

83. Bai, "Post-Race."

84. Jeffrey O. G. Ogbar, *Black Power: Radical Politics and African American Identity* (Baltimore, MD: Johns Hopkins Press, 2004).

85. Sugrue, *Sweet Land of Liberty*.

86. "Remarks of President-Elect Barack Obama—as prepared for delivery Election Night," Tuesday, Nov. 4, 2008, p.1, in author's possession.

87. *New York Times*, November 5, 2008, pp. A1, P. 7.

88. Kurt Anderson, "Obamaism," *New York Magazine*, November 17, 2008, pp. 26–33.

89. *Newsweek*, November 17, 2008, pp. 20–21, 24.

90. *Time*, November 17, 2008, p. 13.

91. *Ebony*, January 2009, p. 12.

92. Luci Baines Johnson, "LBJ, King opened door for Obama's election," November 24, 2008, http://www.cnn.com/2008/POLITICS/11/23/johnson.lbj.obama/index.html?iref=mp storyview.

93. Obama, *Dreams From My Father*, p. 158.

94. Mike Davis, "Obama at Manassas," *New Left Review* 56 (March-April 2009), http://www.newleftreview.org/A2769.

95. See David Garrow, *Bearing the Cross: Martin Luther King Jr. and the Southern Christian Leadership Conference* (New York: Harper Perennial, 1999); Taylor Branch, *At Canaan's Edge: America in the King Year, 1965–1968* (New York: Simon & Schuster, 2006); Thomas F. Jackson, *From Civil Rights to Human Rights: Martin Luther King Jr. and the Struggle for Economic Justice* (Philadelphia: University of Pennsylvania Press, 2007).

96. Eric Foner, *Reconstruction: America's Unfinished Revolution, 1863–1877* (New York: Harper Perennial, 2002); Phillip Dray, *Capitol Men: The Epic Story of Reconstruction Through the Lives of the First Black Congressmen* (Boston: Houghton Mifflin, 2008).

97. Taylor Branch, *Parting the Waters: America in the King Years, 1954–1963* (New York: Touchstone, 1988), p. 875.

98. Remnick, "The Joshua Generation," *The New Yorker*, November 17, 2008.

99. "Remarks of President-Elect Barack Obama—as prepared for delivery Election Night," pp. 1–4, in author's possession. See also Ryan Lizza, "Battle Plans: How Obama Won," *New Yorker*, November 17, 2008, http://www.newyorker.com/reporting/2008/11/17/081117 fa_fact_lizza?printable=true.

100. Obama, *Dreams From My Father*, p. 135.

101. Sugrue, *Sweet Land of Liberty*.

102. Obama, *The Audacity of Hope*, p. 29.

103. *New York Times*, January 21, 2009, p. 1.

104. *Wall Street Journal*, January 21, 2009, p. R1.

105. All quotes are taken from "Barack Obama Presidential Inaugural Address," January 20, 2009, pp. 1–3.

106. *New York Post*, February 18, 2009, p. 12.

107. http://www.nypost.com/seven/02192009/postopinion/editorials/that_cartoon_155 984.htm.

108. Eyes On the Prize, Parts I and II: America's Civil Rights Movement, 1954–1985. Blackside Productions, 2006.

109. "Remarks as Prepared for Delivery by Attorney General Eric Holder at the Department of Justice African American History Month Program," February 18, 2009, http://www .usdoj.gov/ag/speeches/2009/ag-speech-090218.html.

110. Dayo O. Olopade, "Visible Man," *The Root.com*, February 19, 2009; Melissa Harris-Lacewell, "Why Eric Holder's Speech was a Failure," *The Kitchen Table.com*, February 19, 2009.

111. http://www.cnn.com/2009/POLITICS/02/18/holder.race.relations/.

112. Stephen L. Carter, "We're Not 'Cowards,' We're Just Loud," *New York Times*, February 25, 2009, p. A23.

113. See for example, MacFarguhar, "The Conciliator," p. 55.

114. Ibid., p. xlvi.

115. Obama, *The Audacity of Hope*, p. 97.

116. Ibid., p. 72.

117. Ibid., p. 131.

118. Ibid., p. 255.

119. Ibid., pp. 305–306.

120. H. W. Brands, *Traitor to His Class: The Privileged Life and Radical Presidency of Franklin Delano Roosevelt* (New York: Doubleday, 2008), p. 283.

121. David Remnick, "The President's Hero," *The New Yorker*, February 2, 2009, p. 21.

122. Ibid., p. 22.

123. William Jelani Cobb, "As Obama Rises, Old Guard Civil Rights Leaders Scowl," *Washington Post*, January 13, 2008, p. B01.

124. Ifill, *The Breakthrough*.

125. Ibid., p. 58.

126. Remnick, "The Joshua Generation."

127. James Baldwin, *The Fire Next Time* (New York: Dell, 1964), p. 73.

128. James Baldwin, *No Name in the Street* (New York: Dell, 1972), p. 9.

129. Ibid., p. 119.

130. Ibid., p. 97.

131. John Stauffer, *Giants: The Parallel Lives of Frederick Douglass and Abraham Lincoln* (New York: Twelve, 2008), p. 244.

132. "President Obama's Address to the Turkish Parliament," April 6, 2009, http://www .whitehouse.gov/the_press_office/Remarks-By-President-Obama-To-The-Turkish-Parliament/. Obama's well-received speech in Cairo two months later continued this theme by citing his own recent election as proof of America's extraordinary capacity to continually reinvent itself.

America, Obama suggested, sought a new and more constructive relationship with Muslim nations after years of tensions related to the war on terror. Obama deployed his personal biography as a black man who had lived in Indonesia and had family members on his father's side who followed the Muslim religion in order to express his abiding respect for Islamic historical and cultural traditions. See http://www.guardian.co.uk/world/2009/jun/04/barack-obama -keynote-speech-egypt.

133. Obama's July 11 speech before Ghana's parliament, in Accra, amplified this kind of symbolism. Although his speech continued to represent Africa in a largely two-dimensional manner as a continent brutalized by slavery and colonialism in the past and gripped by government corruption in the present, the imagery of a black American president traveling through Ghana's streets and addressing its citizens was extraordinarily powerful. Ghanaians embraced Obama as a kind of living prophet, and he remains incredibly popular in Africa. See http://www.washingtonpost.com/wp-dyn/content/article/2009/07/11/AR2009071101 327.html.

134. *New York Times*, April 27, 2009, http://www.nytimes.com/2009/04/28/us/politics/ 28poll.html?ref=politics.

135. *New York Times*, May 2, 2009, http://www.nytimes.com/2009/05/03/us/politics/ 03race.html?_r=1&hp. See also Jabari Asim, *What Obama Means . . . For Our Culture, Our Politics, Our Future* (New York: William Morrow, 2009).

INDEX